ASIA LOOKS SEAWARD

Asia Looks Seaward

Power and Maritime Strategy

Edited by Toshi Yoshihara and James R. Holmes

PRAEGER SECURITY INTERNATIONAL
Westport, Connecticut · London

Library of Congress Cataloging-in-Publication Data

Yoshihara, Toshi.
  Asia looks seaward : power and maritime strategy / Toshi Yoshihara and James R. Holmes.
    p. cm.
  Includes bibliographical references and index.
  ISBN 978–0–275–99403–7 (alk. paper)
1. Navies—Asia. 2. Warships—Asia. I. Holmes, James R. II. Title.
VA620.Y64 2008
359'.03095—dc22   2007027858

British Library Cataloguing in Publication Data is available.

Library of Congress Catalog Card Number: 2007027858
ISBN-13: 978–0–275–99403–7

First published in 2008

Praeger Security International, 88 Post Road West, Westport, CT 06881
An imprint of Greenwood Publishing Group, Inc.
www.praeger.com

Printed in the United States of America

The paper used in this book complies with the
Permanent Paper Standard issued by the National
Information Standards Organization (Z39.48–1984).

10 9 8 7 6 5 4 3 2 1

CONTENTS

CHAPTER 1

INTRODUCTION

Toshi Yoshihara

Asian waters promise to be a new geostrategic locus of international politics in the coming years. This assertion may seem somewhat jarring or even bizarre to the casual observer of world affairs. After all, successive Asian powers, including China, Japan, and Russia, repeatedly tried and failed to dominate their nautical environment militarily over the past century. Not an Asian great power but Europe's unsurpassed naval power preserved maritime order in the region during the imperial heyday of the nineteenth century. The U.S. Navy succeeded to this role in the Pacific following World War II. Unsurprisingly, then, Asia's abrupt turn to the seas over the past decade has elicited little to no attention from most observers and has been viewed with indifference by many who have taken note. This oversight, however understandable, could cost nations with a stake in the Asian order dearly as the international system undergoes a barely perceptible but momentous maritime shift.

This transition is symbolized by two seemingly unrelated events at opposite ends of the earth: the retreat of European states from the seas and the entry of Asian states into the oceanic arena. The noted world historian Paul Kennedy points to a "remarkable global disjuncture" involving "massive differences in the assumptions of European nations and Asian nations about the significance of sea power, today and into the future."[1] He notes that Western capitals, with the exception of Washington, appear ready to abdicate their status as maritime powers, while Asian leaders seem eager to expend national treasure on building up their navies. As Kennedy readily concedes, the global implications of this apparent divergence are far from clear at the moment. But the regional phenomenon in Asia, where closely clustered fleets of navies are growing at fairly rapid rates nearly simultaneously, raises some intriguing and troubling questions.

What explains this sudden rise of navies at virtually the same time within a specific geographic region? What are the strategic implications of this surge in sea power, especially in terms of the regional balance of power? Are rivalries, crises, or conflicts among the Asian maritime powers more likely as a result of perceived or real imbalances in the relative correlation of naval forces? If so, what can be done to dampen the competitive effects produced by the proximity of increasingly powerful navies to one another? These are some of the key questions addressed by the contributors to this volume.

It is our contention that a more holistic analysis of Asian sea power, something missing for the past decade, is long overdue. The paucity of scholarly writings related to Asian maritime affairs is startling in view of the region's strongly nautical character. The need to fill this gap in the literature is gaining in urgency, moreover, as naval buildups in the region gather speed. Appreciating the oceanic dimensions of Asian politics from the perspectives of geography, history, commerce, and military power is critical.

Geography and History

Even a cursory glance at the map reveals the intensely maritime nature of Asian geography. The Japanese home islands, the Korean Peninsula (essentially a half island), Taiwan, the Philippines, and the Indonesian archipelago envelop the entire East Asian landmass. Though a small nation, Japan boasts one of the longest coastlines in the world. Indonesia, home to the world's largest Muslim population, is also the largest archipelago on earth, encompassing more than sixteen thousand islands. The South Asian subcontinent is one massive peninsula jutting out into the sea. All major cities in East, Southeast, and South Asia are coastal metropolises. According to a report by the Center for Naval Analyses, 40 percent of the four billion people residing in Asia are located within forty-five miles (seventy kilometers) of the coast.[2] An expert on coastal populations claims that 60 percent of Asia's nearly four billion people live within four hundred kilometers of the ocean coast. Of these, approximately one-and-a-half billion, representing roughly a quarter of mankind, live within one hundred kilometers of the sea.[3] These demographic figures are striking by any measure.

Major historical events in Asia have originated at sea. Some of them have helped Asian leaders mold national myths that continue to grip the imaginations of coastal citizens. In the thirteenth century, for instance, Mongol attempts to invade Japan were thwarted in large part by seasonal typhoons, inspiring the now-infamous notion of the kamikaze, or divine wind. Around the same time, Indian Muslim traders began a gradual process of religious conversion through-out Southeast Asia. Admiral Yi Sun-sin's naval victories against the Japanese during Toyotomi Hideyoshi's failed attempt to conquer the Korean Peninsula (1592–98) remain widely celebrated in South Korea.

Chinese historiography too incorporates a brief period of maritime glory and heroism. In 1405, Admiral Zheng He set off on the first of seven major naval expeditions. His voyages spanned over a quarter-century and ranged far beyond China's shores. Equipped with technology that was state-of-the-art for its day, Zheng's massive treasure ships sailed throughout the Southeast and South Asian seas and may have even reached the eastern coast of Africa. To this day, the top Chinese leadership invokes Zheng He's benevolent voyages as evidence of China's "peaceful rise."[4] In contrast, the crushing defeats meted out by the French (1884–85) and the Japanese (1894–95) against the Qing Dynasty's navy form an integral part of the so-called "century of humiliation" narrative that continues to animate Chinese nationalism.

Commerce

The most dynamic and some of the most powerful economies on the globe are concentrated in Northeast and Southeast Asia. The Japanese archipelago is home to the second largest economy in the world. South Korea, Taiwan, and Singapore remain important high-technology and manufacturing hubs of the global economy. China, the most impressive performer of the past decade, is looked upon as the prospective economic juggernaut of the twenty-first century. South Asia's economic prospects are bright as well. India's prowess in information technology is the envy of the world, and there is hope that Indian economic growth will yield spillover effects, aiding productivity beyond the subcontinent.

Statistics on the volume of seaborne of trade in Asia furnish one indicator of the close relationship between commerce and oceanic activity. Consider the case of China. According to the United Nations Conference on Trade and Development (UNCTAD),

> China is by far the world's largest exporter of containerized cargo, with 14.4 million TEUs in 2003. This is expected to grow further to 18.6 million TEUs in 2005, assuming an annual growth rate of almost 18 per cent, which is also the region's highest. China will then account for 24 per cent of the world's containerized exports.[5]

Asia's seaborne trade, as measured in tonnage, is equally impressive. In 1990, total goods loaded in the region weighed in at 585 million tons. Fifteen years later, the figures jumped to 1.6 billion tons, an astounding 280 percent increase.[6]

Shipbuilding capacity is another important indicator. Clustered in Northeast Asia, South Korea, Japan, and China are the three largest shipbuilders in the world. The reality is that the only cost-effective way to move goods in bulk is seaborne transport. As the volume of trade increases, consequently, the demand for shipbuilding will grow proportionately. China appears poised to meet that demand. Foreign observers predict that China will become the world's largest shipbuilder by 2015, surpassing Japan and South Korea.[7] In anticipation of this,

China's largest state-owned shipbuilder, the COSCO Shipyard Group, has launched into a massive effort to build up capacity at all of its shipyards, including the facilities at Zhousan, Nantong, Guangzhou, Tianjin, Shanghai, Xiamen, and Dalian.

Dalian, for example, registered a staggering leap in capacity, on the order of 73 percent, by late 2005.[8] Its shipyard boasts the largest floating drydock in the world, allowing the yard staff to perform hull work on very large crude carriers.[9] That Chinese engineers designed and built the dock is a point of special pride for Beijing. The reasons for this growth include low costs, the meteoric rise in demand, economies of scale, improved quality, and co-location in China (as opposed to the more distributed global networks of shipyards operated by other marine conglomerates).

That Asian economies have an insatiable appetite for energy resources is already common knowledge. Resource-poor countries such as Japan and South Korea depend almost entirely on oil shipped from the Persian Gulf to sustain their economic viability. China has joined these two countries as a major energy importer. In 2003, China surpassed Japan as a consumer of petroleum, moving into second place behind the United States.[10] The U.S. National Intelligence Council projected that Chinese oil consumption must increase by 150 percent by 2020 to sustain a healthy rate of economic expansion. If so, Chinese demand for oil will nearly equal the U.S. demand forecast for that year.[11]

Accelerating seaborne trade and energy dependence, then, will almost certainly heighten national security concerns related to the safety of SLOCs (sea lines of communication). The need to assure an uninterrupted flow of goods on the high seas may compel Asian nations to build up naval power as a strategic hedge against disruptions to energy imports. Recent military trends suggest that this is indeed the case.

Naval Power

While it is beyond the scope of this chapter to set forth a full net assessment of the military balance in Asia, a few illustrations of the martial dimension of maritime affairs in Asia today are in order. Table 1.1 depicts the force structures of the Asian navies (surface combatants and submarines) featured in this volume as they stood in 2006, including those of South Korea and Taiwan. Table 1.2 provides a snapshot of the quantitative changes in these five naval force structures between 1990 and 2006. Including the latter two navies highlights the considerable combat power that even smaller navies in Asia could bring to bear in times of crisis. Table 1.1 also includes the navies of the United Kingdom and France, widely recognized as second-tier naval powers, as a basis for comparison.

Table 1.1 Regional Naval Force Structures

	Aircraft carrier	Destroyer	Frigates and corvettes	Total surface combatants	Conventional submarines	Nuclear attack submarines	Total submarines
China	0	27	47	74	69	7	76
India	1	8	38	47	16	0	16
Japan	0	44	9	53	18	0	18
South Korea	0	6	37	43	20	0	20
Taiwan	0	4	22	26	4	0	4
United Kingdom	3	11	20	34	0	11	11
France	2	12	20	34	0	6	6

Source: Figures on individual navies are drawn from *Jane's Sentinel Security Assessment,* http://www.janesonline.com. For China, see http://www4.janes.com/subscribe/sentinel/CNAS_doc_view.jsp?Sent_Country=China&Prod_Name=CNAS&K2DocKey=/content1/janesdata/sent/cnasu/chins130.htm@current. For India, see http://www4.janes.com/subscribe/sentinel/SASS_doc_view.jsp?Sent_Country=India&Prod_Name=SASS&K2DocKey=/content1/janesdata/sent/sassu/indis130.htm@current. For Japan, see http://www4.janes.com/subscribe/sentinel/CNAS_doc_view.jsp?Sent_Country=Japan&Prod_Name=CNAS&K2DocKey=/content1/janesdata/sent/cnasu/japns130.htm@current. For the Republic of Korea, see http://www4.janes.com/subscribe/sentinel/CNAS_doc_view.jsp?Sent_Country=Korea,%20South&Prod_Name=CNAS&K2DocKey=/content1/janesdata/sent/cnasu/skors130.htm@current. For Taiwan, see http://www4.janes.com/subscribe/sentinel/CNAS_doc_view.jsp?Sent_Country=Taiwan&Prod_Name=CNAS&K2DocKey=/content1/janesdata/sent/cnasu/taiws130.htm@current.

Table 1.2 Force Structure Trends, 1990–2006

	Surface ships (1990)	Surface ships (2006)	Submarines (1990)	Submarines (2006)
China	55	76	93	58
India	37	58	19	16
Japan	68	53	15	16
South Korea	38	43	3	20
Taiwan	34	33	4	4

Source: International Institute of Strategic Studies, *The Military Balance* (London: IISS, 1990 and 2006). We used figures from *Jane's* in Table 1.1 to provide the most accurate, up-to-date snapshot possible of regional naval forces. Table 1.2 relies on the *Military Balance* to chart long-term trends.

What these numbers obscure are the significant technological advances and tonnage increases that characterize the ships that have recently entered service in all of the Asian navies. In Table 1.2, for example, the significant drop in the number of Chinese submarines over this fifteen-year period reflects the mass retirement of obsolete vessels. The concurrent introduction of modern boats, both imported and indigenously built, should in theory more than compensate for the quantitative losses, preserving or enhancing combat power. Similarly, the relative stagnation in the number of Japanese platforms does not account for the fact that cutting-edge equipment has replaced older predecessors. In any event, all five navies have enjoyed varying degrees of recapitalization—portending a highly competitive naval environment in the coming years.

China has undergone the most comprehensive across-the-board modernization, defying even the most extravagant predictions from just a decade ago. The fifth largest fleet in the world, the Indian Navy, aspires to be a blue-water navy in the coming decades. Japan's modestly named Maritime Self-Defense Force plans to put to sea at least two "helicopter destroyers" that are, by even the most restrictive definition, prototypes for aircraft carriers. By the end of this decade, South Korea will become the third country in the region (following the United States and Japan) to deploy state-of-the-art Aegis destroyers. Taiwan will possess four very capable *Kidd*-class destroyers, the precursor to the Aegis warships, by the end of 2007. At nearly 10,000 tons, these vessels displace twice as much as the largest vessels currently in the island's inventory.

Sea-Power Theory and the Asian Maritime Environment

From the brief regional overview above, it should be evident that Asia's entry into the sea is not a passing phenomenon. The geographic, historical, economic, and military imperatives are simply too compelling to be ephemeral. While the specific circumstances facing the Asian nations are crucial to understanding how events will unfold in the oceanic arena in the twenty-first century, a review of sea-power theory will supply a broad analytical framework by which to assess patterns of behavior on the part of the region's maritime aspirants. Insight into their likely interactions at sea will follow.

What does it mean to say Asia is looking seaward? To portray this seaward turn in strictly military terms is not enough. A navy unguided by larger political or economic purposes is little more than a "luxury fleet," to borrow a term from one prominent historian.[12] Nor is seagoing trade and commerce, as manifest in massive tankers and container ships and the terminals that service them, the end-all-and-be-all of maritime affairs. Maritime affairs is an intensely multidisciplinary subject, spanning political science, military strategy, economics, history, and culture, not to mention mathematics, the natural sciences, and engineering.

To gain some purchase on the future of maritime strategy in Asia, accordingly, it is worth asking briefly: what is sea power?

Great seagoing nations have been grappling with this question for over a century. For Alfred Thayer Mahan, the intellectual father of the U.S. Navy, amassing sea power meant more than raising and deploying navies or driving enemy fleets from the high seas. Writing in the 1890s, Mahan portrayed sea power as resting on the "three pillars" represented by international trade and commerce, naval and merchant shipping, and overseas bases.[13] His contemporary Sir Julian Corbett—who scoffed at Mahan's work, terming it "shallow and wholly unhistorical"—preferred the term *maritime,* which carried both military and nonmilitary connotations, to the term *naval,* which was more common in Mahan's writings despite his avowedly broad conception of sea power.[14]

How could an aspiring sea power erect Mahan's three pillars? Mahan famously described a nation's potential for sea power as a function of six broad attributes: (1) geographic position; (2) physical conformation; (3) extent of territory; (4) number of population; (5) national character; and (6) character of the government.[15] Of these, the first four relate to a country's more or less immutable characteristics. Specifically, he asked, does the country have enough people, resources, coastline, and prospective seaports to make maritime power a viable concern? The last two traits, more intriguingly, relate to nonmaterial factors. To what extent is sea power a matter of choice for a coastal state, and to what extent is it a product of material factors?

This is a question worth pondering. Mahan suggests that peoples go to the sea because they have the innate aptitude, or genius, for seafaring endeavors. Acquisitiveness figures prominently in sea power, impelling coastal peoples to enter into maritime trade and commerce. They acquire colonies and warships, the other components of sea power, to further their quest for wealth and security.[16] A recent scholar, Peter Padfield, turns Mahan's argument around, suggesting that proximity to the sea shapes national character, in turn giving rise to a seagoing culture. Padfield ascribes modern Western dominance not to chance or cultural superiority but to "the particular configuration of seas and land masses that has given the advantage to powers able to use and command the seas."[17] Maritime geography, in this view, imprints a mercantile culture on a nation, suggesting that sea power is indeed destiny. Whether sea power is a matter of fate or deliberate policy is an elusive yet essential question for students of Asian maritime power.

Can sea power be quantified? In one recent work, Geoffrey Till offers a set of useful indices for estimating a nation's seafaring capacity. His effort to show how material factors influence nonmaterial factors complements the earlier, more historically inclined work of Mahan. Till defines sea power as "the capacity to influence the behaviour of other people by what you do at or from the sea." The "constituents" of sea power include (1) population, society, and government;

(2) "other means" such as land power, air power, or joint and combined warfare; (3) technology; (4) maritime geography; (5) resources; and (6) a maritime economy. Measuring an Asian country's endowment of these constituents and gauging how they interact with national institutions, traditions, and culture offer a valuable tool for analyzing the future of sea power in Asia.[18]

The benchmarks for sea power put forward by Mahan and Till provide one vantage point from which to survey maritime affairs in contemporary Asia. Second, to what extent will Asian thinkers fair their own historical and cultural traditions into their naval and maritime strategies? Whether aspiring Asian sea powers incline to Mahan's more military-intensive perspective on nautical matters, embrace Corbett's wider perspective, or fashion their own, distinctive synthesis of Western and non-Western strategic thought will say much about the future of the region. What would happen, for instance, should a regional power predisposed to think and act in Mahanian terms square off against a rival indifferent to seagoing pursuits or with a far different vision of sea power? Likely interactions among these powers are worth pondering as the United States and its allies attempt to keep pace with events.

Whether strategic thinkers and decision-makers regard sea power as a universal or a regional phenomenon carries significant implications. This is no idle debate, as twentieth-century Asian history attests. For instance, many Japanese strategic thinkers in the early decades of the century hewed to Mahanian theory—a theory better suited to global maritime powers such as contemporary Great Britain or a rising United States—while Japan's maritime interests were confined to East and Southeast Asia. While imperial Tokyo was indifferent to obtaining the island bases Mahan had espoused, it cast its gaze onto the Asian mainland, with fateful consequences. Similarly, whether seafaring Asian nations see their interests and sea-power potential as local or global is a question of considerable moment for regional stability and peace. A regional power thinking in global terms could upset the Asian maritime equilibrium, as it did during the 1930s and 1940s.

What is the primary goal of naval power? For Mahan, "command of the sea" connoted "overbearing power" that swept enemy fleets from vital waters, choking off the sea lanes to enemy warships and merchantmen while preserving the dominant sea power's liberty to exploit the oceans for its own commercial and military purposes.[19] Corbett, by contrast, deemed an uncommanded sea the normal state of affairs in both wartime and peacetime. He and like-minded strategists such as Charles E. Callwell stressed the interdependence of land and sea power, shifting the emphasis from major fleet actions on the high seas to sea-lane security and amphibious operations.[20] Such views find expression in post–Cold War doctrinal publications such as the U.S. Navy's *From the Sea,* which takes American sea control as a given, devoting its attention to how U.S. naval forces can influence events ashore. Clearly, an Asian sea power of Mahanian inclinations would exert far different influence on regional maritime security than would a sea power that adhered to Corbett or kindred theorists.

Chapter Summaries

This volume brings together essays examining the phenomenon of sea power in Asia from a variety of functional and country perspectives. It is useful to briefly explain the structure and logic of the book. The first three chapters of the volume are designed to supply a historical backdrop to contemporary Asian maritime affairs. Thus, this first section is essentially chronological, tracing the dominant Asian sea powers of the past. The book begins with an overview of China's role in shaping the Asian maritime order since antiquity, providing a baseline for analyzing Chinese maritime ambitions and capabilities today. This is followed by a study of Great Britain's strategic retreat from the Pacific theater during the interwar period. It offers lessons on how a great naval power can adjust to an environment undergoing rapid changes and stresses as multiple maritime states rise simultaneously. This section ends with a chapter on U.S. maritime strategy from the late nineteenth century to the present day. This narrative of America's quest for maritime power in Asia underscores the elusiveness of a stable strategy in a region that has been repeatedly convulsed by unexpected and sudden strategic transitions.

The second part of the volume contains five chapters on national/regional case studies involving China, India, Japan, and Southeast Asia. The first chapter on China conducts a thorough net assessment of the Chinese navy. The second is an analysis of China's oil tanker fleet. The intent of this pairing is to highlight both the military and the commercial/economic nature of Beijing's turn to the seas. The India chapter that follows illustrates how another regional power aspires to assert maritime influence in its immediate environment and possibly beyond. The possibility that New Delhi might cast its eyes beyond the Indian Ocean hints tantalizingly at the potential for Sino-Indian maritime interactions and friction. Japan is in many ways a beneficiary of American maritime dominance since the end of World War II. The final chapter, consequently, is designed to gauge how states with a high stake in the current maritime status quo will respond as they confront the unprecedented, virtually simultaneous entry of two Asian powers into the aquatic domain. The following summarizes the major intellectual contributions of each chapter.

To begin with, John C. Perry introduces some basic concepts for assessing nautical affairs and provides a sweeping historical overview of China's maritime experience. Perry starts by proposing that coastal states enjoy inherent advantages derived from geographic location that continental powers do not. Specifically, the seas provide a medium by which a coastal state can reach key access points around the globe. Yet Perry is at pains to show that geography is not destiny.

Some coastal communities, such as Sicily, consciously choose to be landbound, while other political entities "become seagoing...as a result of a complex series of cultural decisions and attitudes." In this latter category, some maritime states "construct and maintain all apparatus of maritime life," while other seagoing societies "use the ocean as a source of cultural stimulus and a means of artistic expression." In short, diversity rather than commonality characterizes the activities and the relative strengths and weaknesses of coastal states.

The rest of this opening chapter focuses on China's maritime past. Perry's central hypothesis is that "the means were there" for China to erect a maritime-based regional order in East Asia, "but not the will." First, China's riverine civilization tied itself closely to the Yellow and Yangtze rivers, both of which were inhospitable to seaward voyages. Second, even as its southward enlargement helped reorient Chinese civilization toward the Asian seas, the relative ease of coastal commerce had a "corrupting" influence that discouraged an oceanic outlook. Third, the "grasping hand" of government bureaucracy, which depended on fees and bribes exacted from riverine trade, frowned upon maritime activities that were beyond its immediate reach. Fourth, endemic piracy along the East Asian littoral created a twin-pronged problem. Because pirates were motivated by short-term profits, they were never able to forge a longer-term, politically driven oceanic identity. At the same time, piracy generated lasting antipathy toward the seas on the part of the Confucian-based bureaucracy. Finally, periodic oceanic ventures proved short-lived, failing under the Mongols before being superseded by continental threats under the Ming Dynasty. Perry concludes that modern China's turn to the sea, unshackled by the constraints of the past, "surely is one of the great events of our time."

Nicholas E. Sarantakes recounts the critical decisions and debates surrounding Great Britain's strategic position in Asia during the interwar period, when the nation's inability to police Asian waters was becoming increasingly evident. The author's main proposition is that while the British acquitted themselves relatively well in their assessments of maritime Asia, "it was luck...that was the key factor in determining the success of British strategy in the years following World War I." Sarantakes attributes British luck to the behavior of a cooperative adversary, namely Japan. The author begins by thoroughly documenting the indecision and drift that characterized British policy toward Japan. On the one hand, Japanese naval power eclipsed that of Britain after the Great War. Tokyo's ambitions, moreover, increasingly encroached on British interests in Asia, particularly British economic interests in China. On the other hand, no suitable counterweight was available—the Americans were discounted as too unreliable—to balance or deter Japan. London thus was in no position either to challenge Japanese ascendance directly or to enlist third-party assistance to preserve an Asian maritime order favorable to British interests.

Sarantakes also highlights the inconsistencies in British policy and strategy throughout the interwar period. Beginning in the early 1920s, the Admiralty designated Japan as enemy number one, developing plans for defeating the IJN (Imperial Japanese Navy). Yet its plans focused exclusively on naval engagements that were divorced from an overarching strategy for compelling Japan to do Britain's will. Compounding matters, on the home front, the British populace had neither the political nor the financial appetite to adequately support such a maritime endeavor in Asia. Thus ensued a kind of strategic immobility that persisted until the outbreak of the Pacific War. The author portrays the Japanese attack on Pearl Harbor, which helped forge the Anglo-American alliance overnight, as an enormous blunder that rescued the British from their strategic dilemma. Victory nonetheless exacted a steep price: the campaigns in the Pacific permanently shattered the British Empire in Asia. Sarantakes concludes that luck is a poor substitute for sound policy.

Bernard D. Cole reviews the history of U.S. engagement in Asia. Cole depicts U.S. maritime strategy in the region as a makeshift affair, driven by events and needs of the moment more than by systematic evaluation of the strategic environment, U.S. interests, and strategies able to achieve these interests with available resources. Only with the writings and advocacy of Alfred Thayer Mahan and like-minded sea-power proponents did U.S. strategy take on some semblance of rational decision-making. Yet even Mahanian theory created problems for the United States in the region, exhorting Washington to obtain overseas naval bases—most prominently the Philippine Islands—that in effect offered hostages to potent regional sea powers such as Imperial Japan. The author observes that the United States has further expanded its interests in the region since the downfall of the Soviet Union, declaring safe passage through all important Asian sea lanes, geographic chokepoints, and even rivers to be a matter of concern for Washington. Whether the U.S. Navy has the resources to discharge its ambitious new duties is a doubtful prospect, suggests Cole, leaving the navy in the position of trying to augment its resources with those of allies and coalition partners.

Andrew S. Erickson ventures a net assessment of China's growing maritime capacity. Many Chinese officials and military scholars, contends Erickson, espouse "their own universal logic of sea power, with both Mahanian and Marxist undercurrents." Even so, the nation's naval development is seemingly "constrained less by ideology than by capabilities." The People's Liberation Army Navy (PLA Navy or PLAN) is evolving along lines quite dissimilar to other navies in East Asia, including the U.S. Navy. Indeed, Beijing evinces no particular urgency about constructing aircraft-carrier expeditionary groups like those that represent the core of the U.S. Navy fleet. But will the PLA Navy's strategy and force-structure plans allow it to achieve command of the sea, and how will Beijing interpret command of the sea? Will China become a true maritime power any time soon?

Erickson's exhaustive survey of Chinese naval modernization starts by review-ing Beijing's most recent Defense White Paper, *China's National Defense in 2006.* The chapter then evaluates China's military budget before turning to the submarine force; the PLAN's capacity for mine warfare; the surface and amphibious fleets; the naval air force; the navy's command, control, communica-tions, computer, intelligence, surveillance, and reconnaissance capabilities; and its efforts in the area of carrier aviation. Subsequent sections consider China's base infrastructure, training, and doctrine. From this analysis, Erickson infers that China is merging its own history and strategic traditions with those of the West and applying the resulting, hybrid sea-power theory to East Asian waters. Precisely what this portends for regional peace and stability remains unclear.

Gabriel Collins complements Andrew Erickson's appraisal of the PLA Navy with an assessment of the Chinese commercial tanker fleet, rounding out this volume's inquiry into Chinese sea power. Collins points out that the energy shipping business carries political overtones, imparting "a strong national secu-rity flavor to many actions that in other sectors would be considered purely com-mercial." Who is behind the construction of an enormous, Chinese-flagged tanker fleet? The author asks whether China's political leadership is demanding a large national tanker fleet as a way to assure a steady flow of oil and gas supplies, or whether Chinese shipping firms are manipulating political leaders' feelings of insecurity for commercial gain. He inclines to the latter view while also allowing for the geopolitical implications of China's surging maritime trade and its seemingly unquenchable thirst for oil.

Collins observes that Beijing is looking beyond Taiwan as it contemplates the nation's energy security. Protection of the SLOCs "at long range from Chinese shores" could become a major priority for the PLA Navy, if indeed it has not already. In late 2006, no less a figure than President Hu Jintao advocated a "blue-water" navy prepared "at any time" to defend China's nautical interests by force of arms. The Strait of Malacca, the conduit for most of the nation's foreign oil, preoccupies Hu and his advisers. The American, Japanese, and even Indian navies pose concerns for a China worried about its interests at sea. The author nonetheless maintains that security concerns are secondary to commercial imperatives in China's tanker-fleet buildup. The industry's adherence to market principles, the practical difficulties of recalling tankers to national service in wartime, and other factors cast doubt on Beijing's effort to put to sea a national "oil armada."

Turning from East to South Asia, Andrew C. Winner appraises the efficacy of Indian maritime doctrine, strategy, and forces, asking whether and when this South Asian continental power will become a viable seagoing power. Observes Winner, Indian officials and pundits "have begun to speak the language of maritime power," but nevertheless "one searches in vain for a formal Indian maritime strategy document." To discern some of the nonmaterial drivers behind

Indian maritime strategy, the author reviews two contending models of India's strategic worldview. C. Raja Mohan, a well-known Indian commentator, maintains that Indians think in terms of concentric geographic circles, with New Delhi asserting certain prerogatives in each circle. Primacy and the capacity to veto external intervention are top priorities within the inmost circle, while achieving great-power status is Indians' foremost goal in the outermost, globe-spanning circle.

An American scholar, Stephen P. Cohen, portrays the Indian worldview more in philosophical than geographical terms. Rather than concentric circles, Indian strategic thought is shaped by three contending visions, namely Nehruvian, realist, and revivalist. Applied to the nautical realm, each of these schools of thought would see things somewhat differently, with, say, followers of Nehru striking a more cooperative pose in world affairs and revivalists focusing on military preeminence in the Indian Ocean region. Winner evaluates each of the missions laid out in New Delhi's 2004 *Indian Maritime Doctrine* statement—sea-based deterrence, economic and energy security, forward presence, and naval diplomacy—in light of the strategic worldviews posited by Mohan and Cohen. While the author deprecates Indian maritime power as it currently stands, he confidently predicts that the nation will fulfill its potential at sea in the not-too-distant future, regardless of which model best explains Indians' strategic perspectives.

James R. Holmes appraises the condition of maritime strategic thought in Japan today, contending that Tokyo is "allowing strategic thought to atrophy." In prewar Japan, notes Holmes, the IJN revered Alfred Thayer Mahan's works. Japanese naval strategy nonetheless bore at best a partial resemblance to Mahanian doctrine, interwoven as it was with Japan's peculiar geography, the nation's ambitions on the Asian continent, the lessons Japanese strategists learned from the Sino-Japanese and Russo-Japanese wars, the IJN's bureaucratic needs, and countless other factors. In the end, tactics and hardware shaped Japanese strategic thought as much as the ideal relationship among theory, strategy, and force structure did.

Postwar Japan speedily took on maritime duties, largely at the behest of its enemy-cum-ally, the United States. Washington prodded Tokyo to build warfighting capabilities augmenting those of the U.S. Navy, notably in the areas of mine warfare and ASW (antisubmarine warfare). Territorial defense, protection of the SLOCs, and ASW were among the primary missions entrusted to the Maritime Self-Defense Force, and Japanese mariners executed these missions with aplomb. But there was little evidence that Japanese officials thought about these missions in rigorous theoretical terms. Wartime defeat discredited Mahan in Japanese eyes, but no thinker, Western or Asian, has yet taken his place.

Today, says Holmes, the nation's political leadership is thrusting nontraditional missions on the Japanese armed forces under the rubric of "international peace cooperation activities." These missions are intensively maritime in nature, running the gamut from disaster relief to missile defense, but resources are lagging commitments. To keep naval means aligned with political ends, Tokyo sorely needs to revive its tradition of maritime strategic thought, whether by looking to the West or by working out its own synthesis of Western and Eastern sea-power theory.

Finally, John Garofano appraises the security dynamics of Southeast Asia in the context of a rising, energy-hungry China. Garofano distinguishes between the politics of Northeast and Southeast Asia, observing that the nations ringing the South China Sea are less affluent and less well-armed than those to their north. More importantly, they do not share the "historical animosity and related baggage toward a rising China" that suffuses Japan's relations with the giant to its west. The equanimity with which Southeast Asians view China could prove problematic, says the author, particularly once the Taiwan question is settled and Beijing is free to reorient its energies toward other nearby seas. The coming years could witness the emergence of a more assertive Chinese policy toward Southeast Asia, given the critical sea lanes traversing the region and the conflicting maritime territorial claims—including a Chinese claim to virtually the entire South China Sea—that promise to roil regional politics.

Some Concluding Observations

For well over a decade, and more or less breathlessly, analysts have hailed the coming of a "Pacific century." The Asian financial crisis of 1997–98 curbed this enthusiasm for a time. The concept of a Pacific century has regained much of its luster, however, as the economies of the region resume their former vitality with the benefit of China's swift rise. Notably, this concept is premised on the oceanic medium binding the Western Hemisphere to the East Asian littoral. The Pacific-century narrative usually centers on the economic dynamism of Asia and on the prospect of stronger political leadership from Beijing, Tokyo, and other regional capitals. This implies what one of our contributors calls a "saltwater perspective" on regional affairs. Even so, the security implications of Asian ascendancy—particularly implications relating to maritime matters—remain largely absent from such analyses of the past and present. We contend, therefore, that the time is ripe for a broad assessment of the nautical dimensions of the expected (or delayed) Pacific century.

The foregoing analysis suggests that the emerging Asian maritime order could fundamentally challenge the assumptions that have underwritten the security of the region since World War II. In particular, the entry of China and India into the oceanic realm at nearly the same time—an unprecedented event in Asian maritime history—presents both challenges and opportunities. If both states view sea power through the bellicose lens of Mahan, a competitive element could well find its way into Asian politics. It is equally plausible that Beijing and New Delhi will temper their enthusiasm for Mahanian precepts, deploying maritime power as an instrument of regional cooperation. If so, Chinese and Indian mariners could find themselves prosecuting humanitarian, counter-piracy, and counterterrorist operations together. Either strategic pathway would give rise to corresponding reactions from stakeholders such as the United States and Japan. The result could be rivalry or a durable maritime order.

It is important, then, to note that neither Asia's maritime rise nor rivalry on the high seas is fated. The historical record suggests that the trajectory of sea power is rarely linear. Few if any analysts of the mid-1800s would have predicted the rise of American sea power, let alone decades of American dominion over the Asian seas. British sea power was checked and challenged by Spain and France for over a century, and was by no means assured until the downfall of Napoleonic France in 1815. Similarly, externalities or unexpected developments could compel great Asian land powers to modify their naval ambitions, or even frustrate these ambitions altogether. For example, a resurgence of Russia, China's historic rival to the north, could very well force Beijing to divert resources from its navy—slowing any Chinese efforts to assert control over the China seas or build up forces in the Indian Ocean basin. Alternatively, an economic downturn comparable to that of the 1990s would set back political and financial support for naval power in all affected capitals.

Even if observers assume that Asian naval programs *will* expand along a linear path, the question of sustainability will remain. Numbers of ships and even technological wizardry are by themselves insufficient measures of seagoing might. As Mahan counseled, there is far more to sea power than warships and weaponry. Certain coastal nations enjoy innate advantages deriving from geography, natural resources, and territorial extent. Cultural traditions and maritime genius, furthermore, constitute sinews of lasting sea power. To date, neither India nor China has proved it possesses these Mahanian qualities in adequate supply to make itself preeminent in Asian waters.

Critics, moreover, may protest that the economic interdependence resulting from globalization will attenuate the competitive aspects of sea power in Asia. By their logic, Asian governments will avoid destabilizing actions that give rise to naval rivalry or conflict, holding at risk the seaborne commerce so crucial to the region's economic growth. From a rational-choice perspective, weaker naval powers ought to maximize their ability to free ride on the efforts of the U.S. Navy, the current guarantor of freedom of navigation. In other words, the United States provides an international public good that should dissuade other powers from upsetting the existing maritime order. Yet rationality as construed by scholars and analysts is not the sole arbiter of international affairs. National passions count as well. In a previous era of globalization, many pundits proclaimed that war was at once inconceivable and irrational. By 1914, the major powers—the main beneficiaries of interdependence—nonetheless plunged themselves into a disastrous war over questions of honor.

The uncertainties accompanying Asia's turn to the seas, then, demand humility and sobriety on the part of observers. We should neither exaggerate the rise of new naval powers in Asia nor dismiss it out of hand. These extremes would yield policy prescriptions tending to overreaction or inaction. A careful study of the region's seaward orientation supplies ample basis for hedging against the most destabilizing elements of Asian maritime power while embracing—and perhaps institutionalizing—patterns of cooperation on the high seas. This book by no means represents the final word on Asia's seafaring future. We do hope it will jumpstart serious intellectual discourse on a long-neglected subject.

CHAPTER 2

IMPERIAL CHINA AND THE SEA

John Curtis Perry

If you stand on Cape Agulhas, that needlelike promontory at the southernmost tip of Africa, and look out at the ocean, you will see a sign announcing that on the left you are facing the Indian Ocean and on the right the Atlantic. This is a terracentric view of the world. Of course what you face is an uninterrupted body of water, a reminder that the salt-water space of the globe is united in the world ocean. Salt water may separate continents, but itself it forms an undivided whole.

The ocean covers more than 70 percent of the global surface; we are the blue planet, a body of water spinning through space, more accurately called Ocean, not Earth. The sea is outside us, the sea is within us; we ourselves are watery creatures. As John F. Kennedy put it in a speech toasting the Australian winners of the America's Cup sailing race in 1962, "We have salt in our blood, salt in our sweat, salt in our tears." The composition of the human organism is about 70 percent salty water. Thus each of us is the globe in microcosm.

Humanity is drawn to the sea. Eight of the world's ten largest cities lie at the ocean's edge. Nearly one-half of the world's people live within one hundred miles of salt water, and that proportion is growing as people seek out the sea. We are lured to that from which life itself springs.

We can divide the world's land areas into continental and coastal, those that face oceanic space and those that do not—turf and surf, we might say. This is a simple matter of geography. Continental empires have played a vastly significant role in history. One of the greatest was that of the Mongols who swept from Pacific shores almost to the Adriatic, opening a huge area to flows of commerce and culture. But the Mongols' rule was short; their nomadic patterns of life made for political instability and great fluctuations of power and influence.

Other Eurasian societies such as China practiced sedentary agriculture and engaged in a continuing contest with their nomadic neighbors, a struggle between steppe and sown, the man on horseback vs. the man with a plow.

For Eurasia this formed the great rhythm of history over the course of many centuries. Gunpowder weapons would end the era of the horse, but continental space still seemed to hold great advantage, with centrality of position providing a classic strategic asset. Early in the twentieth century, the British geographer Sir Halford Mackinder defined the underdeveloped core of Eurasia as the Heartland, center of what he called the world island. But the centrality was something not yet achieved. Its integrity relied on a transportation network that had earlier been furnished by the horse but was awaiting something to replace it.

The network of railroads such as Mackinder anticipated has yet to be constructed. His Heartland remains undeveloped. Furthermore, it could not be global. Global power demands control of global space. And that control is necessarily maritime.

The continental era now appears to be gone, with the collapse of the Soviet Union in 1989 punctuating its end. Today the world's hinterland nations in Eurasia, Africa, and Latin America are overwhelmingly poor (unless they possess oil and gas deposits) and isolated from main currents of international thought and activity. Not only are they poor, but they are also disaffected, often distrusting of the outside world and its cargo of new ideas. The parts of the world least touched by maritime influences are now the world's most unstable and most unhappy, the most desperate and the most dangerous.

Location would appear to be fixed, a frozen fact of life, offering no element of choice. And yet a coastal location seems to provide something more than the continental. This is access. Here lies a special opportunity for the adaptable, for those who perceive the current of the times and choose to flow with it, even to direct it.

Extrinsic factors may affect location. We know from our study of history that location is not necessarily static and can become dynamic. Changes in technology can affect the significance of location. In the nineteenth century, a revolution occurred at sea when engineers applied the steam engine to the ship to provide a new mode of propulsion. Ships could now operate without relying upon tide, current, or wind, but they became newly dependent upon fuel sources. The coaling station became a key element in transport and changed world oceanic routes.

The British benefited hugely, more so than any other power, from the switch from sail to steam. By 1900, Britain was already a global empire, with ports scattered strategically around the world to stock coal for both merchant ships and warships. These service stations became essential links in what came to be called the "lifeline of empire" that stretched from Gibraltar to Hong Kong, making Pacific Asia a salient of British power and Britain a major presence in those waters.

A second benefit the British enjoyed was their huge home resource of high-quality coal deposits. For Britain, "Welsh Cardiff," an anthracite coal of high caloric efficiency, was both an economic and a strategic asset. It provided a lucrative export commodity and ensured that British shipping would always have an adequate supply of an essential resource in peace or war.

A small island, Britain is by definition a coastal nation, with London both its maritime and its political capital. Some states are both coastal and continental; France and even Germany are such hybrids, torn between opportunities. Their coastal areas may look to the sea and interact with it, but continental influences ultimately prevail. Thus Paris has dominated Marseille, Berlin, and Hamburg. Some states like Japan, and China and Korea too, have fluctuated in their attachment to the sea. In the Tokugawa era, continental influences dominated Japan. In the Meiji period that followed, the coastal seized command, and Japan took to the sea.

I suggest that we can divide the coastal into two subcategories: landbound and seagoing. Coastal states, even islands, are not necessarily oriented toward seagoing endeavors. They may be landbound. This is a matter not of location but of choice. Landbound societies are indifferent to the ocean; seagoing societies embrace it.

Sicily is a prime cultural receptor, enjoying an exceptionally rich cultural experience and providing a longtime delight for the tourist. Sicily is home to a multilayered civilization, but it is not a cultural disseminator. Sicilians are ardent fishermen, but they did not build trading empires. In the words of one of the island's greatest writers, Sicilians perceived the sea as "capable only of carrying away the emigrants and disembarking the invaders." Sicily has remained landbound and never become seagoing.

Or take the case of Bali, a small island that is coastal but not seagoing. Its cultural orientation is toward the mountains, not the sea. The Balinese perceive the mountains as the home of the gods, the sea as a place of demons. Despite the island's many beautiful beaches, the Balinese do not learn how to swim, or they do so only badly. A ferry accident thus becomes a disaster.

Those societies on the sea that transcend the landbound and become seagoing do so as a result of a complex series of cultural decisions and attitudes. Each case is different; perhaps a political scientist could construct a model for this, but historians find differences fascinating, and we are more likely to look for those rather than similarities.

In any case, the remarkable success of seagoing societies as generators of power and accumulators of wealth makes the matter of their character worth exploring. The maritime Mediterranean world springs immediately into mind: Genoa or Venice or, much earlier, Tyre, Sidon, and then Athens. Ringing the Baltic, independent or quasi-independent Hanseatic city-states such as Riga or Bergen bestrode history powerfully at one time or another, as did feisty and outward-looking Aceh at the far western tip of Sumatra. But their impact was regional rather than global, thalassic rather than pelagic.

Perhaps we can divide those seagoing societies actively, using the ocean as source, arena, and avenue, into the maritime and the oceanic. Maritime states construct and maintain all the apparatus of maritime life, including industries such as shipyards, shipping, docks, and warehouses; institutions such as insurance, banking, and brokerage; and the know-how to generate, distribute, and control information relating to these matters.

But some seagoing societies carry their activities into another dimension, the realm of the arts. I would call these oceanic as opposed to maritime societies; they use the ocean as a source of cultural stimulus and a means for artistic expression. Life in Polynesia, for example, is ocean-centered rather than land-centered. So were the original inhabitants of the eastern Pacific coast, today's British Columbia.

In the modern culture of the North Atlantic world, the ocean has been an important presence. Be it in the writings of an English poet like Lord Byron:

> Roll on, thou deep and dark blue Ocean—roll!
> Ten thousand fleets sweep over thee in vain,
> Man marks the earth with ruin—his control
> Stops with the shore.

Or the American Longfellow:

> My soul is full of longing for the secrets of the sea
> The heart of the great ocean sends a thrilling pulse through me.

The pounding of the surf, the cries of the seabirds, the ding dong of the bell buoy, and the roar of the foghorn create a symphony of sounds attractive to the poet and to the composer as well.

These sounds of the sea have inspired musicians as well as writers. Germany's Richard Wagner, France's Claude Debussy, and England's Benjamin Britten all struck oceanic themes in their work. The sailor at his work inspired the simple sea shanty. It made hard labor easier by imparting rhythm to it.

Painters too were attracted to the luminous quality of the light cast by the sea, a result of the refractory combination of sky, water, and saltwater particles in the air. The Dutch were the first great European marine artists, but others would respond enthusiastically, including Monet, Turner, and Homer. They were drawn to the ocean and to what takes place upon it, recognizing that it offered dramatic subjects for the brush. And in this Atlantic culture, many artists across the spectrum have chosen the sea as metaphor, identifying the voyage as life's journey and the sea as a symbol of human interaction and the continuing struggle with the powers of nature.

Why is this so strong in some North Atlantic cultures? Why is it so lacking in East Asian civilization? Few Asian artists from any genre have shown much interest in the sea. Attempting to answer this question lies beyond the dimensions of this paper, but perhaps geography of location has something to do with it. Europe has a lengthy, indented coastline, and it encloses several inland seas. In short, the physical presence of the ocean is overwhelming as compared with East Asia. Parts of East Asia may once have been vigorously maritime, as they are now, but they are not oceanic in a cultural sense.

Uses of the Sea

We can define several ways in which humans use the sea. As source, the sea has provided salt and fish, and fish are still a major source of protein for more than a billion people. Increasingly, the sea is a source of energy. Nearly one-third of the oil and gas the world now consumes comes from the seabed. Methane hydrates offer a future potential energy source. And the sea is increasingly regarded as a source of renewable energy, as humans learn to exploit the fluctuating tides, the movement of waves, and water temperature differentials.

For millennia, the Austronesian world has enjoyed its direct physical encounter with the sea as a source of pleasure. The Atlantic world discovered the beach in the early nineteenth century, first finding it attractive because salt water, both by ingestion and by immersion, was considered conducive to good health. Later the therapeutic yielded to the hedonistic, and the seashore became identified with relaxation and recreation, swimming and boating. With cultural globalization, these pursuits have spread across the world, including Pacific Asia. Missionaries of the nineteenth century discovered the pleasures of Beidaihe; now China's governing elites savor it. Deng Xiaoping even directed that his ashes be scattered offshore there.

Ocean has also played a major role as arena, both active and passive: active as a place of struggle and combat, where navies fight and pirates prey on their victims, passive as moat and strategic buffer. The Taiwan Strait enabled the losing side in the Chinese Revolution to flee to a secure base and make a fresh start in 1949. Taiwan subsequently became rich, tapping a highly successful maritime economy. For the last five hundred years, but not before, the English Channel has served as a protective moat for Britain. It frustrated Napoleon and Hitler, cheating them both of ultimate triumph because they could not move their victorious armies over that watery space. More recently the memory of the great moat served as a psychological barrier to the digging of the "Chunnel."

As avenue the ocean has served as medium for the flow of goods, people, and ideas—until 150 years ago the only such avenue. Today information and people travel largely by means other than salt water, but at least 90 percent of world trade by volume is still borne by the ocean. Coal, wheat, running shoes, computer screens, automobiles, and much else all travel on the oceanic highway. But more than half of the total volume consists of oil.

People, both the highly privileged and the least fortunate, still sometimes travel by sea. Cruises are a high-growth industry. Illegal immigrants travel by sea, often as the final passage in their circuitous routes. The Vietnamese boat people found new importance in the China seas as an avenue for escape. Elsewhere in the world, the desperate are using the sea to flee oppression and poverty in their search for freedom and prosperity.

China's Maritime Past

The impetus to open up the sea routes and to sail the world ocean came in the 1400s from the Atlantic edge of western Europe, at the time the fringe of the fringe in terms of its overall place in global accomplishment. But it was the European genius to enter the unknown South Atlantic and to move beyond, to incorporate known sea regions and known sea routes into a new global network, and in that process to begin to explore and discover new regions and new routes, fusing them into a new global network. Atlantic Europe, using the gunned sailing ship as its instrument of power, rediscovered the New World and brought Pacific Asia into continuing contact with a global community.

The initiative could have sprung out of maritime East Asia; the means were there, but not the will. China has a vibrant if often overlooked maritime history. But oceanic experience was not part of the formative rhythms of the many early centuries that cut the templates of Chinese civilization. Nor was it part of the traditions of the rest of Pacific Asia.

Northern China was a major core of civilization from earliest times. But Chinese historical geography slowly propelled the culture in a southerly direction, with an ultimate shift of the national center of gravity from the Yellow River valley to the Yangzi and farther south. Although the center of politics would largely remain in the north, the economic heart moved to the south, reflecting the suitability of climate and terrain to the growing of rice, a richer caloric crop than the wheat and millet staples of the dry and cool plains of north China.

As long as that great plain and the Yellow River basin remained the key center of power, culture, and wealth—until 900 CE or so—China's focus was riverine, like that of ancient Egypt or Mesopotamia. But, unlike the Nile, the Yellow River was almost useless for navigation because of its heavy load of silt; its fluctuating water levels; and its large, swampy, and shifting estuary. The river lured no one down to the sea.

All along the northern China coast, furthermore, from just below the Shandong peninsula down to the mouth of the Yangzi River, no harbors punctuate the coastline. Even the navigable Yangzi does not thrust voyagers out to sea. Not until the mid-nineteenth century and the stimulus of European presence did Shanghai emerge as a great international seaport.

No major seaport cities would emerge on the Chinese coast to challenge the cultural and political authority of the traditional capitals until modern times. Earlier, the only possible such contender was Guangzhou (Canton), and that was simply too remote from the nation's political heartland to exercise any kind of threat to the existing order.

China lacks an enclosed sea, a Mediterranean or a Baltic, in which seamen might have safely practiced the arts of salt-water sailing. The East China Sea is temperate and was generally kind to sailing ships, except perhaps during typhoon season, but the Taiwan Strait is known to be one of the most dangerous stretches of water in the world. The island of Taiwan, slow to become part of mainstream Chinese culture, has a long coastline, but the coast is characterized by treacherous shoals and has few safe anchorages.

The pattern of winds and currents discouraged Chinese navigators from venturing very far eastward out into the Pacific. Like other mariners operating under sail, the Chinese at once feared the wind and dreaded the lack of it. Typhoons raged from June to November. But one sailor recalled being "becalmed in the ocean for seventeen days and the ship did not move a foot or an inch; the water was smooth as a mirror."

Nearby landmasses do not shelter the China seas from the open Pacific. China's oceanic neighbors, like Japan or the Philippines, are archipelagic. China also lacked nearby overseas trading partners. The nearest Japanese ports were more than five hundred miles away; Luzon was equally remote and, like nearby Taiwan, remained undeveloped.

The peasant farmer spearheaded Chinese expansion. He looked for new lands to cultivate in China's slow, steady southward march into the Yangzi valley and beyond. The push of nomad pressure on the northern and northwestern frontiers and the pull of opportunity offered by the fertile, amply watered, undeveloped, and underpopulated lands of the south combined, motivating the farmer to move in that direction.

The incorporation of southern territories expanded the range of crops for the Chinese farmer. Rice, demanding much water, could supplement the millet and wheat of the north China plains. Silk, reliant upon mulberry leaf to feed the silkworm; tea, grown on sunny hillsides; and porcelain, fired from the rich clays of the south, furnished valuable products for home consumption as well as for export.

Moreover, north China produced no export goods like tea, silk, or porcelain, those luxuries that would come to be so identified with China and so coveted by foreigners. These would be primarily of south Chinese origin and would become important as the south became an integral part of the Chinese world.

An enlarged China enjoyed a variety of topography, climates, and soils that made possible a wide range of products and relative economic self-sufficiency.

China thus stood in sharp contrast to Atlantic Europe. The southward shift of the Chinese state's economic center of gravity would add a new oceanic dimension to the Chinese experience. Thus a "blue," salt-water China of the south could emerge alongside the "yellow," earthbound China of the north.

"In the north go by horse, in the south go by boat," runs the old Chinese proverb. South China has no great coastal plain analogous to that of the north. But many lakes and streams, the aquatic environment of much of southeast China, made it relatively easy to dig canals and to fuse the natural with the man-made into what became, in all likelihood, the premodern world's most extensive water-based system for moving goods. Since land transport of bulk items at any distance was prohibitively expensive, this waterway system conferred enormous economic advantages. Cheap transport thus became the engine for premodern China's great leap into global economic primacy.

The jagged southeastern coast, with its many inlets and harbors shut off from large mainland spaces, encouraged the evolution of many dialects and distinctive cuisines. Local people looked to the sea. Fishing, trade, and piracy all flourished in their outward surge. Fishermen and merchants and their families would sometimes live out their lives in coastal waters. As the poet Po Chu-I wrote of a salt merchant's wife, "wind and waves are her village, her ship her mansion."

Thousands of ships carried grain up the coast to feed the hungry north, venturing out into open sea, but whenever possible hugging the coastline to take advantage of comfortably predictable currents, as well as seasonal winds that blew southward in the winter before reversing in the summer. The ease of sailing with the wind on these north–south voyages may have ultimately been corrupting, encouraging Chinese mariners to confine themselves to monsoonal seas rather than braving adverse weather.

The typical ship was the junk, a sturdy craft that was the product of centuries of continuous improvement. Shipwrights would use nails to hammer the planks together, varnishing the timbers with water-resistant tung oil and partitioning the interior spaces with watertight bulkheads, improving a damaged vessel's chances of survival. Fishermen first devised these compartments in order to flood part of their ship's hold and thus get their catch live to the market. These ships, their sails raised and lowered by pulley and slatted like Venetian blinds with bamboo battens, boasted sternpost rudders, sounding leads, and star charts as standard equipment. Chinese mariners began to use the magnetic compass a century before Europeans did.

Joseph Needham has pointed out the curious fact that whereas Europeans built their ships in the shape of a fish, bulging out from the bow and tapering to the stern, the Chinese built theirs in the shape of a water bird, swelling aft with the mass of the structure at the stern. Like today's giant oil tankers, the superstructure rose far aft, well abaft any masts, leaving ample space for cargo.

Seagoing ships were faster than those coursing inland waterways, but they required much larger crews for the amount of cargo carried than did river craft, and, for all their seaworthiness, they probably suffered many a disaster from the vagaries of wind and wave. Here lay the incentive to find a sheltered route.

Furthermore, the sea lay beyond the reach of the official's grasping hand and was open to private entrepreneurship. The government bureaucracy preferred to see inland waterways used. These they could control, and from them they could illegally squeeze personal profit. Chinese officials were modestly paid but expected to become rich in office. The bribes or "fees" they customarily exacted from the long-suffering populace were traditionally described as being "as numerous as the hairs on the hide of an ox." The complex canal system with its many fees could sustain a large bureaucracy; ocean transport did not.

The Grand Canal ran for more than a thousand miles from south to north, connecting the two great river valleys, Yellow and Yangzi, and linking Beijing with the south. It thus fed the capital district from the centers of greatest food production while avoiding the disadvantages, both perceived and real, of shipment on the open sea. Sometimes human feet moved treadmills turning paddle wheels, but the Chinese never used large numbers of oarsmen; nothing like the Mediterranean galley operated in Chinese waters. Poling, or propelling long heavy oars with a fishtailing motion, boatmen scraped the sandy shallows of the Grand Canal, moving at a maximum speed of two miles per hour but making steady progress. Traffic had to be seasonal, avoiding both the low water and ice of winter and the monsoon floods of summer.

Year round the Yangzi pulsated with east–west boat traffic, even through the gorges. There gangs of sweating trackers pulled bamboo hawsers attached to boats laboring upstream against some of the world's stiffest currents. With painful slowness the men moved along a narrow path carved out of the cliff face, with live rock to one side and death on the other.

Sino-Japanese Clashes

At the turn of the first millennium, the northern capital fell to the nomads following one of their frequently successful invasions of China. In 1135, accordingly, the Chinese established a new capital at Hangzhou, on the coast to the south of the Yangzi mouth. This was the first (and only) seaport to serve as the imperial capital. But it could play the imperial role for only 150 years before the Mongol conquest of all of China. The temporary political shift prompted by the move to Hangzhou did not form new values; it created no new set of attitudes about the ocean.

Foreign hands and foreign ships—Muslims, Arabs, Persians, and Gujerati from northwest India—conducted much of China's overseas trade at the time. The government tried to limit trade to certain ports so it could be more easily

supervised and taxed. By choice of China's rulers, foreign merchants lived under
their own laws, but they sometimes took Chinese wives and adapted to Chinese
ways. It seems that China influenced the foreigner more than the foreigner influenced China.

The Mongols who built a huge though ephemeral Eurasian state in the
thirteenth century—the largest empire ever conquered by men on horseback—
were the first outsiders to take control of all of China, and even they were able
to stay in power for only eighty-seven years. The Mongols moved the capital of
their Chinese realm back to the inland north, close to their own homeland.
But their continental and nomadic origins put them in touch with diverse groups
of peoples, and they had a broader worldview than the Chinese. By incorporating
the Chinese into their world empire, the Mongols enriched Chinese cultural and
economic contacts across Eurasia.

The Mongols attempted to establish a maritime state alongside their continental one by mounting far-flung, ill-fated overseas expeditions to occupy Japan
and Java. After six attempts, the Mongols finally brought Korea to heel (1231–
58). The Mongol next dispatched an envoy to Japan with a letter from the Great
Khan announcing that "we have become masters of the universe," and that the
Koreans "came to us to become our subjects; their joy resembles that of children
with their father." The implication was of course that the Japanese should also
join the happy family.

Khubilai, the Mongol emperor of China, found the Japanese intolerably
impudent for refusing to reply officially. His response was to send a small army
to invade Japan. Khubilai chose Kyushu, close to the Asian mainland and Korea
but far from Japanese centers of power, as his target. The Mongols co-opted the
Koreans to supply ships and seamen for the enterprise. Like the later nomadic
people, the Turks, the Mongols were conspicuous for their readiness to take to
sea by exploiting the talents of others. They themselves did not build and sail
the ships they used as ferries for their warriors.

The first of two Mongol expeditions against Japan in 1274 employed a fleet of
about eight hundred ships, many of them small. The fleet carried about forty
thousand troops and sailors in total. They landed successfully in Hakata Bay,
where they greatly outnumbered the Japanese defenders. The Mongols deployed
an array of weapons, including crossbows and catapults; the Japanese had never
before seen the like of some of their arms, such as poisoned arrows. How the
battle might have gone, we do not know, because the weather began to turn foul.
On the advice of their Korean pilots, the Mongols withdrew to their ships and
prepared to sail away. But they had waited too long. A great storm ravaged the
fleet; one-third of those who had joined the expedition died, many by drowning.

The Mongols resolved to try again, this time with a much bigger, two-pronged
effort. One thrust was to come from Korea, the second from Fujian province,
using Chinese ships and seamen from newly conquered southeast China.

The first squadron was about the size of the entire earlier expedition. The second was even more immense, with 100,000 troops on board, dwarfing any European naval operation for centuries to come. But Mongol success ultimately proved to be only in the logistics of the operation.

The invaders fought on shore for two months, but most of the Chinese soldiers were not Mongols and had little appetite for the struggle, whereas the Japanese were fighting for their own land. Storms again—the divine wind, or *kamikaze,* as the Japanese called it, thinking the gods were responsible—smashed both of these squadrons, destroying much of the fleet and stranding many troops on shore where they were abandoned to the mercies of the defenders. The remaining ships sailed home. Nonetheless, the Japanese could not feel entirely secure. The threat lingered, but Khubilai, preoccupied with other matters, spared Japan.

Another large Mongol expedition, this one directed southward against Java, also failed. The Mongols' willingness to venture out to sea in a serious way at least opened the eyes of Chinese, Koreans, and Japanese to a new dimension of power projection. Three centuries later the Japanese would invade the Asian continent, as they had not for a millennium—giving Yi Sun-sin his moment in history. But long before that, pirates began to turn the brown waters of Pacific Asia into an arena for combat.

Piracy in East Asia

Low-level maritime violence became a common, persistent phenomenon in brown-water East Asia. Using the sea as a springboard, pirates not only harassed the coasts but also fought on land in China and Korea. They even built bases and lay siege to towns, taking ruthless advantage of any local weakness. Pirates pillaged even on the outskirts of Kaesong, the inland Korean capital.

Smuggling and piracy erupted from a desire to break the trade-inhibiting confinements of an official order that frowned on commerce. This gave rise to an international maritime culture in which Chinese, Korean, and Japanese seafarers enthusiastically took part. Pirates became a prime fact of Pacific Asian oceanic life for centuries, a plague in the eyes of the establishment.

Pirates are like nomads; they leave few written records, and so we know little about them. Their history must be pieced together from outside, usually hostile sources. We do know that piratical activity was sporadic and intermittent, but also widespread and continuing. Sometimes pirates began as smugglers. Often they began as fishermen; catching ships was not a big step from catching fish.

Piracy provided a professional opportunity for aggressive individuals of extraordinary talent, but it did not result in the creation and coalescence of independent political entities like, say, the city-states of the Mediterranean world. Pirate bands did not aggregate into something larger. Heavily dependent upon personalities and charismatic leadership, they did not emerge as a sustained, major political force.

The maritime community did not directly challenge official orthodoxies, either in China or elsewhere in northeast Asia. Maritime China could go its own way only at those times when the imperial regime faltered. Pirates, and merchants too, for that matter, never developed a political alternative or indeed any distinctive way of thinking. They were looking for profits, not for political advantage. They attacked any potential victim, of any nationality. These people were pushing no cause except their own enrichment, and China provided the most attractive target.

For a state like China whose governmental institutions were justified by preserving stability and nourishing agriculture, combating the violence and commercial culture that piracy represents became a shibboleth. The public ideology, Confucianism, distrusted, even condemned, the profit motive behind trade, and promoted antipathy toward foreigners. Because foreigners like Japanese and Koreans were often among those participating in piracy, this provided another reason for Chinese xenophobia.

Japanese provided the cutting edge for these warrior bands, the weaponry and the fighting skills to form and galvanize their internal teamwork. Japan, its leadership constantly at war, was for centuries a disunited state. Its southern island of Kyushu, closest to the Asian mainland, lacked strong political authority. Essentially no one was there to assert law and order. After 1350 or so, Japanese pirates found ideal sanctuaries along the island-dotted coasts of Kyushu. From these they could sally forth to attack the nearby shores of Korea or even sail over to China, scuttling back to their home nests whenever they wished.

Eventually pirates, increasingly ethnic Chinese, focused their attention on China, ranging along the coast to the Yangzi delta and beyond. Even far south Guangdong felt their scourge. Sometimes these Chinese passed themselves off as Japanese, who were perceived as particularly ferocious, evoking special terror. What were the pirates after? Anything portable of value, it seemed. They especially prized silk, either raw or woven, but they would also seize mundane items like iron chains and kettles or copper cash. Japan produced not only raw materials such as copper, lead, and sulfur but also folding paper fans, a low-tech Japanese invention for which there was high demand in China. Japanese consumers were eager to acquire Chinese antiques and works of art, notably paintings, porcelains, calligraphy, and Buddhist texts. So these too could find a ready market, and for pirates everything sold at a 100 percent profit.

Ming Sea Power

By the first half of the fifteenth century, when the native Ming dynasty had established itself after tossing out the Mongols, China could have called itself the world's greatest power at sea. This primacy was the fruit of centuries of experience in maritime trade. At the same time the Portuguese were tentatively reaching out along the Moroccan coast and expanding their geographical knowledge of the Atlantic, the Chinese took a new tack, urged on by the vigorous and ambitious Yong Le emperor. From 1403 to 1433, the Ming demonstrated their salt-water power by sending seven interoceanic expeditions, encompassing hundreds of ships, across the Indian Ocean. Chinese vessels ranged south to Zanzibar, north to Ormuz, and west to Jiddah, the port of Mecca, crossing the "savage waves as if. . . treading a public thoroughfare." The scope of the voyages testifies to the quality of the Ming ships, the seamen who sailed them, and the navigational tools they used.

We have little hard information about their commander Zheng He, a high eunuch official, and what we read about his life is more often eulogistic than biographical. Despite his emasculation, he was reportedly a physically imposing man of exceptionally large girth and stature. Eunuchs usually had disagreeably shrill voices; his was described as pleasingly penetrating in tone, "bell-like" in its clarity. He was apparently a popular commander.

Castrated as a child prisoner of war, Zheng He built a highly successful career as a soldier, making a reputation for bravery and loyalty while fighting the Mongols and catching the eye and winning the friendship of a prince who would become emperor. Zheng He's organizational skills, on display as he supervised the construction and maintenance of imperial palaces—earning himself the high eunuch rank of Grand Director—were probably another reason the emperor selected him to command a fleet.

Ming novelist Luo Maodeng declares that Zheng He had been a frog in a previous incarnation. Perhaps this was one reason for his successful career leap from land to sea. But the leadership requirements and fighting skills needed for both domains were quite similar in those days. Yet despite his evident competence and adaptability, Zheng He was always at a disadvantage in the treacherous milieu of court politics. He was not only a eunuch, belonging to a group invariably despised by civil bureaucrats, but also a member of a minority ethnic group; a non-Han Chinese; a professional military man, not a scholar; and a Muslim. In the world of Chinese officialdom, Zheng He would always remain a consummate outsider.

His position was completely dependent upon the favor of his imperial master. As long as the occupant of the Dragon Throne favored costly maritime ventures, they could continue. But because they were both unusual and extravagant, they remained highly vulnerable to bureaucratic criticism and reliant upon the imperial whim.

We should think of Zheng He in action as a collector and recorder of information, more diplomat than explorer. He was not China's Vasco da Gama or Christopher Columbus, as some have suggested. After all, he and his fleets were not charting salt-water space unknown to Chinese mariners. These waters were well-traveled monsoonal pathways of trade with which the Chinese had long been familiar. China's maritime career had really commenced centuries earlier, when the Song dynasty moved south and the Chinese began to link themselves to the wider South China Sea trading world, which extended southward to Indonesia and westward into the Indian Ocean.

Zheng did not seek to conquer, colonize, or convert on behalf of his government. His was at least ostensibly a mission of persuasion, of demonstrating to the world the power and wealth of China and convincing it of China's moral authority. In a speech at Harvard in November 1997, President Jiang Zemin lauded Zheng He as a disseminator of Chinese culture abroad. This was consonant with the Confucian ideal, and casting Zheng He as a player of that irenic role is a way of looking at the past that many Chinese favor today.

But the reality is something else. China's near neighbors would certainly argue any assertion that the Chinese are a uniquely pacifistic people. The Yong Le emperor's maritime ambitions bear comparison with, for example, his expansive continental policies against Vietnam, where he waged a twenty-year war. Zheng He's policy was implicitly one of force. Beneath any moral gloss, his immensely powerful fleets formed what today would be called an oceanic strike force.

The Grand Director's ships were quite ready to shoot their fire weapons if ordered to do so. Their complement was made up overwhelmingly of fighting men, not merchants or priests. The number of military aboard, as Robert Finlay points out, was larger than the entire male population of almost all of the individual seaports the fleet would visit after leaving the Chinese coast. Zheng He's 28,000 men numbered more than the entire army of France at the time; his fleets were far more formidable than any of the Portuguese fleets that entered the same Indian Ocean waters a century later.

The objective of the enterprising, pugnacious emperor who caused the ships to be launched and ordered them to sail was to bring more nations into the tributary system, using the ocean to enlarge China's international sphere of influence—thus reinforcing what the Chinese perceived as a proper relationship between China and the inferior world outside.

The larger ships, called treasure ships, were built on the banks of a tributary of the Yangzi at the city of Nanjing, then the nation's capital. And they were monsters, probably the largest wooden ships ever built anywhere. They were not junks but flat-bottomed and of shallow draft. Edward Dreyer likens them to great barges. They had immense capacity, but they could not have been sufficiently seaworthy to weather the rough oceanic waters of large parts of the world ocean, such as the stormy North Atlantic from whence Europeans first came by sea to Pacific Asia.

The great Ming expeditions ended abruptly and without consequence and therefore may seem a magnificent failure. But they were not as isolated and exotic as it might seem. The ships were constructed and sailed with the benefit of generations of salt-water knowledge behind them. And, although the Chinese state abandoned the sea, the fleets may have opened the eyes of many individuals to new commercial possibilities.

Using fresh water—with lakes, rivers, and canals fused into a vast and efficient network for the cheap carriage of raw materials and goods—made south China the most productive part of the empire, helping make China a major node of global prosperity.

Although salt water became an avenue for a significant, fruitful commercial relationship with Southeast Asia, continental worries kept the government from fully realizing the nation's maritime capabilities. And the incursion of the Atlantic world in the nineteenth century brought further discouragement, posing a profound new oceanborne threat far more serious than any from pirates. The Atlantic world menaced not only the imperial regime but also the very bones of the culture. To contemporary Chinese, the ocean seemed to provide opportunity only for outsiders.

In the late twentieth century, the collapse of the Soviet Union enabled the Chinese to face in a different geographical direction for the first time in their history. Using salt water as the medium to build a flourishing economy based on manufacturing and overseas trade is now enabling hundreds of millions of Chinese to move from desperate poverty to decent prosperity. This surely is one of the great events of our time.

THE LAST DAYS OF THE ROYAL NAVY: LESSONS FROM BRITAIN'S STRATEGIC RETREAT FROM THE PACIFIC

Nicholas Evan Sarantakes

The purposes of this chapter are to examine how the United Kingdom of Great Britain and Northern Ireland responded to the strategic rise of Imperial Japan during the first half of the twentieth century, and to ask whether the United States can learn lessons from the experience of its English-speaking cousin as it deals with similar transitions in Asia in the twenty-first century. Although history never repeats itself, it presents a database for scholars and practitioners seeking instructive case studies. In this particular case, there are some parallels between the British position in Asia and the Pacific then and the situation confronting the United States in the early decades of this new century. These parallels warrant a venture in applied history—which is what this chapter aspires to be.

What are the similarities between the Asia-Pacific then and now? First, Britain in the 1910s and 1920s found itself embroiled in greater and greater disputes with its ally, Imperial Japan. In a similar vein, the United States, though never formally allied with the People's Republic of China, did cooperate with the Asian nation during the second half of the Cold War and now finds itself increasingly distant from the Chinese. Second, the United Kingdom, like the United States now, found itself dealing with this shift during a period when its navy was shrinking in size. Finally, both nations had taken on security obligations they lacked the resources to honor. The British were obliged to protect their colonies in Burma, Hong Kong, Malaysia, and the dominions of Australia and New Zealand. For its part, the United States has assumed responsibility for the defense of Taiwan and, to a lesser degree, South Korea.

The central argument set forth in this chapter is that despite British leaders' fairly reasoned and realistic assessment of international affairs in the Asia-Pacific

region, it was luck—or chance or contingency, to use the more academic terms—
that was the key determinant of the success of British strategy in the years following World War I. While the British ultimately decided that the merits of alliance
and friendship with the United States outweighed those with Imperial Japan,
matters almost took a far different course. And even then, the cost to British interests was high: the conflict that followed destroyed the empire and accelerated the
decline of Great Britain as a world power. As a result, the policies and strategies
British statesmen pursued during this era offer good examples of what not to do.

The British responded to Japan in two very different ways that mark two
distinct periods in Anglo-Japanese relations. First, the two countries were formal
allies during the early decades of the twentieth century. In 1902 the United
Kingdom signed a mutual security treaty with Japan. The two partners renewed
their pact in 1905, on the verge of the Russo-Japanese War, and then again in
1911. The alliance was an important achievement in the history of Japanese
foreign relations. Japan was the first Asian nation to sign a security agreement
on the basis of equality with a European power. The alliance ameliorated some
of the fears that had motivated the samurai who overthrew the Tokugawa
shoguns and drove the modernization efforts of the Meiji era. Many Japanese
leaders worried that Japan would suffer the same colonial degradation as India,
Burma, the islands of the Dutch East Indies, Malaysia, Vietnam, and, most of
all, China. A resolution issued by the Cabinet in 1908 attests to the importance
accorded the alliance in Tokyo: "The Anglo-Japanese alliance is the marrow of
Japan's foreign policy."[1]

This partnership was also important to the British, providing regional security
and stability on the cheap. In the first decade of the twentieth century, the British
and Japanese faced common threats from the French and Russian empires.
The alliance allowed the Royal Navy to withdraw from the region while the
IJN (Imperial Japanese Navy) served as a proxy, protecting British interests.
In 1911 the Committee of Imperial Defense asserted,

> So long as the Japanese alliance remains operative not only is the risk of attack by
> Japan excluded from the category of reasonable possibilities to be provided against,
> but British navy requirements are held to be adequately met if the combined British
> and Japanese forces in the Pacific are superior to the forces in those waters maintained
> by any reasonably probable combination of naval Powers.

The alliance became even more important to the United Kingdom as Germany
began to threaten British naval supremacy in Europe. The British could
concentrate on the threat in their home waters, worrying less about issues on the
periphery.[2]

World War I profoundly altered world affairs, testing the Anglo-Japanese partnership. The Japanese seemed ready for this challenge. In 1912, the Cabinet in
Tokyo approved a resolution that declared, "The alliance is the crux of

the Japanese government's foreign policy and is an object which it will always unflinchingly uphold."[3] Two years later, the British called on Japan to honor the alliance as they went to war with Germany. Japan did so, but a number of scholars argue that they did so in a grudging way that fostered more resentment than gratitude.[4] Timothy D. Saxon's recent multilingual, multinational research challenges this view, showing that Winston Churchill and the Admiralty never shared the views of Sir Edward Grey and the Foreign Office. "I think you are chilling indeed to these people. I can't see any half way house between having them in and keeping them out," Churchill told the foreign minister. "We are all in this together." He also pushed the idea of soliciting Japanese naval assistance: "The Japanese [Government] should be sounded as to their readiness to send a battle-squadron to co-operate with the allied powers in the [Mediterranean] or elsewhere. The influence & value of this powerful aid could not be over-rated." The press of war also convinced many skeptics within the Royal Navy of their ally's value.[5] In the end, though, the only two powers that emerged from the war stronger than they were when they entered were Japan and the United States.

Japan was at war with itself about how to respond to this changed international environment. Frederick R. Dickinson and J. Charles Schencking disagree on the nature of this internal conflict. Dickinson maintains that it was primarily a confrontation between political factions. Field Marshal Prince Yamagata Yoritomo, one of the last remaining samurai of Choshu who had helped overthrow the Tokugawa shoguns, led a group that wanted a Japan in which the nobility, the military, and senior bureaucrats made the decisions. To this end, he favored some type of orientation toward Germany, which was similar in its social structure. Foreign Minister Baron Katō Takaaki, the son of a former Tokugawa samurai, had a different vision. As the leader of a major political party, he wanted a Japan with a government responsive to the public, more along the lines of the U.K. government. For Dickinson, these disparate visions were the principal factor fueling Japanese foreign-policy debates.

Schencking, on the other hand, sees the conflict as an interservice confrontation between the army, with its strong continental focus, and the navy, which wanted institutional and budgetary resources that could only come at the expense of the army. Either way, the result was the same: Japan began pursuing foreign-policy objectives that conflicted with or even directly challenged established British economic interests.[6]

The end of World War I brought two overarching policies British diplomats had pursued over the past several decades into conflict with each other. The first was preserving the alliance with Japan in the Far East. The second was a policy the British had pursued since 1862, when they flirted briefly with intervention in the American Civil War: avoiding conflict with the Americans and perhaps reaching some type of accord, or even an alliance, with their English-speaking cousins.[7] The growth of Japanese and American power during the Great War, compounded by clashing interests in China in the interwar period, seemed to be bringing these two Pacific powers into direct conflict. Sooner or later, officials in Britain's Cabinet were going to have to decide between a nation that was their formal ally—a nation with which they shared a similar approach to world affairs, as well as a good working relationship—and a linguistic and culturally similar nation that wielded real economic power, but remained unpredictable and even, to some degree, hostile to the British Empire.[8]

The British government began debating the question of renewing the alliance with Japan. A Foreign Office memorandum on this topic accurately summarized the basic issue in Anglo-Japanese relations. "Generally speaking the interests of Great Britain and the United States of America in China are similar, whereas they are often in conflict with those of Japan, who in claiming a paramount position in the Far East and especially in China, antagonizes all other countries, including China."[9]

No two nations, even allies, have the exact same interests. London's problem was that Tokyo and Washington were pursuing interests at odds with each other. "Of paramount importance are our relations with the United States of America in the Far East, as elsewhere," the Foreign Office paper declared. "If we were able to count with certainty upon the active co-operation of the United States, the need for an alliance with Japan would not be apparent."[10]

Japan considered the United States the chief threat to its interests.

> From despatches which have reached this Office from Tokio, it appears that in Japanese Military circles at any rate the renewal of the Alliance is desired by Japan in order to have the support of Great Britain in the event of war with the United States. The Japanese Government must know that there could be no possible question of this, but it will have to be made quite clear if the Alliance is renewed.[11]

With those points made, there were clearly good political reasons to sustain the alliance. "In spite of many difficulties and dangers the alliance may be said on the whole to have worked well to the benefit of both parties." Japan had been a good ally up until now. "She kept her word to us faithfully." Anglo-Japanese partnership would protect the United Kingdom against some type of Russian-German rapprochement. Finally, it would give the British a certain amount of leverage over Japanese policy in China. "The existence of some form of agreement with Japan would on the other hand render it easier for His Majesty's Government to keep a watch on her movements in China, to demand of her in her dealings with us a greater measure of freedom and frankness than it would otherwise be possible to expect, and to exercise a moderating influence on her policy generally."[12]

One of the strongest proponents of this view was the foreign minister, Earl Curzon of Kedleston. He argued:

On the other hand, there was an Imperial aspect of the case, which Britain and the Dominions were bound to consider, in relation both to the peace of the Pacific and the future political stability of the Far East. The great majority of opinion certainly held to the view that even though the circumstances which called the agreement into being had ceased to exist, it had nevertheless justified itself, and exercised a tranquillising and pacifying influence in the Eastern world. Should the danger which it had been originally designed to meet, namely, that of an all-powerful Russia in the north and east of Asia, come again into being, and should this phenomenon be strengthened by a German alliance, it might well be that in some such agreement as that between Japan and Great Britain would be found the future salvation of the East.[13]

There were many who disagreed with this view. One of them was Winston S. Churchill. If the purpose of an alliance was for one ally to control the other, the "controlled" nation would be in position to make constant demands in return for proper behavior. The "controlling" nation would have little option but to comply. As Churchill put it, "Getting Japan to protect you against Japan is like drinking salt water to slake thirst." Japan specialists, even those in the Foreign Office, also disagreed with Lord Curzon. Ernest Miles Hobart Hampden had held diplomatic posts in both Yokohama and Tokyo in the 1910s and argued,

> For such an Entente there appears to exist a sufficient though hardly a super-abundant, community of interests, as well as a number of antagonisms calling for composition by agreement; but one ventures to think that no genuine alliance with Japan can in the future be founded upon a main desire on the British side to restrain the other party from a selfish policy in China and from undesirable attachments elsewhere.[14]

There were good military reasons to end the alliance. If the United Kingdom and Japan remained allies, argued Churchill, then "Every naval authority in the United States will press for a two-Power standard against Britain and Japan. It is this danger which I fear more than anything else. It is the most terrible danger, and it is the imminent danger from our point of view." Such a development had to be avoided. According to Churchill, "This would be a disaster of the first order to the world, and we must do everything in our power to avoid it."[15]

There were also good military reasons to keep the alliance. The agreement guaranteed the safety of British territory and interests in the Pacific region, including Australia, New Zealand, western Canada, Hong Kong, Burma, and ships of the British merchant marine operating in Pacific waters. The Royal Navy was also too weak to add the IJN to its list of possible future opponents. "Unless we have a very definite promise of American co-operation & support we cannot afford to leave Japan isolated & thus a potential enemy," declared H.G. Parlett of the Foreign Office in his minutes. The Lord Commissioners of the Admiralty agreed. "Without considerable increase in Naval expenditure, however, they do not see their way to maintain Forces sufficient to support a strong policy involving a possible coercion of Japan," reported one navy official.[16]

The British did explore the possibility of a tripartite treaty among Japan, the United States, and the United Kingdom. In June 1921, Sir Auckland Geddes, the British ambassador in Washington, met with Secretary of State Charles Evans Hughes. The British and American records of this meeting are quite similar. The main difference is a discrepancy over the date the conversation took place. Hughes also comes across as more evasive in the U.S. account than in the British account. He made it clear that the United States was concerned about a future in which Britain was associated with Japan; the American people would like to see the alliance terminated. Taking advantage of Hughes's disavowal of U.S. hostility toward Japan, Geddes proposed a three-way agreement. Hughes toyed with idea intellectually for a few minutes, but in both accounts he makes it clear there was no way that the Senate would ever consent to such a treaty.[17]

In 1921, the issue of naval disarmament became entangled in the complex issues associated with British relations with Japan vis-à-vis the United States. At the Washington Naval Arms Limitation Conference—a gathering hosted by the United States, largely in hopes of preventing an arms race among itself, Britain, and Japan—the British agreed to American proposals regulating the size and number of battleships. The agreement allowed the Royal Navy to maintain its dominant position on the high seas, while the British in return agreed to end their alliance with Japan. The Japanese understood the decision the British were making: naval arms control and avoiding conflict with the United States were more important in British eyes than the long-standing partnership with Japan. "We would only embarrass the British government if we insisted on the alliance being continued. It would be useless and senseless for us to try," observed Shidehara Kijūrō, a member of the Japanese delegation, with palpable resignation. Reflected Itō Masanori, a reporter covering the conference for the *Jiji Shimpō* newspaper,

> It was a forlorn funeral. It was as if only a few members of the wake followed the coffin, with three or four lanterns dimly lit, treading a narrow county lane on a lone winter night. A strong and healthy evergreen tree, which had symbolized peace in the orient for over twenty years, had been felled, crumbling without any resistance when swept by a cold blast of wind.[18]

The Washington Conference reestablished British naval power in the Pacific for awhile, and despite the end of the alliance, the United Kingdom and Imperial Japan maintained cordial relations for the rest of the decade. Even before the formal end of the alliance in 1923, however, Royal Navy planners started treating Japan as the prime enemy they were likely to face in the near future. There were few other contenders. The Imperial German Navy was resting in Scottish waters, at the bottom of Scapa Flow. The Hapsburg Empire was gone, as was its fleet in the Mediterranean. The French and Italian sea services were small and posed no threat worthy of the Royal Navy. The United Kingdom would never go to war with the United States, so planning against the U.S. Navy was unnecessary. The only remaining possible naval threat was Japan.

Bureaucratic self-interest thus played a small role in ending the alliance, but what is more important is how plans shaped British strategy during the interwar period. With little strategic input from the Cabinet, the navy developed plans to maintain a large battle fleet, centered around battleships and cruisers, that would steam to Singapore in the event of war. To allow the city to hold out until the fleet arrived, the British would build a naval fortress able to withstand bombardment by Japan's Combined Fleet until His Majesty's ships arrived and vanquished their one-time protégés in a fleet action.[19] According to War Memorandum (Eastern):

> If Singapore were lost the Fleet would be immobilized for want of fuel and would be incapable of relieving the pressure on Hong Kong in time to save it for also falling into the hands of the Japanese. . . . With Singapore in our possession the situation could be retrieved even if Hong Kong had fallen. . . . *The safety of Singapore must be the keynote of British strategy.*[20]

There were a number of problems with this strategy. The first and most obvious is that it was less a strategy than a battle plan. Would the fleet action actually defeat Japan, or would another effort like a blockade or a submarine attack on merchant shipping be necessary? What if Japan went to war with the United Kingdom as part of a coalition? What if the Royal Navy was otherwise engaged and was unable to send its battle fleet to the Far East?[21]

The navy and its strategy encountered many critics in London. One of the biggest was Churchill. As chancellor of the Exchequer during the 1920s, it was his job to deal limit government spending, keeping it in line with tax revenue. The Admiralty was the biggest-spending government department, and Churchill used his experience as a former first lord of the Admiralty to his advantage. He thought planning officers were exaggerating the Japanese threat. "It seems to me that the Admiralty imagine themselves confronted with the same sort of situation in regard to Japan as we faced against Germany in the ten years before the war. They have a wonderful staff of keen, able officers, whose minds are filled with war impressions," he observed. "What question is pending between England and Japan? To what diplomatic combination do either of us belong which could involve us against each other? There is absolutely no resemblance between our relations with Japan and those we had with Germany before the war."[22]

In fact, Churchill dismissed the chances of war with the Japanese altogether. "I do not believe there is the slightest chance of it in our lifetime. The Japanese are our allies." Even if that were not the case—which by this time it was not—Churchill pointed out that Japan was no Germany. "Japan is at the other end of the world. She cannot menace our vital security in any way."[23] But he understood the bureaucratic reasons why the navy was putting forward these arguments.

The Admiralty seems to be misconceiving the problem which is before them. That problem is to keep a Navy in being which over a long period of profound peace will, taken as a whole, not be inferior to the Navy either of the United States or of Japan. But this does not imply the immediate development of the means on the part of the British Navy to dominate either of these two Powers in their own quarter of the globe.[24]

These arguments were extremely effective. Admiral of the Fleet Earl Beatty, Churchill's former secretary, told his wife, "That extraordinary fellow Winston has gone mad. Economically mad."[25]

Churchill might have made his criticisms for economic and political reasons, but he offered them at the level of foreign policy and grand strategy. The navy also had its own internal critics of its plans for the Far East. In 1924, Vice Admiral Herbert Richmond, commander in chief of the East Indies Squadron, criticized British plans for war with Japan at the strategic and operational level. "It is better frankly to acknowledge our inability," he proclaimed, "than to live in a fool's paradise." Richmond's comments were directed at his colleagues who had developed a strategy that ignored reality. This trend nonetheless became even more pronounced in the 1930s as it became more difficult for the British to meet their foreign-policy obligations. The political will to raise taxes was absent, and the economic strength required to maintain a stronger fleet was weak. "Is it not time that the National Government took the question of the defence of Singapore more seriously?" demanded Sir Maurice Hankey, secretary of the Committee for Imperial Defence, of Prime Minister Ramsay MacDonald.[26]

Another problem was that the fortress at Singapore turned out to be a hollow shell. The armed services were confused about how best to protect the facility. The Royal Air Force and the Royal Navy engaged in a bitter feud about which would be best, fighter aircraft or naval guns, in holding off the Combined Fleet. The British also lacked the political resolve to build the base. Funding was never adequate. At the end of the 1920s, in fact, the dominions and colonies had contributed more to its construction than had the United Kingdom. The Labour government that came to power in London in 1929 decided to cancel the construction of this naval base. As a practical matter, this decision had little long-term impact. Contracts with construction firms for the dockyards had to be honored, and planning work went forward.

Other features like defensive fortifications, however, were not built. With the "ten-year rule" in place—in essence a declaration that great-power war was so unthinkable over the coming decade that the United Kingdom could afford a strategic pause—there seemed little need to pursue such efforts in strenuous fashion. Real work on the base started only after the Manchurian incident of 1931 and the Shanghai incident of 1932. The British Chiefs of Staff Committee assigned a subcommittee of deputies to study the situation in the Far East. The deputies' conclusions were rather pessimistic. They reported that "our present political difficulties in dealing with the Sino-Japanese problem at the present junction arise very largely from the insecurity of our naval bases at Hong Kong and Singapore." The main problem was that the Great Depression had made it impossible for the United Kingdom to maintain enough force strength to defend the base.[27]

The instability following the end of the Anglo-Japanese alliance created other problems for the British. In 1933, the naval attaché at the British Embassy in Tokyo declared, "Our Intelligence Service has found it increasingly difficult to get information concerning their Armed services. Our Confidential Book on Japan is some thirty years out of date. We know little about their warships—they could build a new battleship or aircraft carrier without our knowing."[28]

In Hankey's view, the British government was beginning to reap what it had sowed.

> The real fact to be faced is that over a period of years all the Defence services have been starved; that they have had to sacrifice bit by bit their ability to fulfil their defensive obligations. They can stage Navy Weeks, Tattoos and Air Displays, but cannot sustain a major war. We have but a façade of Imperial Defense. The whole structure is unsound, and repairs on whatever scale we can afford must include the foundations of the Navy, on which the whole Empire depends.[29]

It was quite common in the 1930s for members of the Cabinet to bemoan the loss of the alliance. Sir Warren Fisher, the head of the Civil Service, offered the most realistic view of Anglo-American relations: "We cannot overstate the importance we attach to getting back, not to alliance (since that would not be practical politics) but at least to our terms of cordiality and mutual respect with Japan." His reasons were simple. "The very last thing in the world we can count on is American support."[30]

Foreign Minister Sir John Simon took a different view of the matter. "We are incapable of checking Japan in any way," he observed, "if she really means business and has sized us up, as she certainly has done. Therefore we must eventually be done for in the Far East, unless the United States are eventually prepared to use force." But Simon was skeptical in this regard. "The Japanese are more afraid of the U.S. than of us, and for obvious reasons. At present, however, they share our low view of American fighting spirit. By ourselves we must eventually swallow any & every humiliation in the Far East. If there is some limit to American submissiveness, this is not necessarily so."[31]

Events throughout the 1930s would only prove Sir Warren and Sir John correct in their views of the United States and of British power in the Pacific. The Royal Navy was losing its advantages in both quality and quantity.[32]

In 1935, domestic electoral politics derailed efforts undertaken in Parliament to authorize rearmament. Then the abdication crisis surrounding King Edward VIII drowned it out altogether in 1936. This incident arose when the king informed Prime Minister Stanley Baldwin that he intended to marry

Wallis Simpson, an American divorcee, after her second marriage ended. Baldwin and the Cabinet refused to assent to the match, as British law and constitutional procedures required. They told Edward either to resign the throne or to give up Simpson. The king decided to abdicate.

Winston Churchill tried to develop a scenario that would give the monarch time to reconsider his decision in the hope that he would give up the American. He was deeply troubled at the constitutional ramifications of a Cabinet forcing a monarch off the throne. This issue might have been nothing but froth on the waves of substance were it not for the fact that many thought the unpredictable Churchill was trying to use the crisis as a way of bringing down Baldwin's Cabinet, perhaps creating a King's Party in opposition to the prime minister that would have eliminated the political neutrality of the monarchy. One of Churchill's publishing associates demanded to know of him: "How can you suggest that the present state of things should be prolonged for five months— five months of raging & tearing controversy, quite possibly a King's party being formed against the Government, the Crown a centre of schism tearing Country and Commonwealth to pieces & all this at this moment in world affairs?"[33]

In 1937, with the start of the Sino-Japanese War, Prime Minister Neville Chamberlain admitted that his government "could not put forceful pressure on the Japanese without [the] co-operation of the United States." He had his doubts about the administration of Franklin D. Roosevelt. "The power that [has] the greatest strength [is] America, but he would be a rash man who based his calculations on help from that quarter." With isolationist sentiment quite strong, the options of American officials were limited. Although bitter, Chamberlain's famous observation had a good deal of substance: "It is always best and safest to count on nothing from the Americans but words."[34]

British colonies in Asia and the Pacific were vulnerable—a fact of which British officials were well aware. Admiral Ernle Chatfield, the first sea lord, bluntly informed Sir Thomas Inskip, the minister for coordination of defence: "Imperially we are exceedingly weak. If at the present time, and for many years to come, we had to send a Fleet to the Far East, even in conjunction with the United States, we should be left so weak in Europe that we should be liable to blackmail or worse."[35] Chatfield's view was not an isolated one on the Chiefs of Staff Committee. The Joint Planning Committee warned that a war with Japan would never be a one-on-one contest. Many people in different regions harbored grievances against the British and could be counted on to take advantage of British problems. "This country is never likely to be faced by a situation in which our plans for a war in the Far East can be framed without reference to consequent risks in other areas."[36]

As the 1930s progressed, then, the two major threats to British interests were Japan and Germany. In 1935, the Defence Requirements Committee, a body chaired by Hankey which included the chiefs of staff and a representative of the Treasury, reported,

> We consider it to be a cardinal requirement of our national and Imperial security that our Foreign Policy should be so conducted as to avoid the possible development of a situation in which we might be confronted simultaneously with the hostility, open or veiled, of Japan in the Far East, Germany in the West and any power on the main line of communication between the two.

In that last category were individual nations in the Middle East intent on eliminating British dominance, as well as the Indian National Congress, which was pursuing independence for India. These parties would not make common cause with the Germans or the Japanese; they would simply try to manipulate the larger confrontation to their advantage.[37]

The naval predicament was particularly acute. In a letter to Admiral Sir Dudley Pound, the commander in chief of the Mediterranean Fleet, Chatfield discussed the problems the Royal Navy faced:

> The whole situation as regards the Fleet going East is at present very uncertain; naturally I am averse to sending it if it can be avoided but I am making all preparations as far as I can. Neither am I forgetting the difficult questions of maintenance, ammunition etc. Obviously the fleet that you will have to take out is not very satisfactory, but if it did go out I think we should be certain to have the American Fleet as well and that will make a great difference.

While the Americans were sympathetic and might make good allies, this development was uncertain at best: "All talk, however, of any action by the US is taboo and highly secret, but we won't mention it to anybody else. Anyhow one can never be sure what they will do so we cannot rely on them absolutely."[38]

Starting in the late 1930s, American officials came to see the importance of helping the United Kingdom defend its colonial possessions in the region. By 1941, this conviction was firmly in place within the executive branch of the U.S. government, as well as the armed services. The problem was that such a view would hardly play well in public with the children of the American Revolution. Whether the United States could have gone to war in 1941 or 1942 primarily to protect British colonies is a question that is unanswerable.[39]

The person who had to handle the Japan issue was Winston Churchill. Churchill had always been fairly consistent in his views toward Japan. While he did not want to preserve the Anglo-Japanese alliance if it threatened to pull the United Kingdom into a war with the United States, he had recommended continuing it in some modified form. He also had no problem with Japanese military action in China and Manchuria. Appearing at the Conservative Association at Oxford University in 1934, he was asked whether "Japanese foreign policy threatens the security of our Empire." Churchill explained, according to notes taken by one of the students, "Japan doing in China what England did years ago in India. Manchuko a good thing."

As first lord of the Admiralty during the early days of World War II, Churchill continued to deprecate the likelihood of war between Japan and the United Kingdom. He refused to believe that Japan would embark on such a "mad enterprise." Yes, Britain was relatively weak in the Pacific vis-à-vis Japan, but the distance between Singapore and Japan was equal to that between Southampton and New York. He told the War Cabinet, "Although it is not at present within our power to place a superior battle fleet in the Home waters of Japan, it would be possible, if it were necessary, to place a squadron of battleships in the Far East sufficient to act as a major deterrent on Japanese action so far from home." If the Japanese started a war with Britain, about all they could do was "insult Australian or New Zealand shores."

There was a good deal of truth to these views, but they overlooked the danger to British territories closer to Japan, namely Hong Kong, Malaysia, and Burma. More to the point, Churchill doubted the Americans would just sit and watch the Japanese advance. "It seems very unlikely that the United States would impassively watch the acquisition by Japan of Naval bases west and southwest of the Philippines. Such an act of Japanese aggression would seriously compromise the whole American position in the Pacific." In his public statements, however, he was careful about what he said about Japan: "We have no quarrel with the Italian or Japanese people."[40]

President Franklin D. Roosevelt helped when he told Churchill he would issue a warning to Japan that Washington would regard an attack on British territory as an action hostile to the interests of the United States. "This is an immense relief, as I had long dreaded being at war with Japan without or before [the] United States. Now I think it is all right," he informed one of his generals on December 7, 1941. Yet that same day, the U.S. ambassador to the Court of St. James, John G. Winant, reminded him that only Congress could declare war.[41]

Japan solved this issue by attacking U.S. and British bases. In 1936, the authors of "The Defense Policy of the Japanese Empire" had added the United Kingdom to Japan's list of future potential enemies. There was a good deal of debate in Tokyo in 1940–41 about the strategic connection between the United States and Great Britain. Shigemitsu Mamoru, the ambassador in London, argued, "The policies of Britain and the US are not joint but parallel. So far these parallel policies have not necessarily been in accord in aim or conduct." Planning officers in the IJN pushed the view, which eventually won out, that the United States would come to the aid of the British if the Japanese attacked Malaysia or Hong Kong.[42] Perhaps this would have occurred, but it is at least debatable.

What is clear is that, unlike his predecessors, Prime Minister Winston Churchill got lucky. After the British ended the Anglo-Japanese alliance, they never had the resources in the Pacific to deal with their former ally as a potential foe, and they never managed to acquire the United States as a partner until the actual outbreak of war in the region. This luck also had its limits. The Japanese victories of 1941 and 1942 brought down the British Empire, while the ultimate victory of the Allies in 1945 did little to repair the damage.

What does this account tell us? For one thing, no two historical situations are ever the same. History does not repeat itself exactly, but this work of applied history shows that there are some broad lessons to be learned from the British experience. Specifically,

- *Know yourself, know your enemy, know your allies.* None of the decisions made by British leaders were stupid or unwise. Many of them made sense at the time. Yet these leaders all failed to respond to the major shift in the balance of power that took place in Asia after World War I. Japan had grown stronger, the United Kingdom weaker. The United States had grown stronger too, but it was, as Britons noted, an uncertain ally.

- *A strategy should be a strategy.* The plans the Royal Navy developed in the interwar period were operational plans premised on moving the fleet from one point to another and doing battle. There was never any serious examination of how to defeat Japan. Nor were these plans tied to policy. Churchill was right that no dispute between Japan and the United Kingdom was pressing enough to warrant conflict.

- *Avoid making enemies needlessly.* The Royal Navy developed battle plans against the IJN in large part because it was the only available opponent. The Foreign Office tended to avoid policies that conflicted with those of Japan, but British leaders were ultimately unable or unwilling to give up British interests in China. This finally brought about conflict between the two island nations. In both cases, the British helped turn the Japanese into their enemy.

- *Avoid denial.* Groupthink can be deadly. Astute leaders appraise the international and strategic situations honestly and develop plans to deploy available resources. Misperceptions about the world can be extremely difficult to recover from, and policies and strategies based on them will be counterproductive. Such was the case for the British at both levels.

- *Dissenters are good.* Richmond pointed out flaws in British strategic planning. Having internal critics is a good way of avoiding a pack mentality—if these critics' complaints and objections are listened to and responded to in honest fashion. The problem for Great Britain was that dissenting views never got full consideration from planners in the Admiralty.

- *Alliances are a means to an end rather than a goal in and of themselves.* Most coalitions are developed to respond to specific needs and interests. These partnerships can survive and even endure, but they must be adjusted as international affairs change. It is ironic that the British got this right but were unable to replace their alliance with Japan with an alliance with the United States, and eventually had to depend on luck to bring about an Anglo-American pact.

- *Luck cuts both ways.* Japan was a wonderful enemy for the British in the sense that it unified the United Kingdom and the United States, resolving the British strategic dilemma. In this case, contingency worked in favor of the British, but at the cost of their empire, which was not so lucky after all.

Finally, it is worth noting that the inability of the British to avoid war with Japan in no way guarantees that the United States will face a conflict in the Asia-Pacific. There is a saying that an intelligent man learns from his mistakes and a wise man learns from those of others. Let us hope that today's American officials are wise men—and that they learn from past mistakes on the part of their British cousins.

CHAPTER 4

CLIPPER SHIPS TO CARRIERS:
U.S. MARITIME STRATEGY IN ASIA

Bernard D. Cole

The United States enters the twenty-first century with the strongest navy in the world, one at least equal in global dominance to that deployed by Great Britain in 1815, at the time of the final defeat of Napoleonic France. While the current American naval dominance is global in capability, like that of its British predecessor, it is concentrated on Asian issues, with forces in the Pacific and Indian oceans and their contingent gulfs and seas. This Asia-centric maritime strategy derives from nearly two centuries of U.S. interests in Far Eastern waters, interests that have been primarily commercial in nature but have been accompanied by a surprising focus on religious issues.

Missionaries—almost entirely Protestant—ventured out from the United States in the nineteenth and early twentieth centuries to carry their version of the gospel to the peoples of Asia. These two elements of the American population, businessmen and missionaries, were not hesitant about calling on elected and appointed U.S. government officials for assistance. As the increasingly chaotic conditions of nineteenth-century China devolved into outright revolution in 1911, after the overthrow of the last Qing emperor, demands for military protection rose. The U.S. Navy was the most flexible force available to provide the necessary protection for the nascent American imperialists. By the end of the nineteenth century, U.S. warships were patrolling China's rivers, a mission formalized in 1902 with the organization of the Asiatic Fleet, which came to include Yangtze River and Canton Delta patrol forces.

These naval units were assisted by U.S. Army and Marine Corps units after the 1899 Boxer Rebellion, but it was the gunboats and destroyers that carried the American message of armed defense into the interior of China during the opening decades of the twentieth century. This mission was soon subsumed by the greater task of preparing for a classic naval war against Japan, as that erstwhile ally became the most challenging competitor to U.S. interests in China and throughout East Asia.

Tokyo believed it should represent—that is, have the advantage of—Asian economic interests. The United States not only disagreed, insisting on equal access to those interests, but offered Japan a natural hostage in the Philippines. From almost the beginning of the twentieth century, U.S. Navy planning was focused on possible war with the IJN (Imperial Japanese Navy). Such a contest, it was assumed, would be fought as described by Alfred Thayer Mahan, with a climactic sea battle deciding the conflict.

Hence, the American maritime presence in Asia began in the early nineteenth century with the mission of protecting commercial and other interests. By the early years of the next century, that mission continued, but was secondary to preparing for a great naval war against Japan. A century later, with the global war on terror marking the onset of the twenty-first century, U.S. naval missions in Asian waters seem no less important, but they seem somehow blurred by a lack of focus.

Throughout these many decades, however, U.S. sea power has been projected into Asian waters as the primary vehicle of U.S. foreign policy. Economic, political, and cultural American interests all rode on the back of its warships. The navy in turn constantly strove to design and implement a maritime strategy appropriate to ensure the completion of American policy objectives. This strategy–policy process is always difficult to design and even more difficult to implement. This chapter will explore how successful the United States has been in this endeavor.

Early Maritime Encounters in Asia

The United States established an Asian naval presence even before it had a Pacific coast. In 1832, the 42-gun U.S. naval frigate *Potomac* was dispatched by President Andrew Jackson to Southeast Asia to avenge an act of piracy committed against an American trader, the *Friendship*. As reprisal for the massacre of the *Friendship*'s crew, *Potomac* destroyed some (probably innocent) Sumatran villages and killed over 150 Malays, establishing an American naval presence in Asia that has continued to the present day.[1] A more regular U.S. naval presence was established between 1838 and 1842, when the "Exploring Squadron" cruised western Pacific waters.

Naval warfare, including amphibious assaults, was the primary means by which Great Britain conducted the First Opium War (1840–42) against the corrupt and failing Chinese Qing Dynasty. Beijing had allowed China's once-formidable navy to deteriorate into impotence, and foreign warships faced practically no opposition afloat. Furthermore, their decrepit defensive installations and obsolete equipment severely handicapped the ability of Chinese land forces to resist.

U.S. naval forces were not formal participants in the First Opium War, but Washington was quick to take full advantage of Beijing's discomfiture. On two occasions over the next decade, the senior U.S. naval officer in East Asia— Commander John Kelly in 1854, Commander Andrew Foote in 1856—led combat operations against Chinese forts in their efforts to protect Americans onshore. In both cases, Chinese observers and other eyewitnesses believed that U.S. ships had acted in concert with British naval forces. Hence, from the very beginning of the American naval presence in Asian waters, indigenous peoples of the region viewed U.S. actions as identical to those of the other Western imperial powers.

By the mid-1850s, American missionaries and diplomats had established themselves in China, joined by a flow of businessmen seeking their fortune. Even most U.S. "diplomats" of the age were more merchants than government emissaries, consular agents usually focused on advancing trade privileges. Until 1856, in fact, these representatives received no salary, but were expected to earn a living through private business or by collecting fees. In 1856, Congress began providing salaries for consuls serving at certain posts, but even these officers were permitted to continue collecting fees for services performed.[2]

Best-known of the U.S. naval actions in nineteenth-century Asia was Commodore Mathew Calbraith Perry's "opening" of Japan. Perry's effort to bring about diplomatic and economic relations with Japan succeeded in part because of American naval power, but perhaps even more so because of the dramatic changes percolating within Japanese society and government, which would lead to that country's historic Meiji Restoration.

The pattern thus established—U.S. naval power, diplomats, businessmen, missionaries—repeated itself throughout East Asia during the nineteenth century.[3] It was a continuum that extended both horizontally, among the Americans residing in China, and vertically, between these Americans and their counterparts "at home" in the United States. Most missionaries enjoyed the sponsorship of specific churches or organizations that rarely hesitated to seek congressional support for their representatives in the field. Similarly, businesses and corporations with agents in China frequently sought active support from Congress. This twin paradigm of religious and commercial zeal was—and perhaps remains—in fact close to the core of the nineteenth- and twentieth-century American character, which was eventually codified under the rubric of Manifest Destiny.[4]

The U.S. Navy was the leading military force in practically all efforts to establish and consolidate an American presence in East Asia in economic, cultural and religious, or political areas of concern. The First Opium War was followed in 1858–60 by the Second Opium War, in which the U.S. naval commander in East Asian waters, Commodore Josiah Tattnall, violated his orders, insinuating his ships—and hence Washington—into the fray against the interests and forces of China, a nominally independent state at peace with the United States.

Tattnall had been dispatched to the Far East in 1858 to deliver William Reed as U.S. minister to China. He then joined British and French warships at the mouth of the Peiho. The Western military threat forced the Chinese emperor to sign the Treaty of Tientsin, which opened eleven additional Chinese ports to foreign trade and missionary activity and allowed foreign plenipotentiaries— including Reed—to reside in Beijing. The next year, when the emperor attempted to renege on the treaty, Tattnall rejoined the allied task force in an attempt to force Chinese acquiescence. The American commander famously stated that "blood is thicker than water."[5]

Even more significant than these operations off China's coast was the expedition to "open" Japan in the mid-1850s, under Perry's command. In command of a squadron of the navy's newer, steam-powered warships, Perry employed firm, imaginative diplomacy and the threat of military force to wring an agreement from Japanese leaders to establish formal diplomatic and economic relations with the United States. It was a demonstration of "soft" American imperialism at its most effective in East Asia.

The United States formally inserted itself into China's internal affairs in the late nineteenth century, when American gunboats and other warships began patrolling Chinese coastal and riverine waters on a regular basis. This practice was inaugurated by the 1874 cruise of USS *Ashuelot* up the Yangtze River, and reached maturity with the establishment of the U.S. Asiatic Fleet in 1902.[6]

U.S. naval forces in fact served as the nation's primary vehicle for exploration and surveillance of Pacific waters during the latter half of the nineteenth century. In addition to the operations noted earlier, significant missions included Commodore Charles Wilkes's path-breaking voyages through the South Pacific between 1839 and 1843. In 1871 a force commanded by Rear Admiral John Rodgers journeyed to the Korean Peninsula in an abortive attempt to "open" Korea. A second expedition followed in 1882, under the command of Commodore Robert Shufeldt. These efforts eventually succeeded, but compare poorly with Perry's visits to Japan in the early 1850s, largely because neither Rodgers nor Shufeldt possessed the same diplomatic skill or military imagination.

No distinct maritime strategy was apparent in other U.S. naval and diplomatic forays into Asia at this time, including U.S. naval and military participation in the 1900 expeditions to punish the Chinese "Boxers" who had assaulted Westerners in China. Similarly, U.S. participation in the 1919–20 military operations that sought to overthrow the newly established Soviet government in Moscow came more as an afterthought of World War I and Russia's Bolshevik Revolution than as part of a coherent American strategic maritime construct. In fact, U.S. participation in World War I was limited almost entirely to the Atlantic and European theaters; there was no significant American naval participation in Asian waters, where Japan quickly took control of German possessions.

America's Rise as a Pacific Power: Theory

Although U.S. naval and merchant vessels were sailing Asian waters by the 1830s, American maritime strategy in Asia only gained character at the turn of the twentieth century, after the writings of Alfred Thayer Mahan gained popularity. The latter half of the nineteenth century saw the beginning of U.S. power projection across the Pacific, as acquisition of an Asian colonial empire led Americans to believe in a strategic requirement for a navy able to achieve maritime supremacy.

Mahanian doctrine could also be cited as justification for that colonial empire, the voyage of the Great White Fleet, and the construction of the battleship navy that occurred prior to and during World War I. Mahan's theories continued to provide the basis for U.S. maritime strategy in Asia throughout the first half of the twentieth century. This strategy quickly came to be subsumed under War Plan Orange, the plan for possible war with Japan. While Plan Orange underwent numerous refinements from 1902 to 1941, its central concept—that the U.S. battle fleet would deploy across the Pacific, en route to a climactic battle with its Japanese counterpart—remained constant.

Ironically, Japan's naval theorists followed the same line of thought, and both the American and the Japanese navies instituted maritime strategies during the interwar years that owed much to Mahan's maritime theories.[7] In fact, he influenced naval and political leaders throughout the world, including those in Germany, Great Britain, and Russia. Mahan was a naval officer who fought in the American Civil War, but he made his mark as one of the first professors assigned to the new Naval War College in the late 1880s.

The College was established under the leadership of Commodore Stephen B. Luce, who aimed to apply "modern scientific methods" to the study of naval warfare, to "derive fundamental principles of warfare of general application on land or sea," and to study and teach "the evolution of strategic principles based on naval engagements of the past." This idea of constructing American naval strategy based on both theory and practical experience has remained in force for more than a century, during which the U.S. Navy has become the most overwhelming maritime force in history.

Mahan's theorizing was based largely on his review of the history of Britain's Royal Navy, particularly during the seventeenth and eighteenth centuries. His most important contribution to maritime strategic thought at the time seemed to be that no nation could be a great, global power without deploying powerful merchant marine and naval forces. Mahan highlighted the victory of Admiral Horatio Nelson over a combined French and Spanish fleet at Trafalgar in 1805 as the ideal of how to employ naval forces to safeguard vital national interests.

Despite that emphasis, Mahan's view was built on a concept of global maritime trade. He identified six characteristics as necessary for a nation to become a maritime power:

1. Geographic position: maritime geography, colonies
2. Physical conformation: coastline, borders
3. Extent of territory: harbors, lengthy coastlines
4. Population: large and seagoing
5. National character: commercial
6. Character of government: free, moral

Mahan also identified five geographic key points, the possession of which was crucial to global maritime power:

1. Straits of Dover
2. Gibraltar
3. Singapore/Malacca Strait
4. Cape of Good Hope
5. Suez Canal

Despite Mahan's concentration on British maritime history, both of these lists were directly applicable to the Asia-Pacific. Much more importantly, his general theory relating maritime and national power held direct relevance for the region. Japan certainly made a good "fit" for Mahan's six national maritime characteristics, and all of his key geographic points directly affected seaborne traffic between Europe and East Asia. It was no coincidence that the American president who dispatched the Great White Fleet on its epic voyage was one of Mahan's biggest supporters: Theodore Roosevelt was determined to establish the United States as a global naval power.

America's Rise in the Pacific: Operations

America's naval, diplomatic, and commercial entrance into Pacific Asia reached its ultimate stage in 1898, when the United States relied on naval power to establish a colonial empire reaching from Hawaii to the Philippines. Hawaii, part of the Samoas, and other minor territories were annexed, while the victory over Spain that year led to the colonization of the Philippines, the Marianas, and other island territories in Asia. Washington's determination to ensure an "Open Door" for American businessmen in China led to the permanent assignment of warships and troops to that unfortunate country.

The United States proved to be a rather ineffective imperial power; the colonies almost certainly cost the colonizer more in resources and effort than they yielded in commercial profit or strategic advantage. Guam and the Philippines in particular proved to be a strategic stone around Washington's neck: their militarily vulnerable positions meant that they had to be defended, impairing their ability to serve as a vehicle for execution of a forward strategy in East Asia.

The islands also drove American diplomacy for much of the first half of the twentieth century, which worked to the detriment of general U.S. national security, since efforts to secure the Pacific possessions at once appeased Tokyo and encouraged further Japanese expansion.

The United States emerged as an Asian maritime power following its emergence as a formal colonial power. President Theodore Roosevelt signaled that development dramatically in 1907, when he dispatched a naval task force to circumnavigate the globe. This force of sixteen battleships was informally called the Great White Fleet because of the ships' hull color; it spent five months of its two-year world cruise in Asian waters, including port calls in Japan, China, the Philippines, Australia, and New Zealand. The fleet made a strong impact during this portion of its cruise, particularly during its Tokyo visit. Although Roosevelt apparently took a benign view of a rapidly modernizing Japan, he was worried about that nation's growing naval power, which had been amply demonstrated against China in 1894 and against Russia in 1905. The Great White Fleet had a direct effect on Japan. The fleet's voyage was, quite simply, Washington's announcement to the world that the United States had achieved world power status.[8]

The American naval presence in Asia went hand-in-hand with diplomacy, as the United States signed a series of agreements with Japan, the core of which agreed to that nation's dominance over Korea in return for Tokyo's nominal acquiescence in American colonial holdings in East Asia. The first of these was the Taft-Katsura Agreement of 1905, in which Japan's Prime Minister Katsura Taro stated that his government did not "harbor any aggressive designs on the Philippines," while Secretary of War William Howard Taft acknowledged "Japanese suzerainty over Korea."[9]

This memorandum, approved by President Roosevelt, was followed in 1908 by the Root-Takahira Agreement, which acknowledged Japanese and American spheres of influence in Asia. The agreement, signed in Washington by Ambassador Takahira Kogoro and Secretary of State Elihu Root, emphasized maintaining the status quo in the Pacific and the independence of China. It also reaffirmed the Open Door policy. Japan and the United States agreed to respect each other's territorial possessions in East Asia, which meant—as stated in the text of the agreement—that America acknowledged Japan's right "to annex Korea and its special position in Manchuria."[10]

These agreements formed part of Roosevelt's attempt to effect Asian policy based both on diplomacy and on naval might. They also reflected a belief that the United States lacked the naval force necessary to ensure the security of American possessions and interests in the Far East in the face of any future Japanese hostility. U.S. maritime strategy, which focused on the seemingly imminent threat posed by European powers, further constrained U.S. naval capability in the Pacific. Great Britain's 1902 treaty with Japan no doubt helped delineate the limits of the United States' ability to leverage its still young if growing navy as a vehicle for national security goals in Asia. Naval superiority over Japan in the western Pacific was one thing; superiority over a Japan allied with Great Britain was quite another.

In 1915, however, Washington did object to Tokyo's infamous "Twenty-one Demands," a Japanese effort to overturn previous international agreements and gain dominance over Chinese economic and political matters. China leaked the list, which included a demand that Beijing acknowledge Japanese control of Manchuria and Shangdong Province, to the United States.[11] Washington thereupon insisted that Tokyo withdraw the provisions that would have inserted Japanese advisors throughout the Chinese government. Japan reluctantly agreed, and its ambassador to the United States, Ishii Kikujiro, signed the 1917 Lansing-Ishii Agreement with Secretary of State Robert Lansing. While this agreement met some of Washington's demands, that success reflected more Tokyo's uncertainties than it did an effective U.S. maritime strategy. By 1917, the United States was fully enmeshed in World War I, and its navy was almost totally involved in Atlantic and European waters. Had the Wilson administration desired to lend weight to its demands on Tokyo, it would have had little means for doing so.

The Interwar Period: Arms Limitation and Planning

Imperialist incursions in Asia were a focus of negotiation at the 1921–22 Washington Conference, where most of the remaining Twenty-one Demands were nominally abolished. This conference is best known for its naval arms limitation agreements, but it also addressed wider international issues in Asia. The conference's most significant diplomatic result was the Nine-Power Treaty, yet another attempt to equalize foreign depredations of China while acknowledging existing colonial possessions in the region.[12] Specifically, the signatories—China, Japan, the United States, the United Kingdom, France, Portugal, the Netherlands, Belgium, and Italy—agreed to make the Open Door policy international law and to respect China's territorial integrity.[13] This agreement was of limited effect, however, since it did not cancel the effects of the 1919 Versailles Treaty.[14] Furthermore, the compact was rendered moot almost immediately by Japan's continued depredations on the Asian mainland.

The Washington Conference also produced the Five-Power Treaty, probably the most significant naval arms limitation agreement in history. The signatories —the United States, Great Britain, Japan, France, and Italy—agreed not only to limit the number of battleships in their navies, but also to scrap ships already in service or under construction. The treaty imposed a 5:5:3 ratio for battleships and aircraft carriers among the world's leading sea powers, namely the United States, Britain, and Japan, while France and Italy grudgingly accepted a ratio of 5:1.75 between their battleship and carrier forces and those of the United States and Britain. Naval guns with bore sizes exceeding 16 inches (approximately

406 millimeters) were forbidden for battleships. Cruiser and aircraft carrier main batteries were limited to 8-inch (approximately 200 millimeters) guns. Aside from battleships and carriers, furthermore, no other warships displacing more than 10,000 tons were to be constructed.

This last restriction was particularly painful for Britain, which placed great value on large, long-range cruisers to patrol its far-flung dominions. Of more concern to the United States was the agreement with Japan and the United Kingdom that that "no new fortifications or naval bases shall be established in the [Pacific] territories and possessions [and] that no measures shall be taken to increase the existing naval facilities for the repair and maintenance of naval forces."[15] In fact, Japan began violating this latter provision almost immediately, as the American amphibious assaults against many Pacific islands were later to prove, at a very high cost in U.S. and Japanese lives.

Finally, the Washington Conference of 1921–22 produced the Four-Power Treaty. In this pact, the United States, the United Kingdom, and Japan agreed to respect one another's "insular possessions and insular dominions in the region of the Pacific Ocean" for a period of ten years (ending in January 1931).[16]

The Washington Conference thus concluded with a generally satisfied United States, a reluctant United Kingdom, a resentful France and Italy, and a dangerously split Japan. A sizable swath of public opinion in that nation accused Tokyo's representatives to the conference of sacrificing their honor and Japan's national security interests. This resentment contributed directly to the rise of the hyper-nationalism that played such a significant role in Japan's aggressive behavior against China and the rest of Asia.[17]

In the near term, despite popular Japanese reservations, the 1922 treaty made Japan the dominant maritime power in Asia. In the longer term, however, the United States' already world-dominant industrial capability and economic prowess more than made up for any force-structure deficiencies resulting from Washington's willingness to decommission existing warships and cancel new shipbuilding projects. Indeed, this prowess allowed the United States to brush aside the 1941 Pearl Harbor debacle as a mere six-month irritant.

The Washington Conference left many questions undecided, including how submarines and other naval armaments should be allocated. These, along with foreign rights and actions in Asia, remained a subject of diplomatic exchanges and naval arms limitations talks throughout the remainder of the 1920s and 1930s, terminating only with the onset of World War II in September 1939.

Naval limitations conferences in 1927 (Geneva), 1930 (London), and 1934–36 (London, again) highlighted the almost continuous series of diplomatic exchanges and conferences that marked the interwar years. But these gatherings failed to halt the slide into World War II, which arrived in Asia in 1931 with Japanese military expansion in Manchuria. The primary focus of these conferences shifted to Europe as Germany rearmed, but the United States never lost its concern over Asia, where its determination to maintain an independent China ran afoul of Japanese naval modernization and belligerence. American attempts to negotiate with Japan lasted literally up to the minute of that nation's surprise attack on the U.S. fleet at Pearl Harbor on December 7, 1941.

The interwar period saw continued Japanese assaults on the integrity of China and Southeast Asia, accompanied by the growth and modernization of a powerful IJN. Meanwhile, the foreign naval presence in East Asia—both afloat and ashore—decreased as the result of the 1902 Anglo-Japanese Treaty,[18] the Washington Conference's Five-Power Treaty, and the effects of the global depression that struck the United States in the fall of 1929.

In this environment, the U.S. presence in Asia was supported by a Mahanian "big navy" strategy that lacked the necessary naval forces to carry it out. American possessions and interests were vulnerable to mounting Japanese naval dominance.

The voyage of the Great White Fleet had announced the coming-of-age of American naval power in Asian waters, but by the 1930s, that power was represented only by the small, weak Asiatic Fleet. This force included no capital ships. It was usually composed of a squadron of destroyers, a squadron of submarines, a dozen or so gunboats patrolling China's rivers, and a single obsolete cruiser.[19] The U.S. Navy was organized around just one major battle fleet that before 1940 was usually stationed in the Atlantic.

Throughout the first half of the twentieth century, East Asian waters were dominated first by the navies of Great Britain and Japan, and then by that of the United States. The British presence was markedly reduced following the signing of the 1902 Anglo-Japanese Naval Treaty, and was further minimized through the naval limitations agreements signed in Washington in 1921–22. The U.S. naval presence was limited by the Washington treaties, but the Root-Takahira and Taft-Katsura codicils between the United States and Japan also limited the American naval presence in Asia, as Washington tried to buy Japan's acquiescence in U.S. possession of the Philippines and other Pacific territories by agreeing to turn a blind eye to Tokyo's depredations in Korea and China. Diplomacy in this era attempted to substitute for effective strategy and naval strength, and it failed.

World War II

This failure became evident in 1941. Japan judged that its strategic requirements, particularly access to raw materials, and a determination to dominate the Asian mainland could best be achieved by destroying American naval power in the region. Rarely has a nation made a more self-defeating strategic decision.

The U.S. maritime strategy developed under War Plan Orange preparatory to World War II was effectively carried out in the Pacific after 1941, although the important battles were dominated by air power rather than by battleships. Although many important sea battles occurred between American and Japanese fleets—including the Coral Sea, Midway, the Marianas, and the Philippine Sea—none resolved the conflict, by itself or in aggregate. Instead the maritime war was won by U.S. industrial capacity, more effective training, operational acumen, and superior leadership.

The Pacific War was largely one of air power. The United States built more survivable airplanes (the Japanese Zero's speed and maneuverability was canceled out by its lack of armored fuel tanks), built thousands more than Japan, and pursued a much more effective pilot training program. Under the seas, Japan never made effective use of its submarine force, while the United States destroyed the Japanese merchant marine and effectively blockaded the home islands.

American industrial capacity overwhelmed Japan in all areas of production, from small arms to aircraft carriers, but the war at sea was not won merely by numbers. Even more significant was the greater quality of U.S. naval leadership and operational performance. The maritime war in the Pacific was "bookended" by the great naval battles of Midway, in June 1942, and the Leyte Gulf, in October 1944. In both cases, Japan tried to carry out unrealistically complicated plans overseen by naval commanders who were unequal to their tasks. By 1945, the Japanese navy had been destroyed and the U.S. Navy alone ruled Asian waters.

The U.S. Navy did not have a coherent war-fighting strategy ready for the post-1945 Asia-Pacific, but one did not seem required during the brief hiatus between World War II and the Cold War. The world wars ended in 1945 with Japan a smoking ruin, Great Britain no longer an Asian naval power of significant standing, and the United States dominant throughout this intensely maritime region.

The navy dominated U.S. strategic planning in Asia during the first half of the twentieth century, although the army was a significant partner in thinking about defense of the American island possessions.[20] Planning was steadily conducted by both services from 1902 to 1941, but no satisfactory plan for the defense of the U.S. Asian empire emerged. This was due primarily to the simple mismatch between geography and resources. The Philippines, Guam, and other American colonies were many weeks' steaming time away for the reduced U.S. Navy, while Japan, located in the region, posed the most likely military threat. Furthermore, U.S. adherence to the Nine-Power Treaty's limitations on constructing fortifications in the Far East significantly reduced U.S. forces' ability to withstand Japanese assaults during World War II.[21]

The Cold War Begins

The Navy soon determined that a new maritime strategy was necessary for the new global situation, both to defend the nation and to assure that, in the face of

U.S. Air Force trumpeting of nuclear-armed intercontinental bombers, the navy remained a major participant in the national defense. Hence, a "transoceanic strategy" emerged in the late 1940s.[22] This sought to make maximum use of fleet resources that were very scarce following the massive post-1945 disarmament. The transoceanic strategy postulated a navy based at U.S. home ports in the continental United States and Hawaii. This force would be ready for rapid deployment to the scene of overseas crises that threatened U.S. security interests. The focus was not on fighting climactic battles at sea, but on using a strong navy to project power onto foreign shores.

In the Pacific, this strategy led to the strengthening of the Seventh Fleet, permanently stationed in Japan. This fleet was first formed in March 1943 as part of General Douglas MacArthur's Southwest Pacific forces, but had withered away after August 1945. The reinvigorated fleet's first major challenge was the Korean conflict in 1950–53. The onset of what was perceived as the initial steps in a Soviet global assault on the democracies enabled the navy to recommission hundreds of warships laid up after 1945. It provided the navy with more definite strategic direction: defeating Soviet-inspired aggression throughout Asia and the Pacific. This mission—global nuclear war with the Soviet Union—would underlay the development of American maritime strategy in the Asia-Pacific until the end of the Cold War in 1990.

The U.S. Navy's Cold War strategy in Asia was based on two primary principles. The first was the overseas basing of naval forces; the second was naval participation in nuclear warfare. The latter first manifested itself in the development of carrier-borne aircraft capable of conducting strategic nuclear strikes against Soviet targets far inland. By 1959, however, nuclear-powered FBM (fleet ballistic missile) submarines continually on patrol had largely superseded nuclear-capable aircraft in this mission.

Although now focused on the Soviet threat, U.S. maritime strategy remained constant in certain respects, including forward-deployed battle fleets; FBM patrols, which constituted one leg of the nation's nuclear triad; the power-projection capability embodied in the Marine Corps and carrier aircraft; and defense of the homeland through ASW (antisubmarine warfare), which involved constructing extensive underwater listening arrays. These capabilities were implemented effectively despite periodic fluctuations in domestic political support.

As always, it was not enough for a maritime strategy to look effective on paper, even if proven at sea. This was especially true for the Asia-Pacific theater, which seemed remote from U.S. shores and interests. Political support had to be maintained, both within the Department of Defense and within the larger domestic political arena, if the navy was to receive the resources necessary to execute its strategy. The Cold War was marked by efforts to justify the strategy and elicit the wherewithal to carry it out.

Ironically, the traditional, Mahanian justification for maritime strategy—global trade—disappeared for the most part during this period. The U.S. merchant marine was a global force only during the first half of the twentieth century, while the Japanese merchant marine was destroyed during World War II. The second half of the century witnessed the almost complete disappearance of American-flag merchant ships, accompanied by the reemergence of global merchant marine fleets from Japan, South Korea, and China.

The U.S. Navy remained the dominant military force in Asia during the largely continental conflicts in Korea and Vietnam that marked the Cold War in the region. More important than these hostilities, however, was the overarching, nearly half-century-long conflict with the Soviet Union. In the Asia-Pacific, the Cold War was essentially a maritime contest. The U.S. Navy was the primary vehicle of American policy against Soviet ambitions and would have been the primary means of resistance had Moscow opted to seek its goals in that region by force.

Winning the Cold War at Sea

In the 1980s, Secretary of the Navy John Lehman drove the development of the most important maritime strategy since World War II.[23] Premised on global nuclear war with the Soviet Union, this strategy sought to take advantage of carrier-based air power and nuclear-powered submarines. FBM submarines, also nuclear-powered, provided the core of the nation's nuclear deterrent triad against potential Soviet nuclear attack. The maritime strategy of the Cold War's last decade was effective both as a domestic instrument for modernizing the U.S. Navy and as a strategic instrument for neutralizing the growing Soviet Navy. In Asia, the Lehman strategy included helping Japan prepare its navy—euphemistically called the Japan Maritime Self-Defense Force—for the Cold War at sea and encouraging friendly states such as South Korea to develop potent navies of their own.

This maritime strategy represented the most coherent U.S. effort since the development of War Plan Orange to construct a logical operational and political framework for the pursuit of American diplomatic and military objectives. Although Lehman's "600-ship navy" never put to sea, the strategy it was intended to execute was the primary American vehicle for defeating Soviet campaigns in Asia.

The Pacific Fleet responsible for attaining strategic maritime objectives in Asia faced not only the Soviet fleet but an internal U.S. Navy threat. Operational planners in the 1980s faced a question that harked back to the pre–World War II dispute over which theater—Atlantic or Pacific, Europe or Asia—should take precedence. The navy of the 1980s made the same decision it had in the 1930s and 1940s, to place "Europe First." This meant that the first priority for American maritime resources—even those assigned to the Pacific—would be to defeat a Soviet attack in Europe, not Asia. This "swing strategy," under which Pacific ships, units, and personnel would be reassigned to the Atlantic theater during war-time, represented a significant constraint on the United States' ability to achieve its strategic objectives in Asia, an intensely maritime theater, and Pacific Fleet commanders never ceased trying to reorder those maritime strategic priorities.[24]

The disintegration of the Soviet empire and the laying up of the Russian Pacific Fleet; the emergence of China as a major participant in Asian economic, political, and maritime relations; and the emergence of smaller Asian economic powers led by Japan and South Korea mark the transition from the twentieth to the twenty-first centuries. U.S. naval dominance, however, remained constant during this transition.

Post–Cold War: The 1990s

Since the Cold War ended in 1990, U.S. naval commanders have been seeking—generally without success—a replacement for Lehman's effective maritime strategy of the 1980s. The situation in the early twenty-first century is somewhat analogous to that faced by the navy following World War II, and therefore it should not be surprising that the transoceanic strategy so ably described by Samuel Huntington remains applicable and attractive.

The U.S. Navy and Marine Corps soon realized that the dissolution of the Soviet empire and the disappearance of its big-navy threat had eviscerated the maritime strategy of the 1980s. The first fruit of this realization was a white paper issued by the secretary of the navy in September 1992, titled . . . *From the Sea: Preparing the Naval Service for the Twenty-first Century. From the Sea* sought to reshape U.S. maritime strategy in acknowledgment of the nation's new National Security Strategy and the political changes accompanying the end of the Cold War. It proffered an essential shift in focus from blue-water battles between large fleets to littoral warfare, emphasizing the role of naval forces in joint operations launched from the sea to affect events ashore. *From the Sea* estab-lished a Naval Doctrine Command to formulate and formalize the concept of "operational maneuver from the sea."[25]

From the Sea was followed in 1997 by *Forward. . .From the Sea.*[26] This docu-ment differed little from its immediate predecessor, simply reaffirming the ability of forward-deployed naval forces to project maritime power, influencing events ashore in littoral regions during times of peace and war. This echo of Hunting-ton's transoceanic strategy emphasized the ability of the navy and marines to oper-ate independently of shore-based political constraints. That is, forward-deployed naval forces could carry out the dictates of the U.S. National Military Strategy in near real-time without infringing on another nation's sovereignty.[27]

Applying the concepts encapsulated in *From the Sea* and *Forward. . .From the Sea* to Asian waters was a straightforward proposition, given the continued regional dominance of even the much-reduced American navy of the 1990s.

Simply put, the U.S. Pacific Fleet decreased by one-half between 1985 and 2005, largely as a result of the end of the Cold War and the effective disappearance of the Soviet fleet, the only credible maritime threat of the time. To an extent, *From the Sea* and its successors represented attempts not only to offer naval forces strategic guidance but to justify generous naval funding within the U.S. government.

The Post–9/11 Period

Efforts to frame a vision for the naval services continued into the era following the September 11, 2001 terrorist attacks. Issued in 2002, the document known as *Sea Power 21* sought to incorporate new technologies and organizational reforms as the tenets of a new maritime strategy. It offered three operational initiatives intended to maximize the effectiveness of joint and integrated operations:

- *Sea Strike:* offensive operations by manned aircraft, cruise missiles, marines, and special forces.
- *Sea Shield:* a layered homeland defense, to include sea-based ballistic missile defense, mine countermeasures, and ASW, as well as improved littoral warfare capabilities.
- *Sea Basing:* use of sea-based forces to project power ashore without foreign basing.[28]

Although this strategy attempted to acknowledge the shattering events of September 11, it was essentially dead on arrival. The global war on terror simply does not offer viable targets for aircraft-carrier task groups. Hence, it offers little or no justification for operating fleets at sea, other than in supporting roles. Using nuclear-powered aircraft carriers as transports for army helicopters is hardly how naval aviation aspires to operate, and does very little to justify the existence of these very expensive assets. Indeed, the navy's ship inventory continued to dwindle through the first half-decade of the twenty-first century, a trend that will continue barring renewed—and improbable—determination on the part of the administration and Congress to recapitalize a fleet that lacks a compelling maritime strategy.

In 2005, even as the decline in ship numbers was threatening the navy's ability to dominate Asian waters, the U.S. government issued a comprehensive NSMS (National Strategy for Maritime Security).[29] The NSMS and the putative "1,000-ship navy" are nowhere more applicable than in troubled Northeast and Southeast Asian waters, where allies, friends, and not-so-friendly nations all face common enemies in the form of piracy and terrorism.

This strategy document's stated objective is both far-reaching and Mahanian. It mandates "a comprehensive national effort to promote global economic stability and protect legitimate activities while preventing hostile or illegal acts within the maritime domain." Its definition of the "maritime domain" is even more ambitious than Mahan envisioned, namely:

all areas and things of, on, under, relating to, adjacent to, or bordering on a sea, ocean, or other navigable waterway, including all maritime-related activities, infrastructure, people, cargo, and vessels and other conveyances. Note: The maritime domain for the United States includes the Great Lakes and all navigable inland waterways such as the Mississippi River and the Intra-Coastal Waterway.[30]

This encompasses *all* navigable waters, both oceanic and riverine, and is truly global in scope. It is even more extensive than Mahan's 1890 list of maritime chokepoints. At a minimum, the NSMS encompasses the Taiwan Strait; the Lombok, Sunda, and Makassar straits through the Indonesian archipelago; the Six- and Nine-Degree channels in the Indian Ocean; the straits at Hormuz and Bab el-Mandeb; and the Panama Canal.

The NSMS focuses on combating terrorism, but its eight supporting plans aim at the dangers posed by piracy, international criminal activities such as illegal immigration and drug trafficking, and environmental degradation. These plans are

- National Plan to Achieve Domain Awareness
- Global Maritime Intelligence Integration Plan
- Interim Maritime Operational Threat Response Plan
- International Outreach and Coordination Strategy
- Maritime Infrastructure Recovery Plan
- Maritime Transportation System Security Plan
- Maritime Commerce Security Plan
- Domestic Outreach Plan

In Asia, the NSMS must come to terms not only with the vast reaches of the Pacific and Indian oceans but also with many of the world's largest ports, including Tokyo, Yokohama, Kobe, Nagoya, Pusan, Qingdao, Shanghai, Shenzhen, Hong Kong, Kaohsiung, Keelung, Manila, Singapore, Port Kalang, Laem Chabang, and Mumbai. Additionally, Asia is served by several vital rivers, including the Yalu, Huang, Yangtze, Mekong, Irrawady, Salween, and Brahmaputra. All of these fall under the aegis of the NSMS.

The NSMS poses an insurmountable challenge for the U.S. Navy, given its declining strength and the host of competing missions. In 2006, recognizing this, the chief of naval operations, Admiral Michael Mullen, attempted to rectify this situation by launching an effort to write a "new maritime strategy for the twenty-first century." Mullen's plan is modeled on the 1980s' maritime strategy that proved so effective in building and guiding the navy in the face of the Soviet maritime threat.[31]

Mullen's plan takes account of what he has called three "enduring qualities" of sea power. First, the U.S. Navy can promote free markets and free societies; second, the flexibility intrinsic to sea power allows the navy to undertake a vast range of missions at sea and in coastal regions; and finally, the navy is readily able to forge partnerships with foreign navies.[32] This last insight—which informs Mullen's innovative idea of a 1,000-ship navy, also known as a "Global Maritime Network"—forms the core of the proposed new U.S. maritime strategy.[33]

This does not mean a drastic rise in the number of U.S. Navy ships. It relies instead on the concept of augmenting the approximately 300 ships likely to make up the navy force structure for the foreseeable future with 700 additional vessels from allied and friendly navies around the world. The concept follows the NSMS by charging U.S. maritime forces with ensuring freedom of navigation throughout the Asian maritime domain. Most importantly, the 1,000-ship-navy concept focuses on interactions with other navies. In Asia, resources would come from the maritime forces of trusted allies such as Canada, Japan, South Korea, Australia, the Philippines, and Thailand. Some participation by the navies of other Southeast Asian states, New Zealand, India, and Pakistan might also be expected. Chinese naval participation in the Global Maritime Network could be feasible for specific missions, such as safeguarding the Strait of Malacca and other critical waterways against pirates and terrorists.

A U.S. Navy intent on a 1,000-ship strategy must overcome at least three major problems. First, notwithstanding the global war on terror, naval leaders must describe the maritime strategic environment in terms compelling enough to justify a large, aircraft-carrier-based navy. It may well be that the time of the huge flattop that displaces nearly 100,000 tons is nearing its end, but the nation's already huge investment in ten or more of these $5 billion-plus behemoths will dictate their continued role as the center of fleet strategic and doctrinal efforts.

Second, the navy must convince the other services it has a viable role in the joint, integrated effort against U.S. enemies. This will pose an increasingly difficult challenge as the Department of Defense sets out to recapitalize the U.S. Army and Marine Corps after the strategic misadventure in Iraq.

Third and most importantly, the new strategy must convince Congress to fund continued naval modernization in both technological and quantitative terms. And the latter is just as important as the former: no matter how revolutionary a warship's capabilities, one ship can only be in one place at one time. "Force multiplication" is a valid concept, but remains subject to the laws of physics.

The Next U.S. Maritime Strategy in Asia

U.S. maritime strategy in the twenty-first century faces serious limits on budgetary resources, personnel availability, and national security objectives. The general strategic paradigm is the global war on terror, which pays relatively little attention to the maritime sphere. This in turn drives budgetary and personnel priorities within the defense establishment. Maritime strategy in Asia, moreover, must justify the required investments without an apparent opponent in the region. Japan is now an ally, the Soviet Union no longer exists, and China has yet to offer a credible challenge at sea. The U.S. Navy seeks a maritime strategy in a maritime region without an identifiable naval threat.

Strategic Elements in a New U.S. Maritime Strategy in Asia

The Asia-Pacific region is particularly daunting with respect to the time–distance problem. The United States must take into account the region's geographical vastness and the presence of two major navies and one aspiring navy in any strategic construct. One analyst has estimated that Asian navies will be spending $14 billion on new naval combatants annually by 2009.[34] Most of these ships will be armed with advanced, very capable antiship cruise missiles that are extremely difficult to defend against and that can be launched against opposing surface ships with relatively little targeting information. This potential inventory of modern warships in the Asian theater (defined as the great sweep of ocean from the Kamchatka Peninsula to the North Arabian Sea) attests to the maritime concerns of regional governments.

Admiral William Fallon, formerly the American military commander in the Pacific, provided the U.S. perspective on the Asian naval picture in March 2006. Testifying before the Senate Armed Services Committee, Fallon briefly addressed his major naval concerns: the Korean Peninsula, the status of Taiwan, and terrorist activities in Southeast Asia, particularly in the Philippines, Indonesia, and Malaysia. He cited the completion of "a major strategic review with Japan" as evidence of the continuing strategic importance of the U.S.–Japan maritime alliance. Fallon also hailed the revised "strategic framework agreement" with Singapore as important for giving the United States "access to some very excellent port and airfield facilities." He highlighted the Australian and Thai alliances but described the Philippines more as a source of problems than a source of assistance in accomplishing strategic goals.[35]

Any U.S. maritime strategy in Asia will depend on the U.S. Navy's Pacific Fleet to accomplish its ends. The fleet's area of responsibility is huge, covering more than 50 percent of the earth's surface. It spans just over one hundred million square miles of the Pacific and Indian oceans, from the U.S. west coast to the Persian Gulf. The Pacific Fleet numbers approximately two hundred ships, two thousand aircraft, and two hundred and fifty thousand sailors and marines.

The Pacific Fleet includes two component operating fleets, the Third and the Seventh. Third Fleet ships usually deploy to the western Pacific and Indian Oceans for duty with the commander of the Seventh Fleet or to the Persian Gulf region for duty with the Fifth Fleet, which falls under the U.S. Central Command. These ships deploy following a training regimen that prepares them to carry out a wide number of missions, ranging from humanitarian and peace-keeping operations to full combat operations at sea.

The Third Fleet's area of responsibility includes approximately fifty million square miles of the eastern and northern Pacific Ocean, including the Bering Sea. Major SLOCs (sea lines of communication) in this area are critically important to the conduct of trade and transportation of energy resources throughout the Pacific Rim region, and figure prominently in the fleet's homeland defense mission.

The Third Fleet is also responsible for deterring conflict and carrying out sustained combat operations at sea under the U.S. maritime strategy in the Pacific. This includes defending the western sea approaches to the United States and commanding joint U.S. forces deployed in response to a specific event or contingency in its area of responsibility.

The Seventh Fleet, the Third Fleet's counterpart in the western Pacific, is the largest of the navy's forward-deployed fleets.[36] Some forty to fifty ships, two hundred aircraft, and twenty thousand navy and marine personnel usually fall under its operational control, including forces based in Japan and Guam, as well as those deploying from the Third Fleet. These Pacific Fleet forces operate in the Pacific and Indian oceans, including the Persian Gulf, supporting three principal elements of U.S. maritime strategy: deterrence, forward defense, and alliance solidarity.

Commander, Seventh Fleet is specifically responsible for three missions: first, service as joint task force commander in the event of a natural disaster or joint military operation; second, service as operational commander for all naval forces in the region; and finally, service as the combined naval component commander for the defense of the Korean Peninsula. In the event of hostilities, accordingly, this officer would command all assigned naval forces.

The Legal Dimension

The age-old connection between commerce and naval power continues to shape American policy toward open access to the world's oceans and seas. Post–9/11 exigencies have amended this paradigm by bringing the linkage between maritime power and homeland defense to the fore. Freedom of navigation has long been a principle of U.S. maritime strategy. Thomas Jefferson was among the first to insist on free passage through the world's waterways. This principle is now codified in the 1992 UNCLOS (UN Convention on the Law of the Sea). Although the U.S. Congress has not ratified UNCLOS, American maritime forces abide by its precepts.

UNCLOS lays out four primary maritime zones of interest. All are measured in nautical miles from the coast of each nation bordering the sea. The first of these, the territorial sea, extends 12 nautical miles from the coast. The coastal nation enjoys full rights of sovereignty in this zone. The second, the contiguous zone, extends 24 nautical miles from the coast and provides lesser but still extensive legal rights—maritime law enforcement, the right to enforce sanitary regulations—to the coastal nation. The third zone, the EEZ (exclusive economic zone), varies in breadth. A nation may claim such a zone, within which it possesses almost complete economic rights, out to a range of 200 nautical miles from its coastlines, or, underwater geography permitting, it may claim a continental shelf zone out to a maximum range of 350 nautical miles. This zone is defined not by mileage, but by the measured gradient of the ocean floor. The nation claiming it reserves the rights to exploit undersea mineral deposits, fisheries, and other oceanic resources.

The limits and privileges codified in UNCLOS are not absolute, however, since many of the signatory nations expressed "reservations" about specific provisions. China, for example, expressed six significant reservations. During several maritime incidents involving the United States, moreover, Beijing has seemed to claim sovereign rights even over the continental shelf.

The first of these incidents involved Chinese harassment of the hydrographic survey ship USNS *Bowditch,* which was conducting survey operations in the sea area claimed by Beijing as its EEZ.[37] The second incident was more serious. In May 2001 a Chinese naval F-8II fighter collided with an American EP-3 electronic surveillance aircraft. The EP-3 was seriously damaged and made a forced landing on Hainan Island, while the Chinese fighter crashed into the sea and its pilot was killed. Beijing's actions following this incident conveyed an interpretation of UNCLOS that strongly implied a Chinese claim to sovereign rights over not just the EEZ but possibly over the continental shelf as well.[38] China has voiced its dubious attitude toward the UNCLOS in less formal venues as well, and Beijing's representatives have often repeated these inferences.

Finally, China's apparent views toward island possessions in the East and South China seas reflect claims that may be unusual. If Beijing were to declare clearly that the waters of the SCS (South China Sea) were sovereign Chinese territory, it would provoke immediate objections and almost certain naval intervention from the United States and, conceivably, from at least some of its treaty allies. Any such claim would directly challenge the U.S. principle of freedom of navigation, which is integral to American maritime strategy.

The Economic Dimension

U.S. economic growth is closely linked to the world economy as a whole, with most of the nation's trade carried on the world's oceans. Free trade at sea, moreover, underpinned the burst of Asian prosperity that marked the past half-century. And SLOCs directly affect the ability of the United States to move forces, equipment, and supplies to crisis areas overseas. The Department of Defense has named eight international regions—five of them in Asian waters—as "U.S. Lifelines and Transit Regions," since they contain crucial chokepoints such as

- The Gulf of Mexico and Caribbean Sea, along with the Panama Canal
- The North Sea and Baltic Sea, including the associated channels and straits
- The Mediterranean Sea and Black Sea, along with the Strait of Gibraltar and access routes to Middle Eastern areas
- The western Indian Ocean, along with the Suez Canal, Bab el-Mandeb, the Strait of Hormuz, and the waters around South Africa to the Mozambique Channel
- The Southeast Asian seas, including the Malacca and Lombok straits, among others, as well as the SLOCs that pass the Spratly Islands
- The Northeast Asian seas, including SLOCs important for access to Japan, Korea, China, and Russia
- The Southwest Pacific, including SLOC access routes to Australia
- The Arctic Ocean and Bering Strait

Economic and military issues alike are important in shaping U.S. strategy in Asia, which aims at assuring unobstructed passage through these eight major SLOCs and the associated chokepoints.

According to the American Petroleum Institute, 1994 marked the first year when more than half the oil used in the United States was imported. The largest supplier, Saudi Arabia, provides 18.5 percent of the United States' petroleum needs, with shipments traveling more than eight thousand sea miles via SLOCs connecting the western Indian Ocean to the United States. Disruption of shipping through these waterways would affect not only the United States but the global economy, as the 1980–88 "tanker war" between Iran and Iraq showed.

The region that includes the Southeast Asian seas and the Straits of Malacca, Sunda, and Lombok is the most prominent of the Lifelines and Transit Regions, measured by its volume of merchant shipping. It encompasses the SCS SLOCs, as well as sea lanes traversed by almost half the world's merchant shipping and large percentages of Asian trade. Shipping traffic through the Malacca Strait is several times greater than the traffic through either the Suez or the Panama canals.

Some numbers portray the significance of this region to oceangoing commerce. More than one-half trillion dollars' ($568 billion) worth of long-haul, interregional seaborne shipments passes through these chokepoints, including over half the trade from Japan, Australia, and the nations of Southeast Asia, as well as one-quarter of the imports of Hong Kong, Taiwan, and South Korea. The economic strength of these countries and their trading partners depends on unimpeded passage in the region.

The United States is concerned about the threat to freedom of navigation through the SCS posed by disputed sovereignty claims in the area. Beijing's hints are especially worrisome for Washington. Several nations claim some or all of the Spratly Islands and, by extension, rights over the waters adjacent to the islands. China, Taiwan, Malaysia, the Philippines, and Vietnam have garrisons on some of the atolls.

An associated legal question is Indonesia's declaration of sovereignty over the waters and SLOCs enclosed within its territory, which derives from the novel doctrine of "archipelagic sea lines." Jakarta's apparent attempt to gain control over shipping among its islands poses a serious danger to freedom of navigation, since the straits through the Indonesian archipelago are important for direct, cost-effective maritime activity between the Pacific and the Indian oceans.

Finally, because of oil spills associated with accidents in the Strait of Malacca, the international community has considered regulating shipping to meet environmental concerns and assure maritime safety. There is no way to separate commerce from the defense of U.S. interests in the SCS and nearby waters, and defending these waters requires an effective U.S. maritime strategy.

Conclusions

The three essential components of the U.S. National Security Strategy—peacetime engagement, deterrence and conflict prevention, and fighting and winning the nation's wars—all assume deploying forces to any part of maritime Asia in a timely and effective manner. Forward-deployed U.S. Navy, Marine Corps, and Coast Guard forces ensure that SLOCs remain open so that forces deploying to the region can fulfill their missions. Maritime forces possess an inherent mobility that ensures the ability to deploy from forward locations to potential crisis areas. But naval leaders must take several factors into account if they are to implement U.S. maritime strategy in Asia effectively.

First, the United States has adjusted its military strategy to address the multiple regional interests and challenges of the post–Cold War era. U.S. maritime forces redefined their focus to emphasize power projection. This strategic reorientation found expression in the U.S. Navy and Marine Corps white papers *From the Sea* and *Forward…From the Sea*. The new mode of strategic thought ushered in by these documents forms the basis for the 1,000-ship navy, itself a version of a transoceanic maritime strategy first proposed in the late 1940s. The missions projected in these documents include traditional roles such as presence, strategic deterrence, sea control (SLOC passage), crisis response, power projection, and sealift.

Second, U.S. naval forces are adjusting to the realities of budget cuts and the consequences of stringent fiscal times for naval operations. The navy is reducing personnel and operating expenses by one-third from the "Base Force" established in 1990, which already incorporated post–Cold War reductions. The drawdown will leave a navy of fewer than 300 ships in the near term, less than half of John Lehman's planned 600-ship force. Joint operations with other services, interoperability with allied forces, and a fundamental redesign of seagoing operations will have to offset this decline.

SLOCs remain the sinews of U.S. strategic maritime strategy in the Pacific. They require international respect for the freedom of navigation and overflight, as set forth in UNCLOS. Otherwise, the U.S. military's ability to exercise its naval mobility will be in jeopardy. The response time for U.S. and allied/coalition maritime forces based far from potential areas of conflict could be prolonged in times of crisis, when time is at a premium.

U.S. naval forces will remain inherently flexible and will continue to focus on guaranteeing unhindered SLOC passage, the importance of which is a constant feature of naval support for the National Military Strategy. Although he wrote more than a century ago, Mahan remains relevant to twenty-first-century U.S. maritime strategy in Asia. He linked maritime policies and events to larger national and international processes and in so doing established naval strategy as a conscious, major element within a nation's overall security policy and strategy.

Sea power's prominent role in national strategy remains closely tied to technological and doctrinal developments. While the Asian theater is not susceptible to a purely maritime strategy, the inherently maritime nature of U.S. strategic interests in that theater is undoubted. The American maritime strategy in the Pacific that is emerging with the new century will remain founded on close relationships with allies and friends, deterrence as an instrument of statecraft, and the capability to project power onto distant shores from forward-deployed maritime forces.

Sir Walter Raleigh once observed, "Whosoever commands the sea commands the trade; whosoever commands the trade of the world commands the riches of the world, and consequently the world itself." Unimpeded SLOCs are as important to the United States today as they were to Raleigh and his successors, who created a mercantile empire sustained by the Royal Navy's control of the SLOCs linking England, its colonies, and its trading partners in Asia.

More than 80 percent of global trade still moves by sea, and the United States depends on the free and unimpeded movement of its share of that commerce. The very small merchant marine with which the United States has entered the twenty-first century depends on vital sea lanes. Furthermore, the United States depends on its ability to use the Asia-Pacific seas to ensure its security. This historic need has become increasingly important owing to renewed American emphasis on employing power-projection land forces within a preemptive strategic paradigm that is replete with ideologically based—and hence seemingly unending—international commitments.

Hence, unimpeded SLOCs underpin U.S. National Security Strategy in the Asia-Pacific. Maintaining maritime dominance across that huge region lies at the cusp of this view, increasing the strategic necessity of not just using but dominating the region's critical SLOCs and navigation chokepoints. No matter how described, named, or codified, any effective American maritime strategy in the early twenty-first century must be capable of safeguarding the sea lanes that are essential to the economic well-being of the United States and its friends and allies. In short, guaranteeing the unimpeded flow of seagoing commerce throughout Asia and the Pacific remains a crucial component of national power.

CHAPTER 5

CAN CHINA BECOME
A MARITIME POWER?

Andrew S. Erickson

Despite possessing a coastline some 7,830 nautical miles long and some 3,400 offshore islands, China has pursued maritime development in an atmosphere of considerable uncertainty.[1] The nation has long been a continental power with a feeble navy, but recent assessments suggest that this historic pattern is changing. China appears increasingly determined to create a modern navy. But—while the possibility cannot be excluded outright—it seems that China is not developing long-range power-projection capabilities. Rather, Beijing seems to be constructing a navy geared to achieving asymmetric sea-denial capabilities on its immediate periphery in order to defend its growing maritime interests, and in particular to resolve the volatile Taiwan issue. Nevertheless, its combat potential should not be underestimated.

At least for now, Beijing does not seem intent on fielding carrier battle groups. Therefore, the PLAN is developing very differently from most other large navies, and from the U.S. Navy in particular. Chinese naval strategists seem to embrace their own universal logic of sea power, with both Mahanian and Marxist undercurrents. Despite these foreign influences, however, they insist that China has not, and will not, replicate the martial patterns of the West. Yet, exceptionalism aside, Chinese naval development today seems to be constrained less by ideology than by capabilities. A concerted effort to improve these capabilities is clearly underway and enjoys the sustained support of China's leadership. More relevant questions are, therefore: What kind of force structure will allow China to execute its strategies effectively, thereby achieving its political objectives? How feasible are China's plans for force-structure development, and how long will it take to fulfill such plans? A close examination of these and other developments will furnish insights into how strategic thought influences Chinese maritime strategy.

Particularly uncertain is the extent to which China will seek to project power beyond its shores. Will China seek "command of the sea"? If so, what will be the essence and implications of "command of the sea with Chinese characteristics"? In short, can China become a true maritime power?

This chapter, which selectively surveys aspects of China's naval development in order to elucidate the trajectory of its growing sea power, will proceed in seven steps. A section on latest developments and assessments will survey China's 2006 Defense White Paper Summary and the 2006 U.S. Department of Defense report on China's military modernization. The next section, on force structure, will examine China's military budget; submarine force; MIW (mine-warfare) capabilities; surface ships; amphibious forces; naval air force; command, control, communications, computer, intelligence, surveillance, and reconnaissance (C4ISR) capabilities; and deck aviation ambitions. Subsequent sections will consider China's base infrastructure, training, and doctrine. Inferences about China's naval modernization plan will then be offered, followed by implications for regional naval relations and an overall assessment.

Latest Developments and Assessments

China's maritime potential is clearly being debated in Beijing. A remarkable Chinese government study entitled *The Rise of Great Powers* attempts to determine the reasons why nine nations became great powers. Conceived on November 24, 2003 at a Communist Party of China Central Committee Political Bureau group session and completed in 2006, it draws on the analyses of many top Chinese scholars. *The Rise of Great Powers* suggests that national power stems from economic development, which is fueled by foreign trade and in turn can be furthered by a strong navy. This latter connection is emphasized by Senior Captain Liu Yijian of the People's Liberation Army Navy (PLAN or PLA Navy). Writing in China's foremost military journal, *China Military Science,* Liu states that "Possession of a big and powerful naval force [is] of great strategic importance in defending national security, promoting a nation's economic development, and maintaining a nation's international standing."[2]

PLAN Senior Captain Xu Qi builds on this theme, emphasizing that "China's ...maritime geostrategic relationships...are undergoing profound change.... China's navy must make [important] strategic choices."[3] For Xu, China's strategic future lies at sea. China, with its "very long shoreline, numerous islands, vast administered sea areas, and abundant ocean resources," is naturally a great maritime power. The nation's "coastal seas and continental-shelf areas [combine to] approach 273 million hectares," he points out. "This area is more than two times that of China's total arable land." For China, with "the world's largest population and relatively deficient resources," the sea can thus "serve as a strategic resource replacement area." Rather than envisioning enduring Chinese vulnerability at sea, Xu views China's navy as a vehicle for asserting Chinese sovereignty abroad: "Naval vessels are symbols of state power and authority [which] can act as 'mobile territory' and freely navigate the high seas of the world....[T]heir mission is not limited to offshore defense." For all these reasons, China's navy must "unceasingly move toward [the posture of] a "blue-water navy" [and] expand the scope of maritime strategic defense...."

By contrast, in an unusually explicit acknowledgment of the growing internal debate concerning the purposes and priorities of China's future military development, Beijing University scholar Ye Zicheng maintains that "in the current stage we must regard the building of China's land homeland as the central task and develop land power as the strategic focus, [while] the development of sea power should be limited and should serve and be subordinate to the development of land power." For China, Ye explains, "possession of strong sea power is an inevitable choice...however...strong sea power must be and can only become a component part of China's land power." China's natural status as a land power, Ye writes, means that its development "can only be based on internal land space, and the development of sea space and expansion abroad can only be important supplements." China's strategists must remember "the lesson of the late Qing: When there are major problems in the building of a country's system, it is impossible to become a sea power just by developing maritime military forces." Yet Ye's emphasis on land power "does not exclude the development of China's sea power, because China's sea power is very far from meeting the needs of its land power."[4] This assessment is supported by the 2005 edition of the PLA's first authoritative volume on strategy, edited by two major generals: "...because the borders and coasts are far away from our central inland, some at a distance of hundreds or even thousands of kilometers, it is very difficult for the projection of forces, operations, logistics and supports."[5] Since Beijing is unlikely to issue definitive policy statements concerning these important issues, its recent behavior must be examined for clues as to its actual maritime trajectory.

At a Communist Party meeting held on December 27, 2006, Chinese president Hu Jintao declared, "we should strive to build a powerful navy that adapts to the needs of our military's historical mission in this new century and at this new stage" and is prepared "at any time" for military struggle.[6] "In the process of protecting the nation's authority and security and maintaining our maritime rights," Hu emphasized, "the navy's role is very important."[7] Hu added that China's "navy force should be strengthened and modernized"[8] and should continue moving toward "blue-water" capabilities.[9]

Hu's words followed an incident on October 26, 2006, when a Chinese diesel submarine reportedly surfaced within 8 kilometers of the U.S. Navy aircraft carrier *Kitty Hawk* as the carrier operated near Okinawa. The incident perhaps suggested a new era of skill and confidence among Chinese submariners. Indeed, Admiral William Fallon, then the commander of the U.S. Pacific Command, stated that *Kitty Hawk* had failed to detect the Chinese submarine.[10] While the specifics of this incident remain unclear, at a minimum it highlighted the inherent difficulty in detecting a diesel submarine.

These Chinese naval developments took on larger strategic significance on January 11, 2007, when China reportedly demonstrated a direct-ascent antisatellite capability. A mobile, solid-fueled *Kaituozhe-1* space launch vehicle, probably launched from Xichang Launch Center in Sichuan province, lofted a kinetic kill payload into low-earth orbit aboard a ballistic missile in order to physically destroy one of its (aging) weather satellites, *Feng Yun 1C,* at an altitude of approximately 865 kilometers.[11] Only hours before, Lieutenant General Michael Maples, director of the U.S. Defense Intelligence Agency, had told the Senate Intelligence Committee that "Russia and China continue to be the primary states of concern regarding military space and counterspace programs." Several months before, Dr. Donald Kerr, director of the National Reconnaissance Office, had confirmed that a Chinese ground-based high-energy laser had "illuminated" a U.S. satellite in low-earth orbit without interfering with the satellite's operations.[12]

Taken together, these events suggest that, just as Beijing is determined to prevent the United States and other foreign powers from dominating China's maritime periphery, it will also maintain a strategic stake in the aerospace dimension that is so critical to modern maritime power projection. As James Holmes points out, "Beijing regards the seas and skies adjacent to China's coasts as a 'commons' through which commerce, shipments of raw materials and military power can flow freely. A rising China is increasingly reluctant to entrust the security of this commons to uncertain U.S. goodwill."[13] Senior Captain Xu offers a naval context for this event: "Outer space . . . has become China's strategic interest and new 'high ground.' . . . [This] is beneficial for enhancing the information strength to safeguard our sea power."[14] Senior Captain Liu Yijian adds, "the struggle to seize space superiority will directly affect the course and structure of maritime combat operations, and it will inevitably have a huge influence on the struggle for command of the sea in the future."[15]

White Paper Summary

China's 2006 Defense White Paper states that China's "overall national strength has considerably increased." It supports Hu's call for naval development, stating that China's navy "aims at gradual extension of the strategic depth for offshore defensive operations and enhancing its capabilities in integrated maritime operations and nuclear counterattacks." The White Paper further declares that China's

Navy is working to build itself into a modern maritime force . . . consisting of combined arms with both nuclear and conventional means of operations. Taking informationization as the goal and strategic focus in its modernization drive, the Navy gives high priority to the development of maritime information systems, and new-generation weaponry and equipment. Efforts are being made to improve maritime battlefield capabilities, with emphasis on the construction of relevant facilities for new equipment and the development of combat support capabilities. The Navy is endeavoring to build mobile maritime troops capable of conducting operations under conditions of informationization, and strengthen its overall capabilities of operations in coastal waters, joint operations and integrated maritime support. Efforts are being made to improve and reform training programs and methods to intensify training in joint integrated maritime operations. The Navy is enhancing research into the theory of naval operations and exploring the strategy and tactics of maritime people's war under modern conditions.[16]

DoD Report Summary

The U.S. Department of Defense's 2006 annual report to Congress on the *Military Power of the People's Republic of China* raises concerns about Beijing's lack of transparency concerning the purposes and future dimensions of PLA development. It further states that

> Securing adequate supplies of resources and materials has become a major driver of Chinese foreign policy....China has also strengthened ties to countries that are located astride key maritime transit routes (e.g., the Straits of Malacca). PRC strategists have discussed the vulnerability of China's access to international waterways....China is investing in maritime surface and sub-surface weapons systems that could serve as the basis for a force capable of power projection to secure vital sea lines of communication and/or key geostrategic terrain.[17]

The marked disparity between these Chinese and U.S. assessments of China's military modernization raises pressing questions concerning the extent to which China possesses and will seek to develop naval capabilities, particularly for scenarios beyond Taiwan—for instance, to secure the nation's substantial, rapidly growing seaborne energy imports.

Force Structure

Budget

Annual increases in China's official defense budget averaged 15 percent between 1990 and 2005.[18] China's official defense budget has expanded fourfold in inflation-adjusted terms since 1997.[19] Expenditures on equipment (which includes procurement, and, to some extent, research and development) have quadrupled in inflation-adjusted terms, from $3.1 billion in 1997 to $12.3 billion in 2006.[20] The official 2006 budget of $35 billion represented a 12.6 percent increase over 2005 and a 100 percent increase over the 2000 figure. According to Jiang Enzhu, spokesman for the Fifth Session of China's Tenth National People's Congress, "China's defense budget for 2007 is expected to hit 350.921 billion yuan (44.94 billion U.S. dollars), 17.8 percent higher than that last year. . . ."[21] Jiang justified Beijing's largest military spending raise since the 19.4 percent augmentation from 2002 by stating that "We must increase our military budget, as it is important to national security. China's military must modernize. Our overall defenses are weak."[22]

Regardless of exact budgetary figures, China is clearly developing and procuring the weapons and nurturing the manpower to modernize its military significantly. China's capabilities are clearly growing, but its naval intentions—at least beyond asserting control over its claimed territorial waters, to include Taiwan—remain somewhat unclear. In the absence of authoritative policy statements or specific figures, let us now examine China's naval platforms for more concrete indications of its maritime development trajectory.

China's Submarine Force: Underpinning the Emerging PLA Navy

The heart of China's accelerating naval development is its submarine force. Submarines offer the PLAN a weapon system that is at once a cost-effective deterrent and a highly lethal means of battling even a superior fleet of surface ships. Recently commanded by Admiral Zhang Dingfa, a nuclear submariner who was promoted to the Central Military Commission in 2004, the PLAN is poised to intensify its undersea-warfare capabilities.

The PLAN launched thirteen submarines between 2002 and 2004.[23] These vessels include two new classes of nuclear submarines, as well as the advanced *Song*-class diesel submarines and the *Yuan*-class diesel submarine, the latter of which, according to some reports, represented a surprise for U.S. intelligence.[24] As many as fourteen *Song*-class submarines have been launched thus far, in three progressively refined variants. The *Song* program defied Western predictions that the series would be a failure and that production would halt upon purchase of Russian platforms. The *Song* is designed to carry the potent YJ-82 ASCM (antiship cruise missile).[25]

Considered by experts to be either a "Kilo with Chinese characteristics" or a "*Song* with Russian characteristics," the Type 041 *Yuan*-class submarine could conceivably be equipped with revolutionary AIP (air-independent-propulsion) technology, which allows diesel submarines to operate underwater for far longer periods without surfacing to snorkel. Even if this is yet not the case, constant attention to AIP on the part of Chinese analysts suggests that such technology may be incorporated into future submarines.

By the end of 2006, the PLAN had also taken delivery of eight formidable *Kilo*-class Project 636M submarines purchased in 2002, complete with associated weaponry such as wake-homing and wire-guided torpedoes and the supersonic SS-N-27B ASCM.[26] The new acquisitions added to the two Project 877EKM and two Project 636 variants the navy already operates. Project 636M *Kilo*s are reported to have an endurance capability of 45 days, allowing for a range of

6,000 nautical miles at 7 kt (with snorkeling). Undersea weaponry is a major priority for the PLAN. Accordingly, the new submarines described above are equipped with a lethal mix of Russian and indigenous torpedoes and ASCMs. With wake-homing torpedoes, for instance, it takes much less skill to strike the target, as fire control is vastly simplified.

As more modern diesel submarines join the fleet, China's second generation of nuclear submarines is also making its debut.[27] Two Type 093 nuclear-propelled attack submarines (SSNs) were launched in 2002 and 2003 and may have begun sea trials in 2005 and 2006, with service entry dates in 2007 and 2008, respectively. A third hull, possibly of a more advanced design, is reportedly nearing completion.[28] *Jane's* predicts that three additional 093s will be built in the near future.[29] The 093 is thought to be replacing the five hulls (401 through 405) of China's first-generation Type 091 *Han*-class SSN. It is reported that the 093 may have been constructed in Huludao Shipyard with Russian assistance.

A single Type 094 nuclear-propelled ballistic-missile submarine (SSBN) was launched in 2004, and has been undergoing sea trials since early 2006. The platform reportedly became operational in mid-2007, and its ballistic missiles are expected to do so by 2008–9.[30] A second hull was reportedly launched in 2006 and may be commissioned in 2010. *Jane's* reports that two other hulls are probably under construction and that they may be launched in 2008 and 2010 and commissioned in 2012 and 2014, respectively. It is thought that the 094 might be outfitted with twelve forty-two-ton JL-2 (CSS-NX-5) SLBMs (submarine-launched ballistic missiles). The missiles boast an estimated maximum range of over 8,000 kilometers and a circular error probable of 300 meters. They can be armed with three to eight multiple, independently targeted warheads apiece and equipped with penetration aids. The 094 may be based on the 093's design and share many of its features, but it displaces 2,000 tons more than its cousin, at 8,000 tons.

Scott Bray, deputy senior intelligence officer for China in the U.S. Navy's ONI (Office of Naval Intelligence), states that "a fleet of probably five Type 094 SSBNs will be built in order to provide more redundancy and capacity for a near-continuous at-sea SSBN presence."[31] If operationally successful, the 094 would represent a substantial improvement over China's single first-generation Type 092 *Xia*-class SSBN, which was equipped with short-range (1,770 kilometers) JL-1 SLBMs, is rumored never to have made an extended patrol, and therefore is unlikely ever to have constituted an intercontinental nuclear deterrent.

The trajectory of China's nuclear propulsion program offers one of the best single indicators of whether China seeks to become a genuine global military power. With no need to surface to recharge batteries and no need to refuel—not to mention unparalleled survivability if acoustically advanced and properly operated—nuclear submarines remain ideal platforms for persistent operations in far-flung sea areas. They will form an efficient means for China to project power should it choose to do so. ONI's Scott Bray states that while the 094 "will provide China with a modern and robust sea-based nuclear deterrent force," the 093 constitutes "an effort to improve the PLA(N)'s ability to conduct anti-surface warfare at greater ranges from the Chinese coast than its diesel submarine force offers."[32] A successful 093 program will significantly enlarge the geographic scope of Chinese submarine operations, perhaps ultimately serving as the cornerstone of a genuine blue-water navy. The 094 could take the survivability of China's nuclear deterrent to a new level, potentially enabling Beijing to posture more aggressively in times of crisis. The actual number of nuclear submarines China constructs and deploys thus will offer insight into its naval and nuclear strategies.

Chinese analysts acknowledge that America has long been dominant in undersea warfare, especially since the Cold War.[33] Many Westerners are therefore surprised that China would have the temerity to challenge the United States directly in this specialized domain of warfare. And yet PLAN analysts scrutinize U.S. Navy submarine build rates, which are currently below the replacement level, while carefully probing for potential USN submarine-force vulnerabilities.[34] A 2006 article by a senior PLAN strategist suggests that "China already exceeds [U.S. submarine production] five times over" and that the eighteen U.S. Navy submarines based in the Pacific would find themselves at a severe disadvantage against a fleet of seventy-five or more Chinese submarines.[35] While the author attributes these assessments to an American source, he makes no effort to dispute them.

Chinese Naval Mines: Undermining America's Littoral Presence in Asia?

Most evidence supports the idea that China does not seek to "rule the waves" writ large, at least for now. Rather, it is seeking the much narrower and more realizable objective of dominating the East Asian littoral. To help achieve this more limited objective, the PLAN has to date avoided acquiring costly aircraft carriers and is instead devoting considerable attention to a decidedly more mundane, less photogenic naval weapon: the sea mine.

Unlike their counterparts in most other navies, PLAN surface, subsurface, and air units regularly practice laying mines, as do civilian vessels. This suggests that sea mining is an important component of China's naval strategy. The PLAN is likely interested in sea mining in part because it is one of the less technology-dependent forms of asymmetric warfare—one that can be deployed to good effect today. Operational and informational asymmetries currently favor the use of PLAN sea mines. It is far easier to lay mines than to find and disarm them, particularly in Taiwan's shallow coastal waters. And America cannot expect Taiwan to defeat Chinese sea mines on its own. U.S. mine-countermeasures forces are located far from the fight, while the Taiwanese mine-hunting fleet is small and of uneven quality.

PLAN strategists contend that sea mines are "easy to lay and difficult to sweep; their concealment potential is strong; their destructive power is high; and the threat value is long-lasting."[36] Key objectives for a Chinese offensive mine strategy would be "blockading enemy bases, harbors and sea lanes; destroying enemy sea transport capabilities; attacking or restricting warship mobility; and crippling and exhausting enemy combat strength."[37] For future littoral warfare, it is said that "sea mines constitute the main threat to every navy, and especially for carrier battle groups and submarines."[38] Moreover, this emphasis corresponds to the PLAN evaluation that "relative to other combat mission areas, [the U.S. Navy's] mine warfare capabilities are extremely weak."[39]

China is apparently engaged in a significant effort to upgrade its MIW prowess. MIW capabilities are easily hidden and thus constitute a true "assassin's mace" for the PLAN, to borrow a term some Chinese sources explicitly use to describe this mode of combat.[40] China has amassed a large inventory of naval mines, many of which are obsolete but still deadly, along with somewhat more limited numbers of sophisticated modern mines, some of which are optimized to destroy enemy submarines. China's mine inventory thus not only is extensive but also likely contains some of the world's most lethal MIW systems. A recent Chinese article claims the PLAN possesses over 50,000 mines, consisting of "over 30 varieties of contact, magnetic, acoustic, water pressure and mixed reaction sea mines, remote control sea mines, rocket-rising and mobile mines...."[41] China is on the cutting edge of MIW technological and concept development and already fields some systems absent from the arsenals of advanced nations such as the United States. PLA strategists, moreover, understand the human dimension of modern warfare. Chinese MIW doctrine appears to emphasize speed, psychology, obfuscation, a mix of old and new technologies, and a variety of deployment methods. It targets very specific U.S. Navy platforms and doctrines. And Chinese naval periodicals reveal an impressive MIW training regimen that goes well beyond rote, scripted exercises.

China would likely rely heavily on offensive mining in any Taiwan scenario. If the PLAN were able to employ these mines (an increasingly likely possibility), it would greatly hinder operations, for an extended time, in waters where the mines were thought to have been laid. The obvious means of employing mines is through submarines and surface ships, while the use of civilian assets should not be discounted. But there are growing signs that China recognizes the fact that aircraft offer the best means of quickly laying mines in significant quantity. These aircraft would be useless, however, without air superiority. China's increasingly impressive conventional ballistic-missile force and inventory of SAMs (surface-to-air missiles) and advanced tactical aircraft cast real doubt on the ability of the Taiwanese military to maintain air superiority over both the Taiwan Strait and the island itself. Relying heavily on sea mines, the PLAN may already be fully capable of blockading Taiwan, and even of obstructing crucial SLOCs (sea lines of communication) in the western Pacific area. Indeed, sea mines, used to complement a variety of other capabilities, constitute a deadly challenge to U.S. naval power in East Asia.

Problems in China's defense–industrial complex—which is already showing strong evidence of improvement—will not constrain sea-mine deployment. What China cannot develop indigenously in the near term, it can procure from Russia. Whatever their origin, a significant Chinese buildup of these armaments could conceivably alter the cross-strait military balance in favor of the mainland.

Surface Ships: Gradually Projecting Power

Chinese maritime ambitions are not limited to wielding stealthy submarines, or even sea mines. "While China's submarine force is well suited to interdiction," explains ONI's Scott Bray, "protection of SLOCs with a submarine force is more challenging. To effectively protect shipping, a visible and demonstrable naval capability, generally based on surface combatants with the endurance and range to operate farther from shore for an extended period of time, is preferable."[42] The PLA Navy has recognized its overall weakness in air defense and surface warfare, and has taken impressive steps to overcome those problems. China has produced a new array of frigates and destroyers over the past five years that incorporate numerous advanced design concepts such as stealthy superstructures, vertical-launch air-defense systems (in four of six new destroyers), long-range ASCMs, and phased-array radars. China's three most recent classes of surface combatants all have sophisticated air-search and missile-guidance radars, and also are said to have the advanced, long-range SAMs to afford these ships a respectable area air-defense capability.

China is rapidly upgrading its previously backward destroyer fleet. The PLAN currently possesses sixteen Type 051 *Luda*-class missile destroyers. Built between 1970 and 1991, these relatively old vessels were designed for surface warfare, with limited antiair-warfare and ASW (antisubmarine-warfare) capability. They were refitted in the 1990s to improve their anti-surface-warfare and air-defense capabilities. A single Type 051B *Luhai*-class multi-role missile destroyer, *Shenzhen* (hull 167), entered service in 1998 and was refitted in 2004. Two Type 051C *Luzhou*-class air-defense guided-missile destroyers have been built so far. Based on the older Type 051B hull design, *Shenyang* (hull 115) and *Shijiazhuang* (hull 116) are outfitted with the long-range Russian SA-N-20 SAM system.[43] Two hulls of the Type 052 *Luhu*-class multi-role missile destroyer (*Harbin,* hull 112, and *Qingdao,* hull 113) entered service in the mid-1990s. These were the first Chinese surface combatants equipped with comprehensive surface-strike, air-defense, and ASW capabilities, and also the first Chinese-built warships to be fitted with significant suites of sophisticated Western-designed weapon systems and sensors.

At 154 meters long and displacing 6,500 tons, the two Type 052B *Luyang I-*class multi-role missile destroyers commissioned in 2004 are larger than any destroyers that China has previously built. New indigenous and imported weapon and sensor systems give *Guangzhou* (hull 168) and *Wuhan* (hull 169) enhanced air-defense capability, as well as basic ASW capability. The PLAN's two Type 052C *Luyang II*-class air-defense guided-missile destroyers are based on the Type 052B hull. *Lanzhou* (hull 170), commissioned in 2004, and *Haikou* (hull 171), commissioned the following year, both possess the indigenously produced, vertically launched HHQ-9 SAM system and the phased-array Sea Eagle radar, which resembles U.S. SPY-1 phased-array radars. This last suggests that China may have mastered a potent air- and missile-defense technology that eluded Soviet technicians.

Two Project 956 *Sovremenny*-class missile destroyers, purchased from Russia in 1996 and delivered in 1999 and 2000, are now designated *Hangzhou* (hull 136) and *Fuzhou* (hull 137). Two improved Project 956EM variant vessels (hulls 138 and 139) with enhanced ASCMs, wide-area air-defense systems, and sensors have also been delivered. "The long-range [SA-20] SAM systems [that the *Luzhou* and *Luyang II* destroyers] possess will provide Chinese surface combatants with an area air defense capability as they operate farther from shore and outside of the protection of land-based air defense assets," ONI's Scott Bray extrapolates.

> Under the protection afforded by these advanced area air defense destroyers, which are also equipped with long-range ASCMs, the Chinese Navy can operate combatants such as two recently acquired *Sovremenny* II [destroyers]. These long-range engagement and air defense capabilities now being fielded by the PLA(N) give China a significantly improved capacity for operations beyond the littoral in support of SLOC protection.[44]

China's inventory of frigates has likewise improved substantially in recent years. Starting in the 1990s, China's thirty-two relatively obsolete Type 053 *Jianghu*-class missile frigates have been supplemented by twelve Type 053H2G and 053H3 *Jiangwei*-class multi-role missile frigates. Of these, the last eight vessels of the Type 053H3 (*Jiangwei II* class) possess improved weapon systems and sensors. In 2005, the PLAN took delivery of two new-generation, *Jiangkai*-class Type 054 multi-role frigates, *Ma'anshan* (hull 525) and *Wenzhou* (hull 526). These vessels boast French-made diesel engines and a combination of Russian- and Chinese-made weapon systems, including vertical launch cells and phased-array radars. In early 2007, according to Internet photos, up to four *Jiangkai II*s were being built at two different shipyards, Guangzhou and Shanghai's Hudong. This is the first class of surface warship of which China has built more than two since the 1990s.

China's surface fleet also includes the stealthy *Houbei*-class Type 2208 fast-attack missile craft. Since 2004, several Chinese shipyards have delivered at least four hulls of this high-speed (perhaps 45 knots), wave-piercing catamaran, which boasts several features intended to help it evade detection. Internet photos indicate that additional hulls are being produced in rapid succession. According to Internet sources, as many as six shipyards are now producing the Type 2208, suggesting that it, along with the submarine force, may become a key component of the new PLAN. The mission of these craft would presumably be to destroy Taiwan's surface force quickly in wartime, if indeed that fleet made it out of port. This impressive anti-surface weapon system would be highly effective in attacking surface warships in the waters around China, although the Type 2208's limited endurance would prevent it from operating far from the Chinese coast for extended periods. If 2208s could carry eight ASCMs each, they would have significant firepower, but they are formidable even with their current armament of four ASCMs. The 2208's minimal in-water profile and high speed, moreover, make it a difficult target for torpedoes.

Amphibious Forces

China has made significant progress in amphibious warfare, probably because of its perceived relevance to a Taiwan contingency: "Overall strength is continuously increasing," declares one Chinese commentator, "and already in the near term the number of forces required for combat victory will be attained...for large-scale amphibious operations."[45] Emphasizing this strategic linkage, the Pentagon's 2006 report on Chinese military power states, "PLA amphibious exercises and training in 2005 focused on Taiwan. In September 2005 the PLA held one large-scale, multi-service exercise that dealt explicitly with a Taiwan invasion. China has conducted 11 amphibious exercises featuring a Taiwan scenario in the past 6 years."[46]

The PLAN currently possesses at least fifty medium and heavy amphibious lift vessels.[47] China has constructed nine 4,800-ton *Yuting III* landing ships tank, or LSTs, since 2003, building on significant amphibious construction efforts from the previous decade. Type 63C amphibious armored personnel carriers, operating in concert with several hundred Type 63A amphibious tanks boasting 105-millimeter guns and gun-launched missiles, give the PLA a useful new capability. Meanwhile, the PLAN is building LSMs (landing ships medium), as well as—evidently—its first amphibious landing dock (LPD)-type amphibious assault ship, which is thought to be equipped with transport hovercraft modeled on U.S. landing craft air cushion, or LCACs.[48]

In 2004, a photo of a model of a possible Chinese LPD appeared on the Internet. In the fall of 2006, additional photos became available, showing the transport being built in a large graving dock at Shanghai's Hudong Shipyard. The "Type 071" LPD (as it has been called unofficially) was launched on December 21, 2006, and is currently being fitted out. Richard Fisher describes the Type 071 as "the PLAN's largest indigenously designed combat ship to date."[49]

PLANAF

The PLAAF (PLA Air Force) and PLANAF (PLAN Air Force), which are finally beginning to recover from grave setbacks suffered during Mao's Cultural Revolution, currently possess 2,300 operational combat aircraft. Of these, over 700 are capable of conducting operations against Taiwan without aerial refueling.[50] China still relies on massive imports of Russian planes and their components, particularly tankers and jet engines. The PLAAF uses one hundred twenty H-6 (B-6) twin-engine, medium-range bombers, derivatives of Russia's Tupolev Tu-16/Badger, as its medium- to long-range strategic and tactical air-strike platform, and continues to produce slightly improved versions of this aircraft.[51] The PLANAF uses an H-6 variant for antiship missile attack. Other H-6 variants serve as aerial refueling tankers. These will be supplemented by eight Ilyushin Il-78M four-engine tankers ordered in September 2005,[52] the deployment of which "will extend the range and strike potential of China's bomber and fighter aircraft."[53] Some H-6s also conduct reconnaissance and collect electronic signals intelligence (ELINT).[54]

China is finally beginning to achieve comprehensive domestic production capacity, even as it acquires advanced Russian platforms. A 2006 *Jane's* report concludes, "Since the end of the Cold War, there have been more research and development activities into fighter aircraft in China than anywhere else in the world. There are now at least 16 active purchase, co-production, production or development programmes for combat aircraft and combat helicopters in China."[55] A second *Jane's* report explains that China's "aviation sector is showing the fruits of massive investment," particularly in skilled personnel and cutting-edge production facilities, as well as machine and development tools.[56] The growing stable of modern aircraft resulting from these efforts, along with the increasingly potent weapons these aircraft carry, is increasing China's chances of achieving air superiority over the Taiwan Strait and even the island itself. While coordination between the PLANAF and the PLAAF has long been problematic and subject to speculation, it seems that some of these recent equipment upgrades, coupled with improved training and doctrine, will increase the possibility of effective joint operations in the future, particularly operations against aircraft carriers venturing into East Asian waters.[57] Were the European Union to lift its 1989 Tiananmen arms embargo, China could further step up its progress in these areas.

The PLA accepted shipments of twenty-six Su-27s in 1992, twenty-two in 1996, and twenty-eight in 2002. It has manufactured an additional one hundred of these aircraft indigenously, dubbing them the J-11. The J-11 has served as a test bed for China's indigenous WS-10A turbofan engine, and perhaps for the associated, indigenously built radar and fire control systems and the PL-12 active-guided AAM (air-to-air missile).[58] Ten two-seat, twin-engine Su-30 multi-role fighter aircraft, currently the most capable in the Chinese inventory, were received in 2000, followed by twenty-eight in 2001, thirty-eight in 2003, and twenty-four in 2004, for a total of one hundred Su-30s to date. China's improved Su-30MK2 variant, which boasts an antiship strike capability and an improved electronic-warfare and electronic-countermeasures suite, was developed specifically for naval aviation. An improved engine and new radar have been installed in the Su-30MK3 variant, over and above the improvements to the Su-30MK2. *Jane's* maintains that these latter Su-30 variants offer the PLA "world-class all-weather strike" capabilities for the first time,[59] and forecasts that all China's Su-30s will ultimately be upgraded to the MK2 standard.[60] Thus, China arguably had 266 fourth-generation aircraft in its arsenal by 2004.[61] As many as twenty of China's JH-7 two-seat, twin-engine JH-7 fighter-bomber aircraft, also designated FB-7 or FBC-1 Flying Leopard, are in the PLANAF inventory. Introduced in 2004, the improved, formal production variant dubbed JH-7A is assessed as having achieved the overall performance level of Western fighters deployed from the 1960s through the 1980s.[62]

China's new, indigenous fourth-generation J-10 multi-role fighter is now in serial production and in service with PLAAF units. J-10s have demonstrated their in-air refueling capability through publicly documented exercises. The J-10 is thought to be based on Israel's discontinued Lavi (which itself exploited U.S. F-16 technology) and to approach the performance parameters of Washington's F-16 Fighting Falcon and Brussels's Eurofighter,[63] including a radar detection range of 125 kilometers and the ability to fire active-guided PL-12 AAMs and deliver PGMs (precision-guided munitions).[64] In a sign that Beijing considers the J-10 a breakthrough, the official news agency Xinhua has publicly recognized its designers. This follows eighteen years of secretive effort as a "national key project involving more than 100 research units, more than 20 ministries, commissions and sectors."[65] In a development of potentially revolutionary significance, an indigenous LM WS-10A Tai Hang turbofan engine may be substituted for the Russian AL-31F that currently propels the J-10.[66] China is already in the process of developing further advanced aircraft, including perhaps even a "fifth generation 'stealth' fighter" that some have dubbed the "J-14."[67] China has purchased a variety of Russian PGMs to equip its aircraft, including the Kh-29 antiship missile (10 kilometer range), the Kh-31P anti-radiation missile (110–200 kilometer range), the Kh-59ME antiship missile (115 kilometer range), and the KAB-1500 laser-guided munition.[68]

To bolster the effectiveness of Chinese air power, the PLA is attempting to improve its airborne ISR (intelligence, surveillance, and reconnaissance) capabilities. China is currently developing two major indigenous platforms, improving on previous efforts that derived from modified Ilyushin Il-76 and Tupolev Tu-154 variants.[69] It purchased A-50 AWACS (airborne warning and control system) aircraft from Russia after the United States pressured Israel into canceling a sale of Phalcon AWACS aircraft to Beijing in 2000.[70] China has reportedly been developing the indigenous KJ-2000 AWACS aircraft to conduct surveillance, perform long-range air patrols, and thereby coordinate naval air operations.[71] China's smaller KJ-200/Y-8 "Balance Beam" AEW (airborne early-warning) maritime patrol/electronic-warfare aircraft, with its electronically steered phased-array radar, is said to complement the KJ-2000 by performing tactical AEW and ELINT more economically.[72] Derived from Russia's Antonov An-12/ Cub transport and produced under license by Shaanxi Aircraft Industry (Group) Corporation, China's more than one hundred Y-8s are divided among over twenty variants that perform such additional missions as radar testing, airlift support, and helicopter and UAV (unmanned-aerial-vehicle) transport. Various sources report that a KJ-200 aircraft crashed on June 4, 2006, killing forty people and possibly retarding the program.[73] If successfully developed, however, these platforms could give China an important aerial battle-management capacity.

Helicopters have traditionally been an area of weakness for the PLA. Most platforms in its disproportionately small fleet (roughly three hundred in the PLA, forty in the PLAN) are either imports or copies of foreign models. The PLANAF operates ten to twelve Z-8s, a derivative of France's Aerospatiale SA 321Ja/Super Frelon. A Z-8F variant powered by Pratt & Whitney engines first flew in 2004. The PLAN also operates a naval version (-C) of the PLA's more than two hundred Zhi-9/Haitun (Z-9) multi-role army support helicopters, which are licensed copies of France's Eurocopter AS 365N/Dauphin II. The PLAN also operates ten to twenty Kamov Ka-28/Helix naval helicopters purchased from Russia to operate from its *Sovremenny* destroyers, as well as perhaps from its Type 052B and Type 052C destroyers. The Ka-28's VGS-3 submarine-detecting dipping sonar and sonobuoys, complemented by any new improvements in rotary-wing aviation, will help the PLAN address one aspect of its significant weakness in ASW. China is attempting to further remedy its helicopter deficiency by developing joint ventures with foreign manufacturers such as Eurocopter. Reportedly, CHRDI (China Helicopter Research and Development Institute) is developing an indigenous WZ-10 advanced attack helicopter,[74] with possible army and transport variants.[75]

Having observed the U.S. military's extensive use of UAVs in recent years, China is purchasing foreign models, transforming former piloted aircraft into UAVs, and developing indigenous variants.[76] China's unmanned combat aerial vehicles include J5/7 remotely controlled ground-attack fighter drones and one hundred Harpy antiradar drones obtained from Israel in 2001.[77] China may have reverse-engineered and indigenously produced additional Harpys. These small, stealthy, autonomous flying bombs could destroy Taiwanese air-defense radars.

China's reconnaissance UAVs include Guizhou Aircraft Industry Corporation's new-generation WZ-9 (WZ-2000); BUAA's (Beijing University of Aeronautics & Astronautics) WZ-5 and WZ-5A variants (modeled on the U.S. AQM-34N Firebee); BUAA's VT-UAV vertical take-off/landing UAV; and the ASN-15, -104, -105, and -206 tactical reconnaissance UAVs. While visually similar to General Atomics's Predator, the turbojet-driven WZ-2000 (a prototype of which is reportedly being tested) apparently has "far less endurance."[78] Guizhou is also developing a medium-endurance UAV.[79] The ASN series, developed by Xi'an Northwest Polytechnic University ASN Technology Group Company, includes the short-range multi-role ASN-206, which is capable of conducting ISR operations, electronic-warfare operations, and electronic-countermeasures operations, reportedly making it "one of the most popular and advanced tactical UAV systems fielded by the PLA." Chinese target drones include the TianJian-1 cruise-missile simulation version (which reportedly entered service in 2005); Shaanxi's Chang Kong-1, -1A, -1B, -1C, and -1E versions (of the Soviet Lavochkin La-17C radio-controlled subsonic target drone); and the Ba-2, -7, and -9 (ASN-2, -7, and -9) radio planes. The Ba-9, developed by Xi'an, "was designed for the training of navy antiaircraft artillery (AAA) crews on surface ships."

C4ISR

No overall assessment of China's naval development is complete without consideration of the increasingly important aerospace dimension. Any increase in Chinese naval capability, from access denial to blue-water operations to power projection, will hinge in part on aerospace innovations, from air- and space-based platforms to C4ISR capabilities. By the end of the Cold War, despite major imbalances in this area, China had become the first developing country to achieve comprehensive aerospace capabilities. While China still confronts some challenges, particularly in its aviation sector, it appears to be making rapid, comprehensive progress in producing advanced aerospace platforms. This in turn affords China an increasing range of military operational possibilities.

Beijing has the world's premier sub-strategic mobile missile force. China has positioned 710–90 mobile DF-11 (300 kilometer range) and DF-15 (600 kilometer range) SRBMs (short-range ballistic missiles) in coastal areas opposite Taiwan, constituting an arsenal that "continues to expand at an average rate of about 100 missiles per year."[80] Increasingly capable, accurate, and numerous, PLA SRBMs offer decapitation strike and PGM capability that does not require operationally more-complex manned aircraft. If sufficiently accurate and employed in sufficient numbers, they can render Taiwan's airfields inoperable. SRBMs can also destroy infrastructure nodes, severely disrupting Taiwan's ability to transmit electricity, refine petroleum, and otherwise support its economy and military.

China is fielding a number of new strategic nuclear systems. An upgraded version of China's DF-5 liquid-fueled ICBM (intercontinental ballistic missile) may have a range of up to 13,000 kilometers and may be equipped with multiple, independently targeted warheads.[81] Based on the JL-1 SLBM, road-mobile, and fueled by solid propellant, China's DF-21 boasts a range of 2,500 kilometers and has a variant with improved accuracy.[82] China's DF-31 ICBM (range of 7,250 kilometers) and its DF-31A variant (11,270 kilometer range) are also solid-fueled and road-mobile,[83] making them extremely difficult to target—as would be any JL-2 SLBMs (apparently derived from the DF-31, with a range of 8,000 kilometers) based in Type 094 SSBNs at sea. This combination may finally give Chinese leaders confidence that their nuclear forces are survivable and thus capable of providing a credible second-strike capability. This could significantly alter crisis calculations and stability on both sides of the Pacific.

China may already be developing the capability to target U.S. ships with ballistic missiles such as the DF-21, with its 500–600 kg warhead.[84] "China is equipping theater ballistic missiles with maneuvering reentry vehicles (MaRVs) with radar or IR seekers to provide the accuracy necessary to attack a ship at sea," states ONI's Scott Bray.[85] If supplied with accurate real-time target data, perhaps China's growing family of radar reconnaissance and electro-optical surveillance satellites, terminal radar seekers, and maneuvering warheads could enable Chinese ballistic missiles to complicate or negate U.S. ballistic-missile defense efforts and seriously threaten their targets.[86] If they work, they would be extraordinarily difficult to defend against.

China has acquired hundreds of high-speed track-via-missile-guided S-300 (SA-10) SAMs from Russia. S-300s are capable of covering the Taiwan Strait from their launchers on the Chinese mainland. Beijing may purchase the S-400 (SA-20) system (with a range of up to 400 kilometers) as well.[87] By 2004, according to *Jane's*, China had received twelve battalions (as many as 144 launchers and 576 missiles) of S-300 PMU and S-300 PMU-1 SAMs, the latter which has a range of 105 kilometers. The PLA is reportedly planning to acquire four to eight battalions of S-300 PMU-2 SAMs (240 launchers, 960 SAMs, range of 150–200 kilometers). An initial battalion may have been delivered in 2006.[88] The HQ-9, an indigenous SAM based on S-300 and Patriot missile technologies, is deployed aboard the PLAN's Type 052C *Luyang II*-class guided-missile destroyers. Deployed on Type 051C *Luzhou*-class guided-missile destroyers and controlled by Tombstone phased-array radars, the Russian SA-N-20 SAM "more than doubles the range of current PLAN systems."[89] Moreover, China's first generation of land-attack cruise missiles (LACMs, such as the Yingji-63, with a range of 400–500 kilometers) will reportedly soon become operational, exponentially increasing PRC power-projection capabilities.[90] The Donghai-10, a second-generation LACM with a range of over 1,500 kilometers, has apparently been test-fired.[91]

The combination of range and lethality offered by these missiles has tremendous ramifications for any battle for air superiority over Taiwan.

But China has achieved perhaps its most striking progress in antiship missiles, where the full-spectrum indigenous capabilities it has achieved approach world-class status in many respects. This offers increasingly effective means not only to strike at U.S. carrier strike groups but also to support future missile development financed by robust international commercial sales (and co-development; e.g., with Iran).[92] Every surface warship launched by China in the past decade (with the possible exception of the new LPD) carries long-range, lethal, indigenously developed Yingji-series ASCMs. The C-801 (YJ-8)/802 (YJ-83) series of missiles currently forms the backbone of China's ASCM inventory. Strongly resembling France's MM38/MM39 Exocet, the C-801 is used by the PLANAF's JH-7 fighter and the PLAN's *Song* submarine. A single Chinese-made C-802, which is less capable than China's newer ASCMs, disabled an Israeli *Hanit Sa'ar 5*-class missile boat off Lebanon in 2006, killing four sailors. The C-802 has undergone improvement through a series of variants. Fitted on the PLAN's Type 052C *Lanzhou*-class destroyers, the sea-skimming C-602 (YJ-62) rapidly descends to 7–10 meters above sea level (in waters up to sea state 6), delivering its 300 kg armor-piercing high-explosive warhead at Mach 0.6–0.8, assisted by inertial navigation and GPS. China also has the SS-N-27 Klub supersonic ASCM, which it can launch from its newest eight *Kilo* submarines.

Russia has also been contributing to China's already impressive indigenous missile inventory by selling China weapons for which there is no Western equivalent. China's four *Sovremenny*-class destroyers boast supersonic Raduga 3M80 "Moskit" (SS-N-22 "Sunburn") ramjet-powered ASCMs, which boast a range of at least 120 kilometers, a velocity over Mach 2, and the ability to execute terminal homing maneuvers that seriously complicate a defender's fire-control solution. The PLAN has fired this formidable missile from its four *Sovremenny*-class destroyers. Hulls 138 and 139 may be equipped with a 250 kilometer-range variant of the Moskit.[93] China has also reportedly acquired both variants of Russia's supersonic (greater than Mach 2) Zvezda-Strela Kh-31 (AS-17 "Krypton") sea-skimming missile, which is powered by a ramjet and has a range of 200 kilometers. Kh-31s are being manufactured indigenously as the YJ-91 or YJ-93.[94] The PLAN's Sukhoi Su-30MK2 "Flanker" fighters, as well as perhaps its JH-7As, are reportedly fitted with the Kh-31. Russia specifically designed the Kh-31P passive high-speed anti-radiation (as opposed to Kh-31A active radar) version to assault Western radar systems such as the U.S. Navy's SPY-1. Finally, even Russia itself does not field the Kh-59MK antiship missile it helped develop for the PLAN's Su-30MK2 fighters. This radar-guided, data-linked missile has a range of 250–300 kilometers.[95]

While China's missiles have long been identified as a potential threat to U.S. forces, perhaps some of China's greatest recent progress has occurred in space.

China produces increasingly sophisticated microsatellites weighing 10–100 kg, far less than the average satellite. They potentially permit China to deploy satellite constellations, decreasing costs while increasing reliability, particularly in communications (as opposed to reconnaissance) missions. Should these space-based assets come under threat, the larger numbers in which they could be deployed would make them harder to target and easier to replenish. At 25 kg, furthermore, the Naxing-1 microsatellite made China the fourth country, after Russia, the United States, and the United Kingdom, to launch a satellite approaching nanosatellite designation (i.e., weighing 10 kg or less).[96] China's other satellites have been similarly impressive. Launched in May 2002, the Haiyang-1A ended China's sole reliance on foreign satellites for maritime observation. This marine remote sensing satellite, which monitors China's peripheral seas, was the prototype for a series of Chinese maritime monitoring satellites.[97] According to an official publication, 12 percent of Haiyang-1A's 2003 "satellite data distribution" was "military."[98] A follow-on satellite, Haiyang-1B, with double its predecessor's data capacity, was reportedly launched in April 2007.[99] According to Sun Zhihui, director of China's State Oceanic Administration, China's State Council has approved the development of a series of Haiyang-Bs.[100] In 2001, RAND reported that China had "developed remote sensing satellites capable of transmitting images of the earth's surface in near-real time."[101] Such a capability could greatly improve China's ability to monitor force deployments on its periphery.

In a development that mirrors Western efforts to reduce costs and enhance reliability, satellite buses (standardized platforms) constitute the backbone of China's microsatellite efforts. China is developing at least five variants of three major small satellite buses: CAST968A, B, and C;[102] CAST2000;[103] and CASTMINI (for true microsatellites). CAST968's design characteristics reportedly include a very high subsystem integration rate, good performance, and high efficiency. CAST968 has substantially improved small-satellite development time, cost, and quality. Total development time has been reduced to two years, approaching world standards.[104]

Satellite navigation has revolutionized military operations in every sphere of combat. Chinese missiles may use the U.S. GPS system, as well as Russia's GLONASS system, for navigation. China is also developing its own Beidou geostationary satellite navigation system in order to minimize its reliance on foreign systems. Beidou 1A, launched on October 30, 2000, was stationed over New Guinea. On December 20, 2000, Beidou 1B was placed over the Indian Ocean. Beidou 2A, launched on May 24, 2003, was placed in an intermediary position.[105] China launched a fourth (backup) satellite on February 3, 2007[106] and plans to launch a fifth satellite later in 2007.[107] China has already begun to employ Beidou extensively for both civilian and military applications.[108]

Beijing previously sought substantial access to Europe's nascent Galileo system,[109] which Chinese analysts have scrutinized.[110] While Europe reportedly never planned to give Beijing access to the military component of the system, there was concern that China might be able to penetrate Galileo's PRS (Public Regulated Service) receivers.[111] Due both to such security concerns and to Galileo's importance as a strategic pan-European asset, the Galileo Joint Undertaking (in which China invested $6.5 million as a shareholder, and through which China had agreed to invest an additional $260 million) will be replaced in 2007 by the Galileo Supervisory Authority, in which ownership is solely European. Sino-European disagreement concerning Beijing's access to Galileo has apparently intensified existing Chinese efforts to develop Beidou. Indeed, there are reports that China seeks to purchase hydrogen master atomic clocks—the keystone of an effective satellite navigation system—from Galileo's supplier, Switzerland's Neuchatel Time.[112] While Beidou previously appeared to be rudimentary and perhaps subordinate to Galileo, the launch of additional satellites will increase the system's military applications.[113]

China's official media reports that Beidou will be developed into a full, independent navigation satellite constellation called Compass. Designed to cover China and surrounding regions by 2008, Compass would ultimately use five satellites in geostationary earth orbit and thirty in medium earth orbit to provide global coverage.[114] Compass's commercial Open Service would offer "positioning accuracy within 10 meters, velocity accuracy within 0.2 meter per second and timing accuracy within 50 nanoseconds,"[115] while an even more accurate signal, coupled with system status updates, would reportedly be available to the PLA. There is concern that the radio frequencies used by Compass will overlay both Galileo's PRS and possibly GPS's M-Code, thereby complicating adversary attempts to jam Compass in times of conflict. Improvements in access to foreign and domestic positioning systems increase the accuracy of Chinese missiles and other position-dependent equipment. Development of Compass as a viable independent system could improve Chinese access to reliable signals in conflict.

China's aerospace development has profound implications for the U.S. military. Chinese strategists envision aerospace assets playing a vital role in any future Taiwan scenario. For instance, ballistic and cruise missiles guided by Beidou satellites might be used to target U.S. aircraft carriers. The most fundamental question is whether the PLA will be able to master the developments in air- and space-based platforms and C4ISR needed to support a PLA strategy beyond the East Asian littoral. Such a strategic requirement would necessitate the continued transformation of the PLA, as at present China's current submarine-focused navy and its still-limited air force can only support the more modest strategy of access denial. But just as China was not dissuaded from submarine development in the recent past by American dominance in that area, Beijing also seems unwilling to acquiesce in U.S. aerospace dominance. As China's overall national power continues to rise, its aerospace capacities are likely to rise with it, with significant implications for Beijing's ability to influence its maritime periphery and challenge U.S. hegemony.

Chinese Deck Aviation Ambitions

The most comprehensive and far-reaching question concerning PLAN modernization is the extent to which Beijing will choose between a navy focused on large-deck aviation vs. one based fundamentally on submarines. This is because the former force structure would likely be needed for the PLAN to truly project power into the blue water "beyond Taiwan." According to Huang Qiang, head of the State Commission of Science, Technology, and Industry for National Defense, "China has the capability of building an aircraft carrier, but it is still unknown when one will be built."[116] Another media source of uncertain reliability states, "China could build its first aircraft carrier by 2010 if current research and development proceeds smoothly."[117] While critical datapoints remain unclear, aircraft carriers have already captured the imagination of China's public, and even of some of its strategists. Perhaps because of Beijing's determination to be respected universally as a great power and the nation's growing maritime interests, the PLAN is apparently contemplating various alternatives for developing aircraft carriers. Increasingly numerous and diverse statements and writings on this subject offer critical insights into Beijing's emerging maritime strategy.

To date, Beijing has made significantly greater progress in analyzing and targeting enemy carriers than in building its own. For instance, Taiwan scenarios and how to target U.S. surface combatants, especially aircraft carriers, are reportedly often discussed in PLA internal meetings.[118] As ONI's Scott Bray assesses, "Much of China's military modernization effort of the past five years, and particularly the modernization of the Chinese Navy, has been designed to improve China's anti-carrier capability. China envisions an attack on a carrier strike group as incorporating submarine-launched ASCM strikes and ASBM attacks."[119] Chinese recognition of the increasing vulnerability of carriers, particularly less-sophisticated versions such as China might develop, may thus retard Beijing's indigenous carrier development.

China has already purchased four decommissioned aircraft carriers, to considerable Western media speculation. China's old carriers, especially *Minsk* and *Kiev*, were probably purchased for dissection to inform future indigenous design efforts. *Varyag*, representing the largest and most advanced Soviet carrier design, may ultimately also be used for pilot and deck-crew training and as a "test platform" for general research and development of relevant shipboard systems. To this end, *Varyag* may be retrofitted with an engineering plant, shafts, and screws (which it was said not to have at time of sale to China), so that it can go to sea under its own power. Eventually, a modestly capable *Varyag* might become a centerpiece of PLAN diplomacy, humanitarian operations, and disaster relief.

A small but determined collection of PLA leaders has advocated carrier development. Admiral Liu Huaqing championed the aircraft carrier when he became PLAN commander (1982–88), and subsequently as Central Military Commission vice chairman (1989–97). Whether it makes sense now for Beijing actually to develop an aircraft carrier has apparently been hotly debated in China. Song Xiaojun, editor in chief of *Naval & Merchant Ships,* reports that one PLA faction advocates aircraft-carrier development but must compete with elements urging submarine and aerospace industry development.[120]

A senior Chinese official has stated to the author that although he had "been an advocate of aircraft carriers for many years because we need them," until recently carriers had "not been the best use of national resources," because China "lacks an escort fleet," thereby making any carrier a vulnerable target. China has therefore invested instead in "submarines, mid-sized ships, and fighters [aircraft]." In 2004, this official declared to a group of Western academics that the reigning political and military consensus in Beijing held that the nation should not develop an aircraft carrier. In 2006, however, he stated that "China will have its own aircraft carrier" in "twelve to fifteen years." He explained this rapid shift by stating that over the past two years the subject of aircraft-carrier development had become a "heated internal debate" in Beijing. Chinese national interests had expanded, the security of SLOCs had increased in importance, the likelihood of noncombatant evacuation operations had grown, and Beijing had come to believe "air coverage" was essential to achieve "balanced naval forces."[121] Another indicator of Chinese interest in deck aviation appeared in a 2006 statement from Lieutenant General Wang Zhiyuan, deputy director of the PLA General Armament Department's Science and Technology Commission. Lieutenant General Wang declared that the PLA

> will conduct research and build aircraft carriers on its own, and develop its own carrier fleet. Aircraft carriers are a very important tool available to major powers when they want to protect their maritime rights and interests. As China is such a large country with such a long coastline and we want to protect our maritime interests, aircraft carriers are an absolute necessity.[122]

Ultimately the aircraft carrier itself is essentially a platform for air operations— the system of systems that allows for the projection of air power from the sea. The acquisition of such a vessel for the PLAN would thus be merely one benchmark, and a relatively simple one at that, along a complex continuum that might someday lead to a truly operational PLAN aircraft carrier. Subsequent steps would involve hardware, software, and training. Dramatic improvements in PLAN aerial power-projection capabilities hinge on breakthroughs in sea-based aviation, mid-air refueling, PLAN doctrine, ASW, and PLANAF service culture. Without major improvements in ASW, for instance, any PLAN carrier would be an easy target for competently manned diesel-electric or nuclear-powered attack submarines. China appears to have made no significant progress toward correcting its weakness in ASW. Although its newer, large surface combatants can certainly carry helicopters and might carry ASW helicopters, none appear to have modern hull-mounted or towed-array sonars. There is also little evidence that China is devoting much effort to developing planes equivalent to the U.S. P-3 maritime patrol aircraft. Thus the PLAN's ASW capabilities, while perhaps slowly improving, cannot yet be counted on to provide a reasonable degree of security in open waters.

A PLAN carrier would play little role in a near-term Taiwan scenario, as land-based PLAAF and PLANAF aircraft could perform all required air operations across the narrow Taiwan Strait from airfields on the mainland. Unless China were able to produce a range of carriers and incorporate them into a cohesive and effective concept of operations, it is difficult to envision them as the center-piece of PLAN doctrine in future decades. A senior Chinese official has further emphasized to the author that "China will not try to compete with the U.S. in the open sea. Even twenty PRC carriers cannot compete with U.S. nuclear carriers."[123]

For the foreseeable future, therefore, a Chinese carrier would most likely serve at least one of two major roles. The first would be to support secondary missions in which the most basic motivation is prestige. That aircraft carriers can play a unique role was demonstrated by the 2004 tsunami, after which the PLAN found itself completely upstaged by the U.S. Navy, the Indian Navy, and, most painfully, the JMSDF (Japan Maritime Self-Defense Force).[124] The second role for carriers would be to complement the PLAN's submarine-centered fleet. Missions allocated to carriers might include collective maritime security (e.g., SLOC protection and counter-piracy operations). This would obviously be a secondary PLAN mission, oriented toward friends and rivals in the SCS (South China Sea) and the Indian Ocean. Deployment of an aircraft carrier would also enable the PLAN to project force into the SCS on a modest scale, defending Chinese territorial claims there.

It remains to be seen, however, exactly what place aircraft-carrier development will have in what has been a prolonged, well-publicized, and increasingly success-ful attempt by China to become a maritime power.

Base Infrastructure

Adm. Wu Shengli, commander of the PLA, together with his coequal, Political Commissar Hu Yanlin, leads the 290,000 personnel (12.6 percent of the PLA's 2.3 million) serving in operational submarine, surface, naval-aviation, coastal-defense, and marine-corps units, as well as ten institutions imparting professional military education.[125] Personnel include 25,000 PLANAF members in seven divisions with twenty-seven regiments;[126] 8,000–10,000 marines (whose number can reach 28,000 in wartime); and 28,000 coastal defenders.[127] The PLAN has 97,000 each of officers, noncommissioned officers, and conscripts, with the former being further divided into command, political, logistics, equipment, and technical career tracks.[128]

Like their headquarters, vessel types appear to be organized hierarchically (e.g., with nuclear-powered submarines enjoying higher status than their conventional counterparts).[129] China's North, East, and South Sea fleets each possess two submarine divisions, three destroyer/frigate divisions, and one mine-countermeasures division. Whereas the NSF (North Sea Fleet) has one amphibious division, however, the East and South Sea fleets each possess two. Recent efforts to make the PLAN a leaner, more effective fighting force include base realignment and closure; placement of PLAN forces under the direct command of their respective fleets; establishment of new "high-tech surface ship . . . units"; strengthening militia units and reserve units (particularly those involved in technological, logistical, and equipment support); engagement in "joint operation and systems building"; and consolidation of a "joint logistical support system." China's coastal defense force has also been strengthened and its equipment upgraded.[130]

China's NSF, headquartered at Qingdao (with the Naval Submarine Academy), has other major bases at Huludao (missile testing, R&D, training, and SSN/ SSBN production), Jianggezhuang (SSBNs), and Lushun, as well as at Dalian (Naval Vessel Academy, other facilities) and Yantai (Aviation Engineering College). NSF PLANAF bases are located at Dalian, Qingdao, Jinxi, Jiyuan, Laiyang, Jiaoxian, Xingtai, Laishan, Anyang, Changzhi, Liangxiang, and Shanhaiguan.

Headquartered at Ningbo, China's ESF (East Sea Fleet) has other primary bases at Zhoushan, Shanghai, and Fujan. Located further inland are Nanjing's Naval Staff College and Wuhan's Naval Engineering University. PLANAF bases are located at Danyang, Daishan, Shanghai (Dachang), Ningbo, Luqiao, and Shitangqiao.

The SSF (South Sea Fleet), headquartered at Zhanjiang, with major bases in Yulin and Guangzhou (Naval Service Arms Command Academy), apparently contains several unique assets. A base to support China's new Type 093 and Type 094 submarines is now reportedly under construction on Hainan Island.[131] The SSF is also home to two marine infantry brigades at Heieu (the 1st and 164th). Each brigade includes one artillery regiment, one amphibious armor regiment, and three infantry regiments. The other fleets apparently lack such robust amphibious capabilities.[132] PLANAF bases are located at Foluo, Haikou, Lingshui, Sanya, Guiping, Jialaishi, and Lingling.

The PLAN also operates a variety of research institutes that provide input into its strategy. These include the Navy Research Institute in Beijing, the Command and Staff College in Nanjing, and the Naval Submarine Academy in Qingdao.[133]

Established in 1985, the Navy Research Institute is reportedly the PLAN's "single most important center...for the development of national-level naval strategy, the development of navy operational-level (campaign-level) warfighting concepts, naval tactics, and research and studies that look to the future of naval warfare and the development of foreign naval issues."[134]

Training

Chinese naval planners realize that rapidly improving equipment is useless without corresponding improvement in human performance.[135] This imperative appears to have been solidified in recent official directives, including a June 2006 General Staff Headquarters Plan,[136] and by a December 2006 PLA Comprehensive Military Training Conference that was reportedly attended by more than 150 military training experts.[137] Citing President Hu Jintao's mandate that military training be "raised to a new level through making innovations," a recent *People's Navy* article elaborates, "We should more intensively and extensively carry out battle training...in an authentic environment and in a complicated battlefield situation as a basic form of conducting campaign and tactical exercises so as to enhance the naval units' adaptability in sea battles under the condition of informatization."[138] A companion article stresses, "To ensure winning in wartime, the units should undergo difficult and rigorous training in peacetime according to the requirements of real war, and be tempered under various complicated and difficult conditions."[139] A survey of relevant articles in *People's Navy* suggests that exercises were scripted and rudimentary as recently as ten years ago. Over the past five years, however, they have become far more diverse and realistic.

Current PLAN-wide objectives include "training under real-war situations... employing mobile operations and support...operating in unfamiliar areas and under unknown conditions...training in poor weather conditions...conducting multiple training subjects simultaneously...employing increasingly larger formations...using data links and radio silence [and] operating in an electromagnetic jamming and countermeasures environment."[140] For instance, marine-corps training increasingly involves the use of simulators, and otherwise takes place in increasingly difficult conditions.[141] Shore-based logistics to support naval operations appears to have been substantially improved through computerized inventory management, maintenance and logistics interchangeability, and even outsourcing to the private sector through Internet ordering.[142] To better support an increasing number of operations in unknown areas, China is engaged in intensive surveying and mapping. The National Institute for South China Sea Studies, for instance, has produced China's first-generation "Digital South China Sea" chart. Extensively tested, it brings the PLAN's charts up to international standards and will support the voyages of Chinese vessels.[143]

Training advances will be further consolidated as increasingly well-educated, technologically sophisticated, and internationally aware personnel gain command in the PLAN, thanks to such programs as the ROTC-like National Defense Scholarship Program, curricular reforms, and study abroad.[144] As a *People's Navy* article emphasizes, "The Navy is a high-tech service with a complex variety of specialties. . . . So it is necessary to rely on science and technology and implement scientific management, scientific means, and scientific thinking in conducting training."[145] China's rapid economic, scientific, and technological development supports these improvements in human capacity, although it has simultaneously increased the need for material incentives to recruit talented individuals who enjoy attractive career options in the private sector. The PLAN's enlisted force, while recently reformed, remains dominated by rural males with limited education,[146] and demobilization can still undermine unit cohesion and expertise.[147]

Charged with seizing the initiative in unforeseen circumstances, *People's Navy* reports, PLAN officers are determined to improve the navy's capabilities,[148] to devise new training methods,[149] and to practice in more flexible sequences.[150] At the beginning of 2001, for instance, SSF Minesweeper 814 reformed its system for noncommissioned officers, implementing "training for different grades and levels," making training commensurate with previous experience, and thereby avoiding unnecessary repetition.[151] Minesweeper 852 introduced competition and exams to improve crew evaluations.[152] At the end of April 2005, a PLAN minesweeper unit practiced sweeping and laying mines in an "unfamiliar sea area," under all weather conditions, with the goal of "training as you will fight."[153] These examples stand in stark contrast to the rote, scripted, automaton-like training of only a few years ago.

To be sure, the PLAN is still working to meet its new goals. Malfunctions sometimes occur during exercises.[154] There is still some resistance to PLAN policies demanding that exercises mimic actual combat conditions.[155] And there is even evidence that the PLAN is still experiencing challenges as it makes the administrative transition to a modern professional organization. There is little doubt that the PLA realizes that joint operations constitute a critical element of limited, local warfare under high-technology conditions. The PLA has observed the U.S. armed forces closely, particularly in Operations Desert Storm, Desert Shield, and Iraqi Freedom, and recognizes the need to improve its joint capabilities. The question of how proficient the PLA is at joint warfare, however, is difficult to answer. There are some indications that PLA exercises are moving toward jointness, but it remains unclear how successful the PLA has been at actually accomplishing its goals.[156] To give a sense of the PLAN's latest efforts to address these problems, this chapter will now survey recent exercises in the PLAN's submarine, MIW, and air forces.

Submarine Force

While digital training and simulations can be useful, the only way to become proficient at handling submarines is to take them to sea and operate their weapons. Chinese submarine exercises have increased in sophistication in recent years and currently encompass such categories as command-and-control, navigation, electronic countermeasures, and weapons testing.[157] "Based on the revised [Outline of Military Training and Evaluation] issued in 2002," reports the U.S. ONI, "the PLAN is developing and implementing new and more realistic tactics and combat methods to enable its submarines to be able to attack, survive after an attack, and maintain the capability to attack again at a later time. . . ."[158] Crews strive to conduct a wider variety of increasingly lengthy and challenging exercises attuned to local environmental, hydrographic, and weather conditions.[159] PLAN submarines have gradually increased the amount of red-on-blue adversary training they conduct. In 2002, in the SCS, an "underwater vanguard boat" confronted ASW ships, aircraft, and an underwater minefield barrier. It successfully escaped after firing "a new type of Chinese-manufactured torpedo."[160] The PLAN's detailed arrangements for emergency contingencies, including the training of its personnel to operate multiple weapons systems, are based on the premise that suffering damage during future wars is inevitable.[161]

Submarine-delivered mines appear to take priority in the PLAN training regimen,[162] in part as a critical aspect of future blockade operations.[163] By 2002, mine-laying had become "one of the most common PLAN submarine combat methods and the most basic requirement of submarine warfare."[164] Accordingly, PLAN crews train to handle submarines loaded with large quantities of mines.[165] Drill variants include "hiding and laying mines in deep water"[166] in combination with such operations as torpedo launches.[167] Broad and deep mine-laying against port targets is also emphasized.[168]

PLAN officers recognize the challenges inherent in "penetrating the enemy's antisubmarine forces and laying mines behind enemy lines." According to one PLAN captain, "Secretly penetrating the combined mobile formation deployed by the enemy's antisubmarine forces is a prerequisite to fulfilling the mine-laying task."[169] Submarine detachments have practiced "difficult new tactics like 'mine laying in great depth.'"[170] China's official radio commended Chao Chunyi, a torpedo and mine officer from the PLAN submarine detachment, for cutting the loading time for mines in half.[171] Commander Ma Lixin, commanding officer of *Song* submarine 314 and a celebrity in China's naval press, recently led the efforts of an ESF submarine detachment to "develop tactical innovations." In one year, Ma researched and developed over ten new operational methods, "including how to carry out a blockade and how to lay mines using conventional submarines." In early 2005, Ma "led his unit to participate in live exercises at sea. . . ."[172] In one mine exercise, Ma was charged with evading "enemy" ASW airplanes, a minefield, and—most difficult of all—an adversary submarine, in order to lay mines in a nearby area. He exploited his mastery of the local environment, ordered his crew to proceed at a speed that minimized noise, eluded the adversary submarine and shore radar, and accomplished the mine-laying mission on time.[173] All three of China's fleets, moreover, have reportedly trained with what appear to be advanced mobile mines. In December 2005, NSF sailors were photographed hoisting a "new type of sea mine."[174]

The PLAN has for some time pursued nuclear submarine missions of extended duration. In his recently published memoirs, Adm. Liu Huaqing relates how he raised the priority of long-duration exercises for PLAN nuclear submarines, testing all parameters of these new capabilities.[175] Apparently as part of these expanded activities, the current PLAN chief of staff, Sun Jianguo, reportedly commanded *Han* 403 during a mid-1980s' mission of ninety days,[176] breaking the eighty-four-day undersea endurance record previously set by USS *Nautilus*.[177] Chinese military medical journals demonstrate a very clear interest in undersea medicine, in particular the physical and psychological challenges surrounding lengthy submerged missions.[178]

Based on photos and anecdotal evidence, Chinese submarines go to sea frequently, though not usually for extended periods. But the submarine force seems set to range ever farther afield. According to ONI's Scott Bray,

> China claims that its submarines have conducted long-range patrols almost since the inception of the Chinese submarine force. According to Chinese press reports, PLA(N) submarines have occasionally ventured into the Pacific Ocean and, with some degree of regularity, continue to conduct these "cruises of long duration." Although China has apparently been satisfied with only a handful of these deployments every year, the growing technological capabilities of the PLA(N) submarine force and China's evolving maritime strategy, which calls for an operational capability beyond the littoral in support of an anti-access mission, create the conditions for Beijing to opt for an increased submarine presence in the Western Pacific Ocean east of the Ryukyu Island chain.[179]

MIW Forces

Particularly since 2002, when the PLA issued a new Outline of Military Training and Evaluation, PLAN surface forces have engaged in an array of increasingly realistic, increasingly complex training involving longer at-sea periods and multiple vessels of different classes. These forces, networked through various datalinks, prosecute exercises such as "beyond-visual-range attacks against maritime and shore-based targets." There still appears to be significant room for improvement in air defense and coordination with submarine and coastal defense forces.[180] Improvised exercises have also been carried out recently by sea-mine warehouse officers. An SSF mobile sea-mine warehouse, for instance, has been tasked with "Four Transformations" to improve high-speed, long-distance mobile mine transport.[181] An ESF sea-mine warehouse has conducted independent, mobile all-weather exercises designed to ensure rapid transport of sea-mine components during enemy air raids. During these exercises, officers developed detection systems and testing instruments, then exploited terrain, weather, and darkness for camouflage.[182]

These recent efforts coincide with the new emphasis on MIW as a major surface-fleet mission. The PLAN has stressed automation and electronics that facilitate "all-weather" mine-laying capabilities.[183] *Jianghu*-class frigates have conducted mine-laying as part of their ASW training.[184] Minesweeping units have recently practiced laying various types of moored and deep bottom mines as part of fast-paced confrontational exercises. One SSF minesweeping unit has recently participated in over ten such exercises, involving "network-centric training" and "the intelligization of sea mines."[185] In 2002, an NSF unit including minesweepers 813 and 811 attacked submarines with "both foreign and domestic torpedo sea mines" with a "100% success rate."[186]

Certain units have been hailed for training innovations. An SSF minesweeper unit's "Flagship" 809 was rewarded for achieving repeated PLAN firsts.[187] The unit established a "Night Training Implementation Leading Small Group" to increase the difficulty of training. The unit's officers used GPS, radar, and handheld location systems to arrive in an unfamiliar area within two meters of required position. This use of multiple navigation systems represented a hedge against any one system becoming unavailable under combat conditions. In 2000, ship 809 established a "Warfare and Training Methods Discussion Group," which studied how to counteract electronic interference, counter high-performance enemy sea mines, defeat over-the-horizon missile attacks, and disrupt potential opponents' operational concepts, as well as both deployed and future equipment. Since 2001, ship 809 has developed twelve new tactics to "counter-electronically jam" advanced enemy mines and over-the-horizon missile attacks. In 2003, *People's Navy* reported that ship 809 had conducted the PLAN's first opposition-force MIW exercise. By 2003, the vessel was routinely and successfully clearing all types of mines, day or night and in all types of weather, using on-the-spot decision-making under a wide variety of uncertain and realistic conditions.[188]

A disturbing potential component of PLAN operations in general, and of mine-laying in particular, is the use of civilian assets to supplement military assets. Over the past few years, each navy unit has reportedly organized militia units—which constitute "an important force in future maritime warfare"—into training-equipment, management, applications, and safeguard groups, in an effort to gain experience and develop new methods "to fulfill mission requirements." An ESF exercise using civilian vessels includes a focus on clearing various types of mines.[189] A Chinese naval periodical offers perhaps the first photo available in the West showing how the PLAN might use civilian ships for MIW. In December 2004, a PLAN base mobilized six civilian ships for a drill that involved, among other activities, reconnaissance, "mine laying by fishing boats," and non-pier and at-sea supply of naval vessels in battle.[190] Another report details the equipment requirements (e.g., cranes) for loading mines at remote ports. Such precautions assume that wharves at major naval bases will be destroyed by enemy PGM strikes in wartime, requiring MIW forces to work around battle damage.[191] This training imperative is described in multiple publications as a "non-wharf" exercise.

PLANAF

Since 2002, PLANAF training has been increasingly rigorous, with exercises involving extended duration, increasingly unfamiliar conditions, and on-the-spot decision-making:

> pilots fly more long-distance, over-water, cross-border missions during the day and night. Many of the flights are at minimum altitude (i.e., below 100 meters) or low altitude (above 100 meters) and in poor weather conditions. Vessels with helicopters have focused on helicopter operations during day and night that are gradually moving further from the vessel.[192]

An SSF exercise in August 2002 exemplified the progress of the air force in such missions. Aircrews dropped mines from bombers in an unfamiliar location under "realistic" conditions, while opposed by simulated adversary forces. The exercise involved a combat aircraft group consisting of three bomber groups, an electronic-jamming aircraft, and escort fighters. The electronic-jamming aircraft jammed the enemy's radar, while the combat-aircraft group employed minimum-altitude tactics, quickly dispensing several tens of mines and torpedoes.[193] Another source, probably reporting on the same exercise, relates how adversary "red force" bombers laying mines in the SCS were intercepted and attacked by Chinese "blue force" fighters.[194] During the Sino-Russian "Peace Mission 2005" exercise, Chinese Su-27 and J-11 fighters reportedly escorted naval units, J-8II fighters performed intercepts, and H-6 bombers dropped precision-guided weapons. In the process, the arguably more advanced PLAAF likely gleaned insight into the Russian Air Force's sophisticated air-combat doctrine, tactics, and techniques for long-range strike.[195]

Despite recent efforts, it remains unclear how proficient China's different services are at joint warfare, particularly in an over-water environment. While the educational requirements for PLANAF pilots, which already exceeded those for most other PLAN forces, were granted bachelor's-degree status in 2001, naval aviation has traditionally been poorly funded. PLAN pilots fly only a fraction of the hours that their peers in the United States, Japan, and even India do on an annual basis: "it appears that Naval Aviation combat aircraft pilots average around 125 hours. Furthermore, most units normally fly only three days per week. Each training sortie for fighter and attack aircraft also averages around 45 minutes."[196] Integrating operations between highly regimented, rigidly structured PLAAF units and immature, sea-based PLAN units would require technical and service-culture innovations, as well as exercises that are less carefully scripted than has been the case in recent years, to develop the requisite interoperability and interservice coordination. Significant additional research is required to gauge how much coordination exists among PLAN land-based naval air and surface/subsurface assets. This is all the more critical, as the type and degree of coordination will necessarily vary depending on the maritime mission assigned. China's development and procurement of increasingly advanced aircraft will not automatically solve the lack of practical experience with these platforms. Indeed, as China's experience has demonstrated, mastering them will involve the loss of expensive aircraft and hard-to-replace pilots.

PLAN Doctrine

China's military lexicon contains no term for "doctrine." Depending on the operational level of conflict referenced, it is more appropriate to refer to strategy, campaigns, and tactics.[197] At the strategic level, the PLAN receives guidance analogous to that of the other PLA service branches. The "National Military Strategic Guidelines for the New Period" offers the "highest level of strategic guidance for all PLA military operations during war and preparation for war during peacetime." The most likely scenario Beijing expects to face is "local wars under modern high-tech conditions." As articulated in the Guidelines, the concept of "active defense" instructs the PLA to prepare to undertake a variety of sophisticated offensive measures simultaneously, targeting enemy weaknesses within this larger strategic context. Doctrine has evolved rapidly to address new challenges: the PLAN "has published an entirely new set of revised guidance documents since the end of the 9th Five-Year Plan (1996–2000)." Since the beginning of this decade, the PLA has sought to implement this guidance through its "Two Transformations" program, using informatization and mechanization to transform itself from a personnel-intensive into a technology-intensive force.[198]

It is only at the tactical level, and to some extent at the campaign level, that the PLAN possesses a "doctrine" distinguishable from larger PLA thinking. The PLAN's strategic guidance is currently conveyed by eight Chinese characters that together mean "active defense, offshore operations." The former "four characters" apply more generally to all PLA service branches, informing military strategy and military-strategic guidelines. The latter "four characters" refer to the PLAN's area of responsibility.[199]

The major generals who edited the PLA's first English-language volume on strategy offer a naval context for China's preparations to fight and win local wars under modern high-tech conditions. They foresee possible threats to

China's "sovereignty, maritime rights, and great cause of reunification" with Taiwan. Such threats may necessitate a defensive, "just war" along China's "borderlines, seacoasts, and air spaces." They state that China is unusual in the number and magnitude of its territorial disputes: one million square kilometers of maritime territory, or "one ninth of China's national land territory," remains under contention.[200] The authors discuss energy, a factor that increasingly influences Chinese strategists. To "ensure the security of [the] channel[s] of [our] strategic energy supply," they observe, is "of great significance to our development in the long run."[201] The authors voice concerns that remaining challenges in long-distance power projection, operations, and logistics will make these battlefields very different from "inland war fields," and thereby "disadvantageous to us."[202] To address these disparities, the authors suggest integrating civilian and military forces, combining "regular warfare with guerilla warfare on the sea," employing asymmetric "trump card" weapons, mixing "high-tech weapons with common weapons," and blending military operations with political, economic,[203] and legal measures within the larger politico-military effort.[204]

PLAN doctrine appears to have evolved with both external security threats and China's ability to project power. From its inception on April 23, 1949 until 1985, the PLAN was charged with coastal defense. As a subordinate organization, the PLAN was assigned to support PLA ground forces in what Mao envisioned as a major land war against the superpowers. Following the 1972 rapprochement with the United States, this concern applied solely to the USSR.

During the late 1970s, however, evidence emerged that China might be moving beyond a policy of coastal defense. The PLAN sent submarines into the SCS, as well as beyond the "first island chain" into the Pacific Ocean, for the first time. In January 1977, specifically, submarine 252 performed a 3,300 nautical mile voyage in Pacific waters. In July of that year, submarine 296 carried out successful diving tests in the SCS.[205] By the mid-1980s, the PLAN had developed a broader ability to conduct "offshore operations" as part of its larger naval strategy predicated on offshore defense.

An "offshore defense strategy" was formally approved in 1985 by Deng Xiaoping and the other members of China's Central Military Commission.[206] This major paradigm shift was driven by Deng's assessment that great-power war would not occur for some time and that coastal economic development should take precedence. Increasing concerns over maritime resources and sovereignty—particularly with regard to Taiwan as the island began to democratize in the late 1980s, raising popular questions about its status vis-à-vis the mainland—accelerated the process. Liu Huaqing further articulated and implemented the new strategic paradigm. In 1983, Adm. Liu recalls,

> I stressed that we should achieve a unified understanding of the concept of "offshore" according to Comrade [Deng] Xiaoping's instructions. Our "offshore" areas are the Yellow Sea, East China Sea, South China Sea, the seas around the Spratly Islands and

Taiwan and inside and outside the Okinawa island chain, as well as the northern part of the Pacific.

As with similar terms, "offshore defense" does not relate to specific geographic distances *per se,* but rather to conceptual areas for naval defense and power projection, progressively farther from shore. The distances to which this and similar terms pertain, while relative instead of absolute, do appear to have expanded in scope as the PLAN's warfighting capacity has expanded. This process will likely continue apace. At present, the extent of offshore defense appears to be "as far as the PLA Navy's capabilities will allow it to operate task forces out at sea with the requisite amount of support and security. For many PLAN officers, this is still a function of the operational reach of the PLA's landbased aircraft and the PLAN's antisubmarine warfare capabilities."[207] To date, however, perhaps to preserve strategic flexibility, Beijing has refrained from publicly and precisely defining these terms, making it necessary to examine PLAN capabilities in order to gain insight into China's intentions.

Island Chains—Benchmarks of PLAN Force Projection?

How then to demarcate China's progress in projecting power farther from its shores? As Senior Captain Xu Qi of the PLAN emphasizes, China's "passage in and out of the [open] ocean is obstructed by two island chains. [China's] maritime geostrategic posture is [thus] in a semi-enclosed condition."[208] The authors of the PLA's first English-language volume on strategy likewise believe that despite its 18,000 kilometer coastline, China is currently constrained by the world's longest island chain, centering on the strategically, politically, and economically vital territory of Taiwan: "If Taiwan should be alienated from the mainland...a large area of water territory and rich reserves of ocean resources will fall into the hands of others.... China will forever be locked to the west side of the first chain of islands in the West Pacific."[209]

Adm. Liu and others have defined the first island chain, or the current limit of most PLAN operations, as being formed by Japan and its northern and southern archipelagos, South Korea, Taiwan, the Philippines, and Indonesia (from Borneo to Natuna Besar). The second island chain, which Liu envisioned as being in range of future PLAN operations, runs from the Japanese archipelago south through the Bonins, the Marianas (including Guam), the Carolines, and Indonesia.[210] The first two island chains thus "encompass maritime areas out to approximately 1,800 nm from China's coast, including most of the East China Sea and East Asian SLOCs."[211] While a 2004 issue of China's official *People's Daily* mentions only two "island chains," the first and the second,[212] some unofficial Chinese publications even refer to a "third island chain" centered on America's Hawaiian bases, depicting this as a "strategic rear area" for the U.S. military.[213]

as submarines are used to deploy sea mine barriers in the water channels outside of enemy ports to blockade them."[225]

Active-defense concepts allow for offensive actions even in a Chinese SLOC-protection campaign. For instance, "active and initiative local offensive operations are an effective measure to reduce and limit enemy capabilities for transportation sabotage combat in a transportation defense campaign."[226] Specifically, "in order to weaken and limit enemy capabilities for SLOC attack, we sometimes need to attack and blockade enemy bases and airports."[227] The authors argue that China's level of offensive measures in a SLOC defense campaign should vary both with relative capabilities and with the operational situation: "[W]hen one has a stronger operational force, launch an active offensive to attack the enemy's SLOC attack force.... [W]hen one does not have the ability to conduct an active attack and the enemy does not attack us, we start to launch transport activities under concealment.... [W]hen the enemy has started blockade and attack activities, we start the campaign with various anti-blockade and counterattack combat activities."[228]

Despite emphasizing offensive fleet action throughout the chapter, however, the authors acknowledge that the dispersed nature of combat and fleet operations today makes obtaining a single decisive battle difficult.[229] The authors' Mahanian approach, which equates to "the best defense is a good offense," appears difficult to reconcile with a strategy for the protection of friendly shipping—a difficult, asset-intensive, defensive mission. Not surprisingly, the authors appear to have struggled with this dilemma as much as Mahan did, as all of Mahan's disciples have, and as the U.S. Navy does today. The authors acknowledge that protecting shipping is a defensive mission and that scarce assets will likely limit a navy's ability to protect all shipping.[230] But when it comes to presenting a solution for this dilemma, they fall back on the primacy of offense. This is highlighted by the authors' caveat that "Generally speaking, the SLOC protection campaign is a defensive campaign. Nevertheless, active and initiative local offensive operations are an effective measure to reduce and limit enemy capabilities...."[231] The rest of the paragraph advocates seizing opportunities to attack first whenever they present themselves, even when performing a "defensive" mission. This dovetails with Mahan's theory that the best way to protect one's own shipping is to seek out and destroy the enemy's fleet, sweeping his flag from vital waters.

"Naval Campaigns" urges both sophisticated knowledge of the strategic and campaign/operational levels of warfare and an integrated air/surface/subsurface approach to planning. Despite this exhortation, however, a warning about friendly fire considerations[232] suggests that PLAN strategists harbor some doubts about the navy's ability to coordinate complex operations. Friendly-fire deconfliction severely challenges even the best navies (especially in ASW), so the authors' comment that blockading forces "must not trespass" on other friendly forces' areas is rather telling. Numerous references to both "hard" and "soft" means of defeating a naval adversary indicate that they appreciate the value of electronic warfare and of tactical and operational deception. The authors routinely stress the need for good intelligence and reconnaissance in support of naval operations. The level of ISR the authors require seems to exceed current PLAN capabilities even seven years later, however, and thus may represent advocacy on behalf of increased capabilities.

The authors repeatedly discuss the need for air superiority, and in each section they provide recommended guidance for the employment of fighter aircraft. This would be relevant for a Taiwan scenario, but, since the PLAN currently lacks carrier-based aircraft, not for missions beyond the range of land-based air. The authors are either discussing Taiwan or implicitly lobbying for a PLAN aircraft-carrier capability or both. The section on "Organization and Covering Transport Ships to Load and Unload and Leave Port" seems to contemplate a naval expeditionary task force assembling to steam to one common objective, as opposed to an ordinary convoy of merchant/cargo ships cruising along the Chinese coast.[233] While these statements need to be compared with those in other PLAN doctrinal writings as they become available outside China, it seems reasonable to conclude that Beijing will not accept a maritime energy blockade and is already developing serious countermeasures.

Inferences About China's Modernization Plan

China's evolving platforms and weaponry point to an access-denial strategy that is wholly consistent with Beijing's focus on the Taiwan issue. There is no doubt that the PLA is fully committed to dominance of the littoral battlespace around China, with an intense focus on the waters and airspace around Taiwan. Everything the PLA is developing, with the exceptions of its ICBM force, its SSBNs, and perhaps its SSNs and LPD, seems to be devoted to this cause. Some of the PLA's more modern ships and aircraft will allow it to extend its combat power slightly farther, into the SCS, and to a limited extent into parts of the western Pacific. The PLAN is also capable of sending limited numbers of warships on occasional transoceanic cruises. These deployments, however, are severely limited by the navy's limited number of replenishment vessels. While China's shipyards are fully capable of building vessels that could perform at-sea replenishment operations, they evidently are not doing so. This suggests that, at least for the time being, China is limiting its military focus to matters closer to home.

Specifically, China's power-projection capabilities are focused on a Taiwan contingency. There is little evidence to show that the PLAN is developing the capabilities necessary to extend its ability to project power (as the United States would conceive of it) much beyond China's claimed territorial waters. Granted, PLAN ships carry sophisticated long-range ASCMs, and some of their aircraft can carry LACMs. The newest SSNs might be similarly equipped as well. But the PLAN does not have the capability to deploy to distant areas and establish an oceanic sanctuary from which it can conduct military strikes against opposing navies or targets ashore.

However, such an interpretation does not capture the full range and potential ambition of China's naval development. "China's maritime strategy is evolving along two paths," explains ONI's Scott Bray. "First, China is focused on a regional anti-access capability, which is principally applicable in preventing third-party intervention in a Taiwan scenario. Second, China is simultaneously expanding its maritime strategy to include a mission to protect China's growing dependence on maritime commerce for economic development."[234] China's growing surface forces could well support missions beyond Taiwan. Indeed, many of China's amphibious craft are based at Zhanjiang in the SSF—rather distant from the Taiwan Strait. Increasing air-defense capabilities hint at genuine blue-water ambitions, since land-based aircraft have sufficient range to cover most missions associated with Taiwan contingencies. After all, PLAN ships would benefit from land-based air cover when operating near the Chinese coast. In a similar vein, rumors of Chinese aircraft-carrier development have intensified and even reached quasi-official status.[235]

Here it is useful to reflect on the challenges the United States faced as it sought to accurately understand Japanese naval development prior to World War II. In a sobering essay, Thomas G. Mahnken, now the U.S. deputy assistant secretary of defense for policy planning, demonstrates that, despite the U.S. Navy's making war with Japan its primary planning contingency, allocating considerable resources to analyze this contingency, and exploiting the large amount of relevant information in open sources (95 percent, in the view of the U.S. naval attaché in Tokyo),[236] mirror imaging, ethnocentric assumptions, and lack of imagination caused U.S. analysts to miss revolutionary Japanese tactical and technological innovations. Because of such shortfalls, the U.S. Army and Navy "repeatedly discounted credible reports that Japan had achieved a capability that the United States lacked, whether it was the Type 91 long-range armor-piercing naval shell, the Type 93 oxygen-propelled torpedo [which boasted not only a minimal wake but also a range over four times that estimated by the U.S.], or the Type 0 fighter."[237] As one former head of ONI's Far East Section, Arthur H. McCollum, recalls, "The tendency was to judge technical developments on the basis of our own technology and on the assumption that our technology was superior to any other. So if something was reported that the Japanese did have and we didn't then, obviously, it was wrong."[238] Of course, one hopes the United States never enters into a conflict with China along the lines of the Pacific War with Japan. These lessons are nonetheless vital to understanding China's rapid if complicated maritime development and its rise as a great power in East Asia and the world.

The United States, China, and Regional Naval Relations: Competitive Coexistence

The evolving contest for East Asia's seas will loom large on the Asia-Pacific security agenda for the foreseeable future. The interaction of threat perceptions, strategies, and force structures among China, other Asian nations, and the United States will make for both cooperation and competition. Chinese analysts view their nation's actions as inherently defensive. They conceive of naval forces as performing a deterrent function, independent of these forces' combat role: "The challenge that China's maritime sovereignty faces is not a problem of actual combat strength between 'Number Two' and 'Number One.' It is rather a problem of effectively deterring the enemy from carrying out provocations."[239] With respect to Taiwan, a senior Chinese official told the author, "We can win a war with the U.S. without nuclear weapons [because the] U.S. is coming to us."[240] In a landmark study, John Wilson Lewis and Xue Litai conclude that despite the continuing difficulties China confronts as it seeks to match Western technology and even organization, Taiwan's importance to Chinese identity, strategic value, and position as a bellwether of national territorial integrity justify extraordinary expenditure of blood and treasure. Moreover, China's military planners appear to believe that by investing selectively in asymmetric weapons, they can reconcile these conflicting realities without fuelling an arms race and hence mutual insecurity.[241] With a burgeoning shipbuilding industry and maritime commercial sector, not to mention an intensifying dependence on foreign sources of natural resources, PLAN admirals find it easier and easier to persuade their civilian leadership that the PLAN should take its place as a major instrument of Chinese power.

Rapid development and acquisition of submarines, naval mines, missiles, and other anti-access weapon systems appear to be part of a larger Chinese effort to prevent the United States from operating effectively in the East Asian littoral, particularly in the event of a crisis in the Taiwan Strait. While U.S.–China relations have improved considerably since September 11, 2001, which helped to ameliorate Chinese resentments concerning the April 2001 EP-3 incident and the May 1999 bombing of China's embassy in Belgrade, emerging trends concerning Taiwan suggest the lingering potential for conflict. U.S. naval planners must prepare for a variety of disturbing Taiwan contingencies, including a decapitating missile strike and a PLAN blockade that relies heavily on submarines and naval mines. As Thomas Christensen writes: "The proximity of Taiwan to the mainland...Taiwan's massive trade dependence...the inherent difficulty in clearing mines, and the extreme weakness of American mine-clearing capacity, particularly in [the Pacific] theater...all make blockade a tempting...strategy for...China. ..."[242] The end of the Cold War has also shifted the thrust of U.S. naval operations from force projection on the open seas to joint operations in easily blocked littorals—thus greatly increasing the importance of mine countermeasures for coastal states that might find themselves the targets of U.S. naval action.

A war between China and the United States over Taiwan should be avoidable—provided the United States honors its commitment to the "One China" principle by consistently opposing Taiwan independence and Beijing addresses the concerns of Taiwanese voters understandably determined to safeguard their democratic way of life. Unfortunately, current Taiwanese president Chen Shui-bian, who has a history of provoking Beijing, has recently made a series of extremely dangerous pro-independence statements. On March 4, 2007, Chen publicly declared that Taiwan has "Four Wants and One Without": (1) "Taiwan wants independence," (2) "Taiwan wants rectification of the country's name" (i.e., changing it from "Republic of China" to "Taiwan," including in the case of local firms whose names currently contain the word "China"), (3) "Taiwan wants a new constitution," and (4) "Taiwan wants development." The "One Without" is "Taiwan does not have a left-right political problem"; it has a national identity problem, and the question is independence or unification with China.[243] These statements, which threaten to cross redlines that Beijing has clearly drawn, directly contravene Chen's 2000 election pledge of the "four no's and the one won't," in which he committed "not to declare independence, change Taiwan's name or hold a referendum on the independence issue."[244]

In a sign that Chen is far from enjoying a monopoly on Taiwanese public opinion, the Nationalist Party, or KMT, disavowed the president's machinations as a "disaster for Taiwan." The People's First Party, a KMT ally, "filed a civil lawsuit...charging Chen with sedition" because "his remarks could lead to war, impacting Taiwan and other parts of the world," according to party spokesman Lee Hung-chun.[245] The bottom line is that Washington cannot let Taipei declare independence, which would be a disaster for all involved. Lest U.S. concerns about free riding continue to increase, Taipei will also need to do more to "tend to its own defenses."[246] In a larger strategic sense, the United States and China will need to develop a positive but realistic understanding of their respective roles in the Asia-Pacific that might best be termed "competitive coexistence."

Perhaps even more difficult to reconcile in the long run will be Japan's regional maritime role and its relations with China. While Japan's defense and foreign policy have changed dramatically since it opened up to the world in 1853, SLOC security has endured as a primary national security concern. Official Diet testimony holds that "the greatest cause of [Japan's World War II] defeat was the loss of shipping" to Allied interdiction efforts.[247] These persistent concerns have been raised anew by China's reemergence as a sea power. A key indication is former Prime Minister Hashimoto's worry that "many commercial flights and aircraft [were] forced to divert around those areas affected" by China's March 1996 missile tests, during which "some of the missiles landed in waters only 60 km from [Japan's] Yonaguni island...."[248]

As a result, Japan is gradually strengthening its maritime-defense and power-projection capabilities. In October 2004, the JMSDF and Coast Guard led Northeast Asia's first Proliferation Security Initiative exercise. In the Indian Ocean in 2006, the JMSDF fuelled allied vessels to support operations in Afghanistan. Meanwhile, Japan is struggling to assert control over its exclusive economic zone, some of which is in dispute. Japanese policymakers, motivated by increasingly "realist" threat perceptions, are exploring new directions in their pursuit of SLOC security. The extent to which these emerging impulses can transcend funding constraints imposed by demographic and economic challenges, as well as constitutional questions over the use of force on the part of the Japanese armed forces, remains a pivotal question for both Chinese planners and for East Asian maritime security.

Overall Assessment

The authors of the PLA's first English-language volume on strategy describe the current age as an "era of sea" in which maritime states, like their predecessors, will employ Mahanian and other strategies to "actively develop comprehensive sea power" and "expand strategic depth at sea."[249] China seems to be adapting to the seas by applying various strands of Western thought to its own unique understanding of and experiences with sea power, as well as its larger history and strategic traditions. For example, Mahan's emphasis on trade following the flag is accepted in China long after falling out of favor in the West, but aggressive power projection is rejected as being alien to Chinese strategic culture. Long-range influence is described as peaceful and nonmilitary in nature, while "for military circles in China, command of the sea means one side in a conflict having control over a specific sea area for a specific period of time."[250]

As Chinese strategists look seaward, they seem in particular to invoke the thinking of Mahan. It is difficult to determine, however, how sophisticated their appreciation of Mahan is, as aspects of his teachings seem to have been adopted rather uncritically, for rhetorical purposes at least. Perhaps Mahan's thought represents a model of Western—particularly American—success in developing comprehensive national power, especially in the maritime realm. This model can serve flexibly as a touchstone for China's own sea-power aspirations, much as the Ming Dynasty mariner Zheng He's legacy now serves as a sounding board for Chinese maritime ideology and conceptions of maritime moral exceptionalism, independent of the exact historical details of his voyages.

An Oil Armada? The Commercial and Strategic Significance of China's Growing Tanker Fleet

Gabriel Collins

> ...once oil imports exceed [1.5 million barrels per day], it becomes necessary to use economic, diplomatic, and military means to secure the safety of one's oil supply.[1]

The energy shipping business is globalized to the hilt. It is not uncommon to find, say, a Norwegian ship owner whose company is registered in the Bahamas running a Panamanian-flagged tanker with an Indian captain and a Ukrainian and Filipino crew, carrying Saudi oil to buyers in Singapore and China.

The oil shipping business lies at the intersection of commerce and the high politics of oil security. Unlike wheat or iron ore, oil is a highly political commodity. Oil's inherently strategic character imparts a strong national security flavor to many actions that in other sectors would be considered purely commercial. In the case of the PRC (People's Republic of China), it is at first glance tough to ascertain the country's "real" reasons for wanting a large domestic oil tanker fleet. Some believe it is so China can "ensure" the security of its oil imports. Others are convinced that the security issues are window dressing and that Chinese tanker operators are content to manipulate the government's oil insecurity for commercial gain.

In this author's view, the buildup is driven primarily by commercial factors. However, the geopolitical implications of China's growing maritime trade (which could reach $1 trillion per year by 2020) and its growing oil demand (which could reach 12 million barrels per day by 2020) necessitate a close look at the factors behind China's desire to increase its presence in the world tanker market.

Beyond Taiwan

The global oil shipping system successfully transports oil from some of the world's most unstable areas. It has functioned through wars, hurricanes, embargoes, canal closures, and other adverse situations. Yet maritime oil transport's fundamental flexibility and adaptability depend largely on global freedom of navigation, which is upheld by the U.S. Navy. Without secure seas, the commercial sector cannot unleash its ingenuity. Most oil importers are content to free ride on U.S. naval protection. But some, such as China, are not. Thus, while tanker operators engage in apolitical pursuit of profit, the process of ensuring the free navigation that makes their operations possible is a highly geopolitical affair.

China's tanker-fleet plans will have significant geopolitical effects if China makes protecting oil and other resource shipments a major priority for the People's Liberation Army Navy (PLA Navy or PLAN). Many Chinese naval analysts' writings emphasize the need for the capacity to protect sea lines of communication, or SLOCs, at long range from Chinese shores. To date the Chinese naval modernization drive has been heavily Taiwan-centric, but it is readily conceivable that protecting maritime resource supply lines could become a key "beyond Taiwan" raison d'être for the PLAN.

China needs secure resource imports to sustain economic development. Speaking at a Communist Party meeting on December 27, 2006, President Hu Jintao bluntly stated that China needs a "powerful" "blue-water" navy prepared "at any time" for military struggle to uphold its interests. This may entail creating a long-distance SLOC protection capacity.[2]

China's 2006 Defense White Paper, *China's National Defense in 2006*, supports President Hu's assertions. The White Paper, the most authoritative public statement of Beijing's appraisal of the strategic environment and the proper responses to that environment, states that China's navy "aims at gradual extension of the strategic depth for offshore defensive operations and enhancing its capabilities in integrated maritime operations and nuclear counterattacks."[3] Clearly, Beijing's perceived need to secure seaborne energy supplies may become an important post-Taiwan driver of Chinese naval modernization.

Chinese analysts advocate strengthening the PLA Navy so that it is capable of "long range rapid responses and interventions in trouble spots" such as the Strait of Malacca.[4] Indeed, Wu Lei, a prominent Chinese energy expert, explains that "the fear that the U.S. might cut [energy shipments] off as a result of the deterioration of Sino-U.S. relations over the Taiwan issue drives much of Beijing's modernization of its navy and air forces."[5] As such, identifying and analyzing the strategic rationale behind China's state-led tanker-fleet expansion may help illuminate China's maritime policy and strategy.

Why Does China Want an Expanded Tanker Fleet?

China's share of total world oil consumption is set to more than double in the next fifteen years. For the foreseeable future, moreover, China will receive most of its imported oil by sea, notwithstanding a much-touted new pipeline originating in Kazakhstan and similar pipelines planned for Russia. Driven by feelings of energy insecurity, China's leadership desires control over the entire oil supply chain in order to guarantee the nation's oil supply during times of crisis.[6]

Accordingly, Beijing advocates building a national tanker fleet capable of hauling up to three-quarters of Chinese oil imports by 2020.[7] In August 2003, the Chinese government established a "tanker working group," providing a clear sign that the fleet buildup enjoys high-level support.[8] By 2010, China intends to transport 40–50 percent of its oil imports in PRC-flagged tankers. By 2020, it hopes to carry 60–70 percent.[9] Chinese analysts predict that the country will need more than forty VLCCs (very large crude carriers) by 2010, each of which can carry 1.5 million or more barrels of oil.[10]

The tanker-fleet buildup is driven to some extent by security concerns, but its biggest effects will be on the commercial side. As Chinese shipyards produce an increasing number of VLCCs, this will affect both shipping rates and the ship market itself.

China aspires to be the number one global shipbuilder by 2015. Its plans for doing so are laid out in official policy statements and are rapidly being implemented.[11] South Korea in particular faces a major competitive threat from Chinese tanker builders hungry for work. Figure 6.1 shows global long-haul tanker builders with total orders exceeding 2 million DWTs' (deadweight tons) worth of shipping. It also depicts these firms' home countries' total share of new construction for global long-haul tankers.

The Malacca Dilemma

The "Malacca Dilemma" lies at the heart of Chinese security analysts' feelings of oil insecurity. Chinese analysts believe that whoever controls Malacca also controls China's oil security, since more than 90 percent of Chinese oil imports pass through Malacca. They fear that these bottlenecks could be easily closed by terrorism, piracy, or the navies of the United States or regional powers in the event of a conflict over Taiwan or some other serious Sino-American crisis. They believe that China's inability to secure the Strait would be "disastrous" for national security.[12]

In Chinese eyes, the U.S. Navy is not the only threat to China's maritime energy supply lines. Chinese planners worry that the rapidly modernizing Indian Navy could use its naval superiority vis-à-vis China in the Indian Ocean to gain strategic leverage.[13] Beijing also casts a suspicious eye on the Japan Maritime

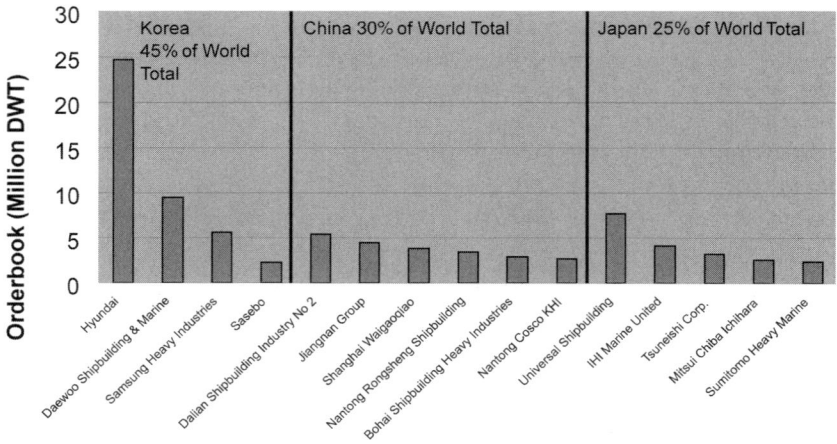

Figure 6.1 Main global long-haul tanker builders.

Source: Lloyd's Sea-Web.

Note: "Long-haul" means tankers greater than 100,000 DWT; percentages rounded to the nearest percentage point.

Self-Defense Force (JMSDF), since Japan competes with China for energy resources in Russia and the East China Sea, and because the JMSDF cooperates with both the U.S. and the Indian navies.[14]

The Malacca Dilemma is reportedly garnering significant high-level attention in Beijing and may be driving China to search for alternative oil shipment routes. This could mean laying a pipeline through Myanmar to China's Yunnan Province or a "Malacca bypass" pipeline across southern Thailand's Kra Isthmus.[15] Nevertheless, China is likely to rely on oil shipments through Malacca for the foreseeable future, simply because of the steep cost of establishing new shipping routes.[16]

Commercial Factors

Despite the Chinese tanker buildup's statist overtones, shippers will likely resist taking orders from the government. The nature of the Chinese government's relationship with the tanker operators is conveyed by a Chinese phrase that loosely translates as "government builds the stage and the companies play." That is, the government "stage master" can set certain ground rules, but the "actors" enjoy substantial freedom to pursue their own commercial objectives once the "stage" is built and the "performance" begins.

Table 6.1 Chinese Energy Shipping IPOs

Company	Amount Raised	Date	Exchange
China Merchants Energy Shipping	$727 million	November 2006	Shanghai
China COSCO Holdings	$1.22 billion	June 2005	Hong Kong

Source: Lloyd's Sea-Web.

Managers of shipping companies appear generally content to let the central government promote the shipbuilding/shipping industry at the broad policy level. Yet, like the state oil companies, they may resist government meddling in their daily operations. If the economic returns from other common tanker market practices—such as chartering tankers out to national and private operators worldwide —trump those of pooling up and serving the Chinese national oil companies, shippers will favor the more profitable approach. Similarly, if the national energy companies find it easier or more cost-effective to have foreign tanker operators haul their oil, they may oppose a forced marriage with Chinese oil shipping firms.

Chinese analysts lament the lack of coordination between state energy producers and state energy shippers.[17] However, the Chinese government will probably have to give Chinese tanker owners economic incentives such as low-interest loans and/or tax breaks to entice them to work more closely with China's national energy companies. At present, an estimated 90 percent of China's oil shipping capacity, or more than 10.8 million DWT, is serving foreign clients.[18] It is likely that this is driven largely by the fact that the shippers realize the greatest profits by evaluating business on its commercial rather than political merits.

Several Chinese shipping firms, all of which either specialize in energy shipping or have substantial positions in the business, have held IPOs (initial public offerings of stock) within the past three years. This may be regarded as yet another indicator of the fundamentally commercial character of Chinese firms' energy shipping operations. Table 6.1 shows major Chinese energy shipping IPOs over the past three years. Much of the global shipping IPO activity of the past two years has occurred in the dry-bulk sector, but strong tanker markets have driven a number of energy shipping offerings as well. It appears unlikely that Chinese firms (particularly state-owned enterprises) will sell controlling shares. Rather, they will sell minority stakes to raise cash while still retaining full control.

Shipping Sector Parallels with Oil Company/Central Government Relations

Understanding the relationships between China's national energy companies and the government will help elucidate how relations between tanker operators and the central government may unfold. Erica Downs of the Brookings

Institution has noted that Chinese national energy companies' parochial interests often influence major high-level energy policy decisions.[19] It is widely believed that much of the initial impetus behind China's "go abroad" oil field acquisition push actually came from the China National Petroleum Corporation, or CNPC.

While powerful elements of China's central government advocate "wellhead to gas pump" control of the oil supply chain, with the idea of shipping Chinese firms' overseas oil production back to China, the managers of national energy companies often operate along more traditional "market" principles. Chinese oil marketers state that transporting equity oil produced from distant fields back to China is too expensive.[20] Instead, they favor selling production locally and acquiring crude closer to home for Chinese use. For example, had the China National Offshore Oil Corporation, or CNOOC, successfully acquired the American producer UNOCAL in the summer of 2005, it would likely have continued selling UNOCAL's Gulf of Mexico production on the U.S. market because it made greater economic sense to do so.

On the whole, China's state shipyards and shipping companies appear to be following the path of its state oil and gas companies. In peacetime, state-controlled oil carriers will pursue profit. Yet Chinese strategic thinkers believe state-owned vessels would stand ready to be pressed into service in times of crisis.[21] Potential flaws in this logic will be discussed shortly.

China's Shipbuilding Industry

Beijing has powerful economic incentives to bolster its shipbuilding sector. A large-scale shipbuilding program aids domestic shipyards, the steel industry, and the metallurgical and machine-tool sectors. Judging by recent experience, it takes Chinese yards approximately 884,000 man-hours to complete each VLCC.[22] Chinese sources calculate that every 10,000 DWT built can create 100,000–200,000 man-hours of employment for Chinese workers.[23] Fifty-seven VLCCs are currently on order with Chinese firms. If twenty of these are undergoing construction simultaneously, this would create some 60 million man-hours of employment, or enough to employ 20,500 people, full time, for one year. Thus, on the basis of job creation alone, China's leadership finds a strong argument for supporting its shipbuilders.

Chinese ship owners and operators presently control eighteen VLCCs. Most other vessels in the Chinese fleet are small, old tankers better suited for the coastal trade than for international oil carriage. Meng Qinglin, a senior manager of Dalian Ocean Shipping Company, estimates that Chinese tankers are not only 30 percent older than their international counterparts on average but also much smaller, averaging only 20,000 DWT (as compared to a typical 300,000 DWT VLCC).[24] Figure 6.2 compares China's current VLCC fleet to those of other major oil importers.

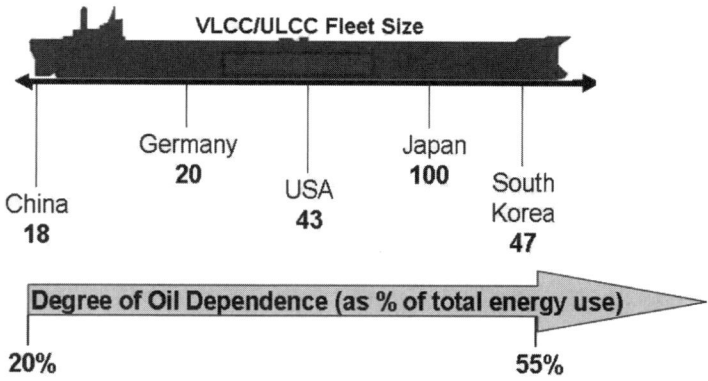

Figure 6.2 Tanker Fleet Size vs. Oil Dependency.

Source: Lloyd's Sea-Web, BBC.

Note: Figures based on ownership by group owners, registered owners, operators, ship managers, and DOC holders.

China has launched an aggressive tanker-building campaign and is now one of the world's leading tanker builders. Indeed, Chinese shipyards have captured 30 percent of global orders for VLCC construction. Tankers form a major portion of Chinese yards' output and will continue to do so, as shown in Figure 6.3.

The figures bear witness to the success of Chinese firms. Of the 21 million DWT of Suezmaxes and VLCCs currently on order and under construction in Chinese yards, roughly 13 million DWT are being built for foreign operators. Although China lags behind the very advanced Japanese and Korean yards technologically, the large number of foreign tanker orders seems to be a resounding vote in favor of the Chinese shipbuilding industry's increasing quality. Table 6.2 summarizes Chinese shipbuilders' relative strengths and weaknesses.

Broader Effect on the Tanker Market?

Some observers worry that China's aggressive tanker-building program could outstrip demand, driving tanker rates down. Chinese analysts suggest acquiring secondhand tankers as a way of avoiding this problem. Strong global oil demand growth and increasing reliance on long-haul African and Middle Eastern oil supplies will help prop up the market for some time to come. Long-haul product exports from the Middle East will also create incremental VLCC demand in the coming years.

In addition, if Chinese builders can capture a share of the tanker market at a rate exceeding the overall growth in demand, this will lower the risk of

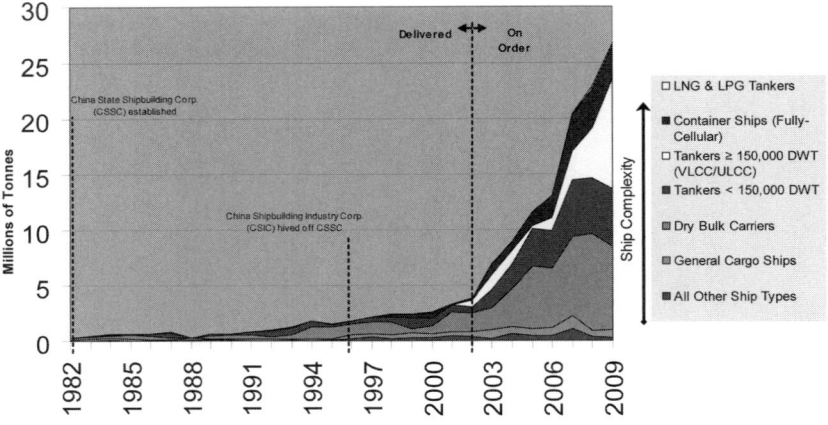

Figure 6.3 PRC Shipbuilding Production by Deadweight, 1982–2009.

Source: Lloyd's Sea-Web.

overbuilding. Changes to the market for ships may also increase China's market share without causing undue downward pressure on shipping rates. Industry observers interviewed by the author have indicated that Japanese heavy industrial firms are considering making a gradual exit from shipbuilding. This would open market share for the Chinese, possibly allowing them to accelerate their construction efforts without overbuilding.

Benefits for Other Maritime Industries

As its need for seaborne oil imports grows, China is also expanding its port facilities and onshore oil handling infrastructure. China is quickly developing large deepwater facilities that can better accommodate the large tankers that haul its oil imports from Africa and the Middle East. In 2005, only three ports— Qingdao, Zhoushan, and Shuidong—could accommodate tankers displacing 200,000 DWT or more. Consequently, China is rapidly preparing specialized facilities to handle large energy/oil tankers, especially in major ports on China's southeast coast. Ningbo is undergoing harbor enlargement to accommodate 200,000 DWT ships, while Zhoushan and Quanzhou ports are constructing platforms to accommodate 250,000 DWT tankers. After these projects are completed, Qingdao, Ningbo, Zhoushan, Quanzhou, Maoming, and Shuidong will all be able to accommodate 200,000–250,000 DWT tankers.[25]

To further facilitate the transport of energy within the country, Chinese analysts recommend rapidly upgrading China's oil transport system of pipelines,

Table 6.2 Chinese Shipbuilding Industry vs. Main Competitors

PRC	Japan/South Korea
Bulk of ships built are of low complexity.	More proficient at high-value ship construction.
Lower price	Higher prices
Gaining technological proficiency, but still behind state-of-the-art.	Main yards are technologically state-of-the-art.
Relatively weak domestic innovation capacity.	High domestic innovation capacity.
Willing to customize ships.	Emphasize series production, little customization.
Low labor costs.	High labor costs, but partially offset by higher technical proficiency.
Has significant land area for physical expansion.	Must build yards overseas and outsource, since space for expansion is scarce.
Extensive co-siting of commercial and military shipbuilding.	Commercial and military shipbuilding separated. Much less military shipbuilding activity at present.
Quality control problems.	Excellent quality control.
Problems with on-time delivery.	Timely delivery.
Weak marine equipment industry (only 40 percent of ship equipment is domestic).	Japan has strong marine equipment industry (95 percent of ship equipment is domestic); 85 percent of South Korean ship equipment is domestic.
Lower degree of integration between shipbuilding and supporting industries such as steel and marine equipment.	Higher integration due to old industrial groupings (keiretsu and chaebols).
Shipbuilding seen as a "pillar industry" in all three countries. The idea is that the industry can promote wider industrial development.	

harbors, ships, shipyards, and oil transport lines, along with the governing laws and regulations.[26] In particular, improving China's domestic oil pipeline network would enhance energy security. Robust capacity to shift oil supplies rapidly between major demand and import areas would introduce a degree of redundancy in case an incident closed one or more major VLCC-capable ports. An improved pipeline network would also bolster the effectiveness of China's growing strategic petroleum reserve by allowing for a rapid infusion of supplies into an integrated market in the event of a crisis. By 2010, Chinese companies plan to expand the country's pipeline network for oil, gas, and other products from 40,000 to 65,000 kilometers.[27] In essence, China has three port zones capable of accommodating VLCCs. The first encompasses the Bohai Gulf area, with Dalian and Tianjin as the main ports. The second lies near the Shanghai area, with Ningbo as the primary port. The third is in the south, with Guangzhou as the main VLCC-capable port. Connecting these zones with users throughout the country has become a major priority for Beijing.

Can a National Tanker Fleet Ensure Oil Security?

As noted previously, China is strengthening its oil transportation capacity in a bid to ensure uninterrupted oil deliveries in times of crisis. But there are no guarantees. First, a national tanker fleet cannot protect oil importers from the internal security problems endemic to many oil-exporting countries. Civil war, terrorism, or many other factors could prevent supplies from ever reaching Chinese tankers. Second, instability in producing countries generally does not affect oil shipments once they get offshore, but many Chinese analysts fear that the U.S. Navy and allied navies will blockade energy shipments to China in a showdown over Taiwan or some other crisis.[28] Chinese "hawks" believe the PLAN must modernize because its ability to secure vital SLOCs and ensure the safety of China-bound shipments "seriously lags" behind China's growing import demand.[29] In their view, a national tanker fleet would bolster the security of the nation's oil supply if PLA Navy units escorted Chinese tankers through contested areas.

Some Chinese analysts nonetheless believe that Chinese-operated tankers can secure oil shipments from unstable areas such as Africa and the Middle East.[30] While internal problems in the supplier country may be unavoidable, the rationale behind these analysts' view seems to be that an importer with its own fleet enjoys greater ability to ensure energy security once the oil leaves the exporting country. Protecting tankers and downstream infrastructure (refineries and distribution networks) is usually simpler than trying to protect oil fields in distant countries jealous of their sovereignty. Protecting an oil or gas field in a country thousands of miles away would entail a large, rapid joint military deployment that is beyond the capability of nearly all oil importers other than the United States. And, even if an importer boasts substantial force projection ability, its response would likely come too late to prevent a supply cutoff.

Tanker Protection Options

Efforts to protect tankers fall into two primary categories. The first is convoying and escorting tankers. Shippers resist convoy operations because it hinders their flexibility and adds costs. Naval officers also tend to dislike escort missions, which cede the initiative almost entirely to the enemy while providing little opportunity for glory. Convoy duty, moreover, is highly asset-intensive, particularly in a threat environment characterized by possible aerial, surface, and subsurface threats. A simple calculation quickly reveals that convoying would stretch China's navy very thin, as the PLAN currently possesses far fewer modern antiair-warfare- and ASW-capable vessels than it would need for a surface escort mission.

Assuming that two VLCCs per day would be needed to meet Chinese oil demand, the logistics of implementing such a convoy system would overwhelm the PLAN. Each group of two VLCCs would require round-trip steaming time of thirty-three days from the Persian Gulf to China, plus a two-day turnaround period to take on supplies and cargo. This thirty-five-day cycle, repeated daily, would correspond to a need for at least seventy escorting surface warships.[31] Logistics ships would be necessary to refuel the escorts on both the inbound and the outbound legs of the voyage (since the Chinese VLCCs would be vulnerable to attack when transiting the Indian Ocean after off-loading in China). Additional ships would likely be required to perform maintenance and repair on the escorts. This is a rough calculation—if anything, it underestimates the force requirements for the PLA Navy—but it does give a basic idea of the assets required. In all likelihood, even if the navy acquired sufficient surface combatants in the coming years to perform sustained convoy operations, China's leadership would still be forced to choose between escorting tankers and keeping enough forces in the main theater of conflict to win the fight that triggered the U.S. blockade. Indeed, a number of Chinese analysts write that it will be some time before China can realistically defend distant energy supply lanes.[32]

The second strategy for protecting shipping is the offensive Mahanian strategy, which entails taking the fight to the enemy, attacking his bases, and driving him from the fight. The pattern of Chinese naval acquisitions in recent years suggests that Beijing would incline toward such a tanker protection strategy. In essence, China would employ its growing modern submarine force, new LACMs (land-attack cruise missiles), long-range strike aircraft, and formidable ballistic-missile force to attack enemy bases and punish any country that imposed a blockade or lent its support to the blockading power. At present, China is simultaneously building or purchasing four classes of attack submarine (*Yuan, Song,* Type 093, and *Kilo*). This construction program is unmatched in the contemporary world. These submarines could conceivably launch the land-attack variant of the Russian Klub cruise missile, which boasts a range of 300 kilometers, as well as the Dong Hai-10 LACM, which can strike targets 1,500 kilometers distant. Finally, the PLA's 2nd Artillery commands a force of more than 900 short- and medium-range ballistic missiles.

Calling the Opponent's Bluff

Unless the PLA can attain outright naval and air superiority in a given sea zone, carrying oil in Chinese-flagged tankers during wartime might render the PRC *more* vulnerable to interdiction of its energy supply, because—at least in theory—foreign navies could easily determine which tankers were permitted to reach China. It might seem, then, that absent a substantial blue-water naval capability—a capability which may be decades away—China is making itself a target by constructing a state-controlled, Chinese-flagged tanker fleet.

If so, Beijing's best option might be to rely on private third-party tanker operators, whose deliveries could be effectively stopped only by a close blockade of Chinese ports—in turn exposing the blockading state's naval forces to a wide range of military threats and almost certainly sparking a larger conflict whose repercussions would presumably exceed any likely political gains for that state.[33] Alternatively, reflagging PRC-flagged tankers to Liberia, Panama, or another flag-of-convenience state would also make these ships back into "private operators," placing the burden of proof on interdicting forces.

Nonetheless, because of international legal norms, having a Chinese-flagged tanker fleet import oil for the government might indeed help ensure China's energy security during a crisis. This is because China could assert "sovereign immunity" for its tanker fleet during times of crisis, in hopes of deterring an adversary's navy from interdicting oil tankers bound for China. Under international law, a PRC-flagged tanker in government service would enjoy sovereign immunity. If an outside power interdicted such a vessel, China would have grounds to claim that its sovereignty had been breached sufficiently to threaten its national well-being, thereby justifying a serious armed response. The escalatory barrier created by putting state-flagged vessels into government service would thus deter adversaries from interdicting PRC oil shipments unless hostilities were either imminent or already underway.

It should be noted that PRC-flagged tankers hauling oil for any of the state-controlled Chinese oil producers would likely meet the criteria for sovereign immune status. During a crisis, furthermore, oil not already being shipped on behalf of PRC state-owned oil companies could rapidly be resold at sea to any number of PRC government entities, thus creating the necessary legal condition to assert sovereign immune status for the PRC-flagged tankers in question.[34] Figure 6.4 depicts China's increased propensity to place its VLCCs, which would be the primary vessels hauling oil through the Indian Ocean and other potentially vulnerable sea lanes, under the Chinese flag.

Interdicting private tankers at sea would be difficult in practice, moreover, because at any given time the ship's bill of lading might not accurately reflect the true end destination of an oil cargo.[35] In normal commerce, cargoes may be bought and sold dozens of times while still on the high seas. Bills of lading can also easily be falsified, a technique regularly used by smugglers. Finally, unless the blockading power was willing to risk environmental disaster by disabling or sinking uncooperative tankers, it would likely lack sufficient military assets to board and take control of such ships, as fifty-two oil tankers pass through the Malacca Strait alone on a daily basis.[36] For all these reasons, a domestically flagged tanker

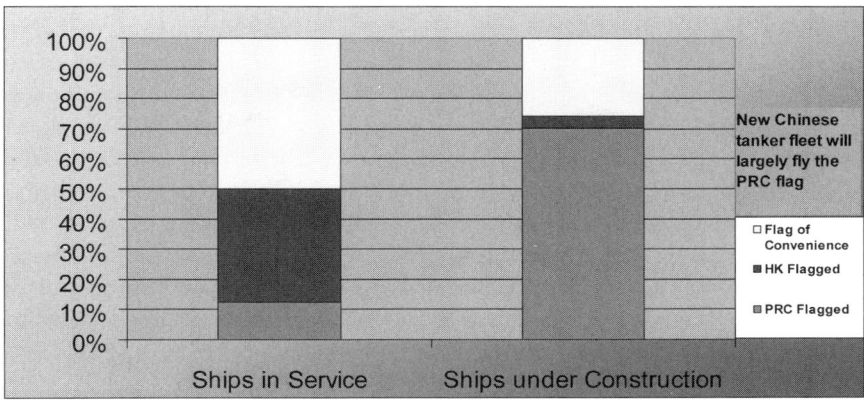

Figure 6.4 PRC Tanker Flagging.

Source: Lloyd's Ship Register.

fleet does in fact make some strategic sense, at least from Beijing's security-focused perspective.

Security Implications

Not all security contingencies threatening Chinese energy security would involve a Taiwan conflict. A terrorist attack on a Saudi export terminal that suddenly tightened world oil markets, for example, might be sufficient to trigger a government "call" on state-run tankers. It might prove difficult for Beijing to press PRC-flagged tankers into state service during a crisis, however. Assuming PRC tanker operators follow normal peacetime operating principles, their VLCCs could be chartered out to shippers in places as far afield as Nigeria, Venezuela, or northwest Europe. Given the distances involved, it might take thirty days or more for these vessels to reach Chinese ports, even if they immediately diverted from their charters and headed for China.

If it had some advance warning, the Chinese central government might notify tanker operators ahead of time and preposition them for crisis oil deliveries. However, numerous commercial observers carefully track tanker movements, meaning that even covert preparations on the part of the PRC would likely be noticed quickly. Other major powers would rapidly become aware that China was marshalling assets, and might see such an action as a sign that Beijing anticipated hostilities. Consequently, rather than helping ensure national security, Beijing's decision to call on PRC-flagged tankers during times of major tension could well cause other actors to assume the worst—thereby precipitating a more serious crisis.

China's leadership needs to understand that for the time being, the world oil market is a far better guarantor of energy security than a state tanker fleet protected by a blue-water navy. It would be very difficult to interdict private tankers bound for Chinese ports at a distance from China. The global oil market is highly fungible; ship destinations are unclear, since cargoes are often resold at sea; and oil can be transshipped to China through third ports in the region. The same logic applies to the Strait of Hormuz and other chokepoints. In addition, the number of tankers transiting key chokepoints would likely far exceed any potential blockading navy's physical ability to take control of uncooperative ships, unless that navy was willing to apply disabling fire—and accept the ensuing diplomatic and military headaches.[37]

Conclusions

While China is building a large number of VLCCs and other long-haul crude tankers, Chinese tanker operators will work almost exclusively within the framework of the existing global tanker market, at least during peacetime. It is highly unlikely that China will try to circumvent the existing global tanker market system entirely, because the opportunity costs of doing so would be very high. Energy subsidies illustrate the cost of working outside the market, even to a modest extent. China already pays its state oil companies billions of dollars in subsidies annually to compensate them for losses they incur when buying oil at market prices, only to be forced to sell products made from that oil at government-capped rates within China. Tanker operations driven by economic opportunity are more profitable than those driven by state directives. Moreover, commercial deals struck by Chinese shipyards and shipping companies with foreign operators are likely to further integrate Chinese firms into the global oil shipping sector.

The precedent set by China's national energy companies also favors the adoption of a largely commercial approach to tanker-fleet operation. Although China has spent billions of dollars on overseas equity oil acquisitions, the flagship state firm CNPC sells the majority of its equity oil on the international market.[38] In sum, China appears to be profiting from shipbuilding and tanker operation during peacetime while hedging its bets against future threats to oil shipments. China will not build an "oil armada." Security concerns are undoubtedly shaping Beijing's plans to have Chinese tankers haul Chinese crude imports, but given the many shortcomings of this plan, its implementation will be driven almost entirely by commercial concerns.

CHAPTER 7

INDIA AS A MARITIME POWER?

Andrew C. Winner

India is not the first country that comes to mind as a likely Asian maritime power. While Indian national security officials and thinkers have begun to speak the language of maritime power, one searches in vain for a formal Indian maritime strategy document. In 2000, one well-respected Indian maritime analyst called for the Indian government to develop and promulgate a maritime security policy as a precursor to a maritime strategy for the IN (Indian Navy) and the national security apparatus.[1] In 2005, the Indian CNS (chief of naval staff) stated in a speech that a maritime strategy was indeed under development, but no such document has yet been issued publicly.[2]

A very brief IN vision statement did appear in May 2006. That four-page document consists of a colorful cover, a half page of introduction (complete with a colorful map of the Indian Ocean), a classic corporate-style "vision statement," and some general guiding principles that provide the reader little insight into how the IN—or indeed the Indian nation as a whole—is seeking to use the maritime realm to advance its security.[3] The IN did release an *Indian Maritime Doctrine* statement in April 2004, but this document—as shown in more detail below—is extremely limited in both scope and depth.[4]

To be sure, the lack of a formal document outlining a nation's maritime strategy does not mean a government is unserious about using maritime power to achieve national objectives. Nor does the lack of such a document mean that a state cannot become a maritime power. One can argue that the United States has not had a formal, publicly promulgated maritime strategy since the mid-1980s, when the Reagan administration unveiled its vision of how to defeat the Soviet Union at sea. Since that time the U.S. Navy has published various other documents that could be called strategies (although none were), while other official documents and policies supplied elements of a strategy, furnishing a modicum of strategic direction. The United States has certainly altered its approach to maritime strategy since the height of the Cold War, and it has done so not once but several times. Any student of U.S. grand strategy and military strategy could identify the major inflection points: the end of the Cold War and the September 11 attacks. Like his Indian counterpart, the former U.S. chief of naval operations, Admiral Michael Mullen, directed the U.S. Navy to develop a new maritime strategy. During the course of 2006–7, a relatively open process to do just that has taken place.[5]

Even absent a formal maritime strategy document or an open process to develop a document that can be mined for information, it is possible to glean the outlines of present-day Indian maritime strategy and to see how India is thinking about and going about becoming a maritime power. This chapter will look at the current state of Indian thinking about maritime power, examine how this mode of thought fits into larger Indian views of national security and India's place in the world, and analyze India's current and future capacity to become an Asian and indeed a global maritime power.

The chapter will look first at how maritime power can support Indian national security objectives and, more broadly, how it can mesh with or support predominant Indian worldviews, as manifest in the major schools of thought on Indian national security. Maritime power may not conform neatly with these views. If not, any gaps and issues will be identified and assessed. Next, the chapter will compare current IN and national security views of maritime power with Indian maritime facts on the water. It will size up the nation's naval and coast-guard capabilities, identify the types of missions New Delhi deems critical and has actually undertaken, and appraise the government's plans for future procurement, organization, and operations.

A First Look at Indian Security Objectives

For quite some time now, the Indian government, and in particular the defense establishment and the IN, has been thinking about how best to use maritime forces to advance the national interest. That intellectual ferment, and the procurements and activities to which it gives rise, has intensified over the past four years. As discussed below, India has often scanted the maritime realm, focusing instead on security challenges emanating from land. It is not surprising, therefore, that India has not yet become a maritime power, either in Asia or beyond. This could change in the coming decade or two, but New Delhi must surmount a number of significant hurdles before it can use its burgeoning maritime power flexibly, consistently, and effectively.

The concept of maritime power implies something broader than naval power. It connotes both the will and the capability to influence events in the nautical commons, well beyond the nation-state's territorial waters, and even beyond its EEZ (exclusive economic zone). If a state has both the capability and the will to become a maritime power, it will almost invariably have an impact on other coastal states, either because of these states' own use of the seas or because of its ability to project power into their littorals. In other words, maritime power is a tool of grand strategy and should serve national-level security goals. As noted in appraisals of past U.S. strategy documents and in studies of what constitutes good strategy, a clear linkage to national-level objectives is a critical determinant of strategic success.[6]

A first pass through New Delhi's national security objectives, accompanied by a brief discussion of how maritime power may (or may not) support each of these objectives, will indicate whether and how maritime capabilities are worth the investment of effort and resources as India contemplates the future. The national security objectives New Delhi has made public are listed on the Ministry of Defence Web site. The first—defending the country's borders as defined by law and enshrined in the constitution—is confined to the territorial sea. Indeed, given India's history of border wars with China and Pakistan, it appears largely concerned with events on land. In all likelihood, only Pakistan would be both willing and able to contest for control of Indian territorial waters over the short term, and even then, it would do so only in very limited circumstances. In the medium to long term, as China's naval capabilities expand, India may confront another challenge to its home waters. Some Indian analysts argue that, in view of its extensive military presence in the Indian Ocean, the United States is the naval power most able to infringe on India's maritime borders. But the current upswing in U.S.–Indian relations, particularly in the domain of naval co-operation, renders such contingencies improbable.

India's second national security objective—protecting the lives and property of its citizens against war, terrorism, nuclear threats, and militant activities—is fairly broad. Nevertheless, how maritime capabilities contribute to each of these areas of concern is fairly straightforward. The IN has taken part in past wars with Pakistan, most notably the 1971 war that led to the creation of the state of Bangladesh. Protecting the lives and property of citizens, however, connotes actions well beyond India's frontiers. This implies that New Delhi might need to project maritime power, sometimes in the course of protective missions, sometimes to strike at threats before they reach Indian shores.

How robust this power-projection capability should be depends on how Indian officials size up the threat from distant states. While India faces a multitude of terrorist and nuclear threats along its immediate borders, these problems may also originate far from its shores, requiring fairly extensive reach. One time-tested way to protect against nuclear threats, moreover, is to amass a retaliatory capability that resides in either land- or sea-based delivery systems. Protecting against terror-ism and militant activities requires guarding the nation's borders from infiltration, both land- and seaborne. India's history and geography have focused attention primarily on land, but the nation's lengthy coastline and increasing maritime traffic and trade should call attention to the seaward approaches.

India's third national security objective—protecting the country from instability, radicalism, and extremism emanating from neighboring states—appears more suited to nonmilitary tools of power, with the possible exception of the border security function mentioned above. Border security involves ideas and information as much as it does a physical attack demanding military or law-enforcement action.

The fourth national security objective—securing the country against the threat or use of WMD (weapons of mass destruction)—is a more defensive, narrower construction of the second national security objective. It involves WMD, not just nuclear weapons, and the "securing" language carries defensive connotations. It also envisions defending the country, a physically confined area, rather than citizens and property, which could be anywhere in the world. Securing the country against the use or threat of nuclear, biological, chemical, or radiological weaponry could involve direct defenses such as missile defenses or protective gear. Very little of this is specifically maritime in character. But the capacity to interdict sea-based platforms used to deliver WMD—submarines, specifically—would require seagoing capabilities.

The fifth national security objective—development of an indigenous defense research, development and production base, among other things to overcome restrictions on international transfers of defense items—has a direct maritime component, as much of the IN is foreign built and supplied. This objective is less about how India will advance its national security than about how it will do so differently in the future.

The next national security objective—promoting further cooperation and understanding with neighboring countries, and implementing mutually agreed confidence-building measures—can be seen more as a way to achieve security than as an end in itself. Regardless, maritime forces can contribute significantly to this objective. Cooperation between maritime forces (both naval and law enforcement) on common issues of security, safety, and stewardship has a long history and is often possible with fewer political overtones or concerns. Cooperative measures, humanitarian and disaster-relief missions, and even port visits can build understanding, confidence, and generally good-neighborly relations.

The final Indian national security objective—pursuing security and strategic dialogues with major powers and key partners—again appears to be more of a means to an end.[7] Maritime forces can play an indirect role in achieving this goal. Security dialogues can certainly include or even revolve around discussions of maritime issues, which are often easier to address first in efforts to improve an overall relationship. The 1972 Incidents at Sea, or INCSEA, agreement between the United States and the Soviet Union stands out among such initiatives. In and of itself, however, a discussion of maritime issues rarely constitutes a complete security or strategic dialogue.

In sum, maritime power generally, and certain types of maritime missions—maritime security operations, power projection, and naval diplomacy—provide significant, and in some cases unique, support among the various tools of national power available to the Indian government. Publicly announced national security objectives, however, are only so useful in an examination of Indian maritime strategy. Such objectives are, by their nature, political objectives. They reflect the views of the current political party or parties in power. This means that they are changeable with the group in power; in India's case, they might take a very different form under a government led by the BJP (Bharatiya Janata Party). In addition, the public nature of these objectives means that their edges have probably been softened. Specific countries are not named. Seldom are specific war scenarios or the need to hedge against close neighbors discussed openly.

Thinking about Maritime Power

To assess comprehensively how maritime power and strategy would best support India's evolving grand strategy, therefore, it is useful to examine Indian strategic worldviews. This type of approach, drawing on categorizations by scholars and other analysts, helps identify the range of views held within the Indian body politic, suggesting how maritime power might serve different governments. It also allows country names to be named and more detailed, more controversial scenarios to be examined—something nongovernmental analysts are more prone to do than government officials.

Two long-time analysts of Indian national security, Stephen P. Cohen and C. Raja Mohan, have developed useful, but different, ways to depict Indian worldviews related to national security. They provide two lenses through which to examine how elements of Indian maritime strategy and power contribute to Indian national security.

Mohan divides Indian grand strategy into three concentric geographic circles.[8] He posits grand strategic goals for each circle, stating Indian national security objectives somewhat more neatly than does the official list discussed previously. His innermost circle consists of India and its immediate neighborhood. Within that geographic area, Mohan maintains that India's twin goals are to seek primacy and to veto detrimental actions undertaken by outside powers. Primacy in India's immediate neighborhood can probably be best defined as New Delhi's ability to impose its will and significantly influence the actions of others, including in the military arena.[9] From a military perspective, primacy translates into the ability to defeat the nation's neighbors in wartime and to pursue diplomacy free of coercion in peacetime. An aggressive form of primacy might see India use its military might to compel neighbors to do its bidding. In the nautical realm, this means fielding warfighting capabilities able to dominate Pakistan's navy, supporting joint warfare against this traditional antagonist. If Indian naval forces were capable of defeating Pakistan, they would presumably suffice for other clashes in India's immediate environs. While China is India's neighbor, it might not qualify as being in the nation's immediate neighborhood as defined by Mohan. Accordingly, it will be examined below in the discussion of the outer circles.

The second goal, vetoing detrimental actions by outside powers, is more challenging, both in general and from a strictly maritime perspective. Outside powers likely to infringe on India's interests in its immediate neighborhood are few and far between. Western nations with significant power-projection capacity—the United States and, to a lesser degree, France and the United Kingdom—and China probably exhaust the list of such powers. Russia could return to this category but probably will not for the foreseeable future. Discerning specific circumstances under which India would need to veto Western military action in its waters is difficult to imagine, but not impossible. China, by contrast, might render assistance to Pakistan in some form or another during a future Indo-Pakistani conflict. New Delhi might also see the need for a general naval hedge against China's rise, but this would fall into one of Mohan's outer circles.

For the IN, vetoing detrimental actions would consist of sea-control and sea-denial operations in Indian littoral waters. Close proximity to Indian territory would make this far easier than asserting sea control on the high seas. Land-based assets would be readily available, as would ships, carrier aircraft, and submarines. Indian military forces, moreover, would presumably be more familiar than any adversary with their home waters.

Mohan's middle circle (largely a maritime milieu) consists of what he calls India's "so-called extended neighborhood," covering a rather large, amorphous area that encompasses the rest of Asia, as well as the Indian Ocean littoral. He posits that India's strategic goals within this vast, differentiated region are to "balance the influence of other powers and prevent them from undercutting" India's interests. The "interests" here are ill-defined in Mohan's work, aside from assessing how India should respond to the rise of China. With regard to the sea, the author discusses how India could involve itself more vigorously in peacekeeping and humanitarian missions if it resolves its problems with Pakistan.

Again, several maritime considerations are at work in this second circle. One is the safety of commerce, particularly energy-laden shipping from the Persian Gulf (part of the Indian Ocean littoral) to India. Protecting merchant vessels from pirates in the Straits of Malacca and off the Horn of Africa represents another maritime mission, although the severity of this threat remains in question. Piracy, furthermore, is largely a law-enforcement issue, best combated within a country's territorial waters. Policing Indian territorial waters (a mission for the Indian Coast Guard as much as for the IN) and cooperating with neighboring states to train their forces, transfer equipment, and share information are central tasks.

Low-key security cooperation would probably be more acceptable to neighboring states than IN vessels patrolling near their shores. Mohan fails to specify how New Delhi can advance its interests in the second circle, but he phrases most of the objectives in negative terms, seemingly deprecating the prospect of cooperative endeavors at sea that support Indian goals.

A second set of missions in the middle circle involves counteracting activities that could contribute to or evolve into strategic threats. Counterterrorism and counterproliferation are prominent among these missions. Maritime interdiction is one method of performing such missions. Again, Indian forces could undertake such operations unilaterally but would probably benefit from international cooperation, at least in terms of information sharing. India's political-level decision to demur from the Proliferation Security Initiative thus could impair its proliferation-related interdiction activities.[10] A third mission in this larger region is forward presence, both to demonstrate political interest and to balance the growing presence of other Asian maritime powers such as China. To hedge against Chinese pretensions, India must consider how it can counter Chinese naval power in the Indian Ocean should hostilities break out (a prospect Mohan considers remote). At a minimum, as in the inner circle, the IN would need the capacity to prosecute sea-control and sea-denial operations. Farther out from its coasts, India must consider how it would conduct anti-surface warfare against Chinese combatants in the Indian Ocean.

Finally, Mohan's third, "rest of the world" circle envisions India taking its place as a great power and a key player in international peace and security. This would involve high-order maritime operations. Long-range power projection would demand capabilities ranging from amphibious warfare to land attack to strategic nuclear deterrence. Protecting or evacuating Indian citizens abroad would also fall under the rubric of power projection. For instance, the IN conducted its first NEO (noncombatant evacuation operation) off Lebanon in the summer of 2006. To prosecute missions of this complexity on a global basis requires the ability to impose sea control far from Indian shores, coupled with substantial underway-replenishment capabilities. In short, power projection may entail high-end warfare, but it also involves peacekeeping, humanitarian, and disaster-relief missions—critical efforts if India wishes to position itself as a leading defender of international peace and security.

Mohan's view of Indian grand strategy, particularly the goals New Delhi should seek in each concentric circle, exhibits a realist bent. In 2001, Stephen Cohen posited that there are three general worldviews among Indian elites: Nehruvian, realist, and revitalist.[11] Mohan is clearly a member of the elite class, and he falls most neatly into Cohen's realist category. By contrast, the traditional Nehruvian view Cohen outlines represents a mix of realism and liberal internationalism—a mix which U.S.-schooled international-relations theorists may find it difficult to fathom. On the one hand, Nehru believed that the world was a dangerous place and that self-help was crucial to the state's survival, but on the other, he believed that "states can rise above 'the rigors of anarchy and fashion at least seasons and locales of peace and cooperation.'"[12]

Applied to the maritime aspects of Mohan's concentric circles, the traditional Nehruvian worldview gives rise to slightly different uses of maritime power. Within the innermost circle, Indian leaders of Nehruvian inclinations would probably still emphasize using maritime forces to deter and if necessary defeat Pakistan in joint operations. In the second circle, however, they would likely place greater emphasis on cooperative endeavors with neighbors in the Indian Ocean littoral. Combined exercises, training, and operations would assume high priority. This would represent a sensible seaward extension of the Gujral Doctrine, which sought to reassure India's smaller neighbors of New Delhi's benign strategic intentions in the region. Cooperative endeavors would also extend to various Asian sea powers, notably China, Japan, the United States (to the degree these powers operated at sea in the Indian Ocean basin), and perhaps even Russia. It is not clear, moreover, that a modern Nehruvian thinker would share Nehru's distrust of China that sprang up after the 1962 war. Finally, leaders possessed of this worldview would use maritime forces to help balance other great powers, refraining from too-close ties with any of them—particularly the United States.

On the world stage, a Nehruvian grand strategy would likely emphasize the cooperative dimension of power projection, with humanitarian assistance and disaster relief holding pride of place. A "recessed" nuclear deterrent—that is, a deterrent that was not always at sea and ready to fire on short notice—would form the nuclear component of a Nehruvian strategy.

The realist view would vary only slightly from the more militant Nehruvian strain described by Cohen. Given realists' faith in the market, using maritime forces to ensure the security of seagoing trade—something presumably to be encouraged under a market-friendly worldview—would likely take high priority. Realists would orchestrate wide-reaching cooperative endeavors, and they would accept navy-to-navy contacts and maneuvers with the United States more readily than would Nehruvian officials. As Cohen notes, one of the main proponents of realist policies, Jaswant Singh, has argued on behalf of looking well beyond India's borders. If New Delhi inclined to Singh's view, it would become far more active in the Mohan's second and third circles, amassing capabilities for maritime power projection and nuclear deterrence.

Finally, the revitalist strain in Indian strategic thinking, prevalent among the Rashtriya Swayamsevak Sangh supporters of the BJP, would reserve its energies primarily for Mohan's innermost circle. The principal goal of a revitalist grand strategy would be to secure the Indian homeland and nearby areas where Indians reside. The latter might include Indian diasporas in the Middle East and, to a lesser degree, in Southeast Asia. Leaders animated by this somewhat inward-looking gaze would pursue maritime security operations dedicated to vanquishing terrorism and defending against Pakistani efforts to "break off other pieces" of India, as they describe the 1947 partition.

Regardless of which worldview or combination of worldviews predominates in India over the coming decade, putting maritime power into action requires both capabilities and an operational and tactical sense of how maritime forces should be deployed. A maritime strategy—if a clear one were in evidence—would furnish some guidance on these matters. But doctrinal concepts, associated procurement strategies, and national security policies and processes that link maritime capabilities to diplomatic, economic, and military levers of national power are likewise critical. India has taken one necessary step in this direction in recent years.

Creating and Using Maritime Power

In April 2004, specifically, India issued its first formal Maritime Doctrine since independence. The doctrine built upon the IN's first Strategic Defence Review, an internal IN effort undertaken in 1998. That it took fifty years for the navy to conduct a strategic review and another six to formulate a doctrine tells part of the story of why India has not yet become a significant maritime power, even in its own region, let alone a global politico-military entity to be reckoned with. As noted above, however, this is all changing very rapidly.

The Strategic Defence Review identified four major roles for the IN: sea-based deterrence, economic and energy security, forward presence, and naval diplomacy.[13] Each of these roles is broad and conforms to the traditional roles assigned to navies in medium to large states with maritime interests and capabilities. How New Delhi chooses to carry out these roles, however, could carry significant consequences for the security and stability of what India regards as its own waterway—the Indian Ocean region—and beyond. As it attempts to fulfill its roles and associated missions, the IN will interact more extensively with Asian navies both small (Singapore and Pakistan) and large (China and Japan), as well as U.S. and European maritime forces. As noted above, the nature of these interactions could vary considerably depending on the worldview and resultant policy choices of India's leadership.

Each role staked out for the navy can be examined in terms of (a) current capabilities; (b) future capabilities and associated acquisition strategies; (c) roadblocks and challenges to acquiring these future capabilities; (d) current and future operations/exercises; (e) limitations, hurdles, and unexpected consequences; and (f) potential interactions with other Asian navies that result from each role. Regardless of how these roles evolve and which worldview predominates in Indian foreign policy, the IN will face issues it has known before but will continue to plague it at least into the next decade.

The IN has faced three significant challenges since its founding that have constrained its ability to reach its full potential as a potent, flexible instrument of national power. The first is the nation's colonial legacy. On the one hand, the IN has benefited from its historical connection to the world's most successful navy, the Royal Navy. Indian naval officers trained and were educated at Royal Navy institutions immediately following independence. New Delhi thus developed a capable officer corps more rapidly than it could have if forced to build indigenous education and training programs from scratch starting in 1948. Moreover, the British officers in charge of the RIN (Royal Indian Navy) before and during World War II began working with their Indian counterparts to lay the groundwork for a sea service for an independent India.

On the other hand, the division of the RIN into Indian and Pakistani navies was devastating for the service. The RIN was far more ethnically integrated than the army, meaning that the partition broke up cohesive units as well as splitting platforms and infrastructure between the two new navies. Early planning for IN roles and capabilities, moreover, bore the stamp of British policy in the Cold War. Early IN requests to the U.K. government for assistance revealed divided views: the British accentuated the support Commonwealth nations could provide in Cold War contingencies, while the new IN staff focused more naturally on Pakistan.[14]

C. Raja Mohan has suggested that an unusual piece of India's historical legacy could be of real value to Indian maritime strategists if they can only break habits of thinking developed since independence. He urges Indian strategic thinkers, particularly those interested in maritime strategy, to rediscover Lord Curzon, viceroy of India at the turn of the last century. Mohan notes that Curzon provides the kind of thinking necessary to place Indian affairs in a maritime context, looking out to the Indian Ocean littoral and beyond.[15]

The IN did an admirable job of shedding its colonial legacy in terms of outlook and planning, but it still faced a challenge that continues to haunt it today: resources.[16] India boosted defense resources significantly after the 1962 Sino-Indian war. Five-year defense plans were drawn up for each of the armed services, but every one of these (through 1997) had to be deferred or restructured before it was completed, owing largely to resource constraints. In 1964, a base force of fifty-four principal combatants was established for the IN. The service has never reached this goal.[17] The reasons for this strategy–policy mismatch are threefold. First, as Rahul Roy-Chaudhury notes in the second of his studies of Indian maritime issues, the five-year plans were often the services' wish lists. They were neither connected to broader national security goals nor compiled with resource limitations in mind. Even if the services' plans were constructed without realistic budgets in mind, various shortfalls and crises in the overall Indian economy nonetheless made the shortfalls even more dramatic.

In addition to absolute deficits in available resources, the IN has traditionally been the most sparsely funded of the three armed services. India has traditionally seen itself as a continental power, and its primary security threats throughout its modern history have been land-based: China and Pakistan. The Indian Army and Air Force have each generally received more than twice the percentage of the aggregate defense budget that has gone to the IN, and it is unlikely that this will change significantly in the near to medium term. The 2007 Indian government defense budget, for instance, allocated 16,500 crore rupees for the air force, 11,374 crore rupees for the army, and 10,000 crore rupees for the Navy.[18] While at times the navy's procurement budget has been augmented, the plus-up compared with the other services has remained in force for too short a time to allow the IN to reach its goals in terms of numbers and types of platforms. As will be discussed below, the IN competes not just with its sister services but also with the DRDO (Defence Research and Development Organization) and, at least in government-wide budgetary terms, with the Department of Atomic Energy and other agencies which support India's now-overt nuclear-weapons capabilities. Depending on the IN's choice of roles and missions, the resources of these other defense-related organizations may either add to or subtract from navy capabilities. By way of example, the 2007 DRDO budget is slated to consume just over one-third of the entire IN budget.

In addition to resource constraints, the IN—like the other armed services— has struggled with slow, inconsistent, and cumbersome availability of defense technology. Even when relying on Indian-derived technology, the defense establishment has learned over the decades that delays and underperformance are routine. One reason is, again, India's postcolonial legacy. New Delhi had to spend considerable time and resources developing its own, indigenous technology base capable of supporting advanced defense platforms and systems. Second, India's decision to follow a strongly nonaligned path meant that it was unwilling —fortunately, at times—to become dependent on a single foreign supplier of military technology. Each superpower used arms sales and other forms of security assistance to help bring countries into its camp during the Cold War. While India eventually decided to rely most heavily on the Soviet Union for military supplies, it never made the political decision to join the Soviet camp or become wholly reliant on Moscow. India learned firsthand about the fickleness of foreign suppliers during the 1965 war, when the United States and the United Kingdom slapped an arms embargo on both India and Pakistan in an effort to pressure them into halting hostilities. U.S. embargoes came and went after India's nuclear tests in 1974 and again in 1998. Finally, India suffered greatly from the breakup of the Soviet Union, when its main supplier of weapons systems, parts, and spares essentially disappeared for several years. In part because of steady Indian demand, supply chains were reassembled in the former Soviet Union in the mid-1990s.

Even today, though, India remains worried about the quality of supplies delivered by the Russian military–industrial complex.[19]

The post–Cold War interruption of the supply of defense goods and technologies from the former Soviet Union redoubled New Delhi's determination to attain self-reliance in areas critical to national security. However, this focus on indigenization, which now represents the core of the IN's modernization program, has the potential to cut both ways. Over a number of years, on the one hand, it could make India largely independent of other great powers for major combat systems, spares, and service for its equipment. On the other, the Indian defense industry's history of delivering quality military platforms in a timely manner has been spotty.[20] Despite brave talk, the Indian government appears to have realized that DRDO needs reorganization and closer oversight if it is to spearhead the drive for indigenous weapons development and production in the future.[21]

Sea-Based Deterrence

It was a good assumption, even as far back as the May 1998 nuclear tests, that the sea-based deterrence role mentioned in the 1998 document was primarily a nuclear one. Since the nuclear tests in 1998 and New Delhi's open declaration of its nuclear-weapons status, there has been open discussion about the size, shape, and basing of India's nuclear deterrent force. The Draft Report of the National Security Advisory Board on Nuclear Doctrine, eventually adopted by the Indian government as a broad outline for India's nuclear doctrine, is not explicit about platforms and systems, but it does contain parameters that seem to point to a sea-based leg for Indian nuclear forces. These parameters include a no-first-use declaration and the concomitant requirement for secure, survivable retaliatory forces.[22] Since the Draft Report was promulgated and ultimately adopted by the Indian government, there has been relatively little public discussion of the specifics of how or when India will go about acquiring such a capability.

Over time, however, information has begun to trickle out. The most authoritative indication that India will pursue a sea-based nuclear capability to date is the 2005 annual report of the Defence Ministry, which indicates that India needs a mix of air, land, and maritime capabilities in the nuclear realm.[23] The IN itself is less shy about what it would like and the reason it believes this is necessary. In the 2004 Maritime Doctrine document, service leaders are very explicit about their view of the need for a submarine-based nuclear deterrent force: it "has become an unstated axiom of the post Cold War era that an independent foreign policy posture is inexorably linked with this [a submarine-based] deterrent capability." The document notes that all of the great powers have such a capability: the United States, Russia, the United Kingdom, China, and France.[24]

As is fairly typical in Indian strategic discourse, a retired senior officer has dropped additional hints at the direction of India's sea-based nuclear force. The officer in question, retired Admiral Arun Prakash, is conversant with the facts. He has stated explicitly that "development work is reported to be under way," deftly reporting the existence of a program without running afoul of laws forbidding the disclosure of classified material. Admiral Prakash also contended that India "must have a small number of SSBNs," or nuclear-powered ballistic-missile submarines—thereby revealing his personal preference for platform and weapon type. In the same interview, finally, he hinted about possible deployment patterns for such a weapon system: "When this platform becomes operationally available, we will need suitable areas in the distant reaches of the Indian Ocean from where it can be safely deployed to pose deterrence to our adversaries."[25]

The reason for this relative lack of public discussion of a submarine-based nuclear deterrent may have to do with the difficulties India has encountered so far in this endeavor and some of the regional consequences of this capability once it is at sea. A maritime nuclear capability can take a number of forms, namely surface ships, naval aircraft, or submarines armed with ballistic missiles, cruise missiles, or gravity bombs. But, as Admiral Prakash averred, the mix of platform and weapon system most likely to produce the survivable second-strike capability India appears to desire is a nuclear-powered submarine equipped with ballistic missiles. Over the past twenty years, India has taken halting steps toward acquiring its own nuclear-powered submarine and developing ballistic missiles capable of being fired from submarines. In 1988, India leased a Soviet *Charlie I*-class nuclear attack submarine as part of a program to develop an Indian-manufactured nuclear reactor suitable for submarine propulsion. The leasing experiment was not renewed, although recent reports indicate that India may try again in a bid to move its indigenous reactor program ahead.

This program, called the ATV (Advanced Technology Vehicle), has made halting progress over the years. Until early 2006, indications were that the ATV had not advanced beyond land-based testing of a prototype reactor.[26] Recent reports, however, indicate that the reactor has successfully been tested. One report in late 2006 declared that the system was "fully online."[27] Although some analysts had estimated that a nuclear-powered submarine would be deployed as early as 2007, this was very optimistic.[28] The latest estimates show the system achieving initial operating capability around 2012, and this is likely optimistic as well.[29]

Now pending, India's acquisition of six French-designed *Scorpene* diesel-electric submarines could supply a substitute platform, allowing New Delhi to put to sea a nuclear deterrent force at an early date. This too would raise some operational issues.[30] For one, what weapon system would conventional submarines carry? The *Scorpene* was not designed to house massive ballistic missiles, and whether it could be retrofitted is doubtful. *Scorpene*s are capable of launching 3M-54E Klub ASCMs (antiship cruise missiles), as well as French-built Exocets, from their torpedo tubes. It is unclear, however, whether either missile is suitable for delivering nuclear payloads: their range is limited, and it remains dubious whether India has the ability to miniaturize a nuclear weapon sufficiently to mount on either of them. Similarly, India's Russian-built *Kilo*-class submarines, which are being refitted to carry the Klub and the indigenous Brahmos missile, could conceivably provide an interim nuclear platform. Again, however, it is unclear whether the Klub and the Brahmos boast either the range or the ability to carry a nuclear warhead. Nor is it clear whether diesel submarines have the range, endurance, and survivability necessary to mount a serious deterrent effort.

India's other short- to medium-term option is to mount nuclear delivery systems on surface ships. The IN has test-launched a naval version (Dhanush) of the army's short-range Prithvi ballistic missile from a ship on two occasions.[31] The issues raised by this ungainly platform/delivery-vehicle combination are fairly obvious. First, the Dhanush has a range of only 250–350 kilometers, meaning that the launch platform would be extremely vulnerable to conventional counterstrikes by an opponent. Second, surface vessels, even modern ones with stealth characteristics, are nowhere near as survivable as submarines—impairing their credibility as a deterrent. Finally, the safety issues associated with launching liquid-fueled missiles on the high seas, particularly during heavy weather, remain to be determined.

Even if it can speedily resolve the engineering woes its submarine reactor project has encountered, India will still face the question of developing a weapon system with the right technical characteristics and enough destructive potential to pose a credible deterrent. Some of the ASCMs mentioned above could be modified for nuclear strike missiles, but ideally India wants a SLBM (submarine-launched ballistic missile). While reporting is scanty, it is reasonable to assume that DRDO, which has spearheaded the research and development effort vis-à-vis ballistic missiles, is heading up such a project. The secrecy shrouding weapons programs prevents outsiders from gauging DRDO's progress. Past problems with systems such as the land-based Agni missile, however, suggest that technical challenges will keep the SLBM initiative from reaching fruition for a decade or more.

The range of a future SLBM is critical if the maritime leg of India's strategic triad is to be an effective part of nuclear deterrence. While some Indian analysts argue that New Delhi needs intercontinental-range missiles to deter the United States, allowing the nation to pursue a truly unfettered foreign and security policy, Pakistan and China provide a more realistic pair of drivers for Indian deterrence parameters.[32] To deter Pakistan, an Indian SLBM could have a range of less than 1,000 kilometers, assuming that India would want its submarines to be able to patrol and fire from standoff distances from the Pakistani coast.

In the case of China, India has two choices, each of which poses its own difficulties. First, if the goal of an Indian maritime deterrent is to reach Chinese soil, the navy could accept ballistic missiles with shorter ranges—that is, missiles that are less challenging to develop and build—and occasionally send its SSBNs on patrol in the SCS (South China Sea). The downsides of such deployments are twofold. On the political side, deployments of nuclear-powered, nuclear-armed submarines to the SCS could be politically objectionable to littoral states, particularly in Southeast Asia, where India is trying to forge stronger defense relations. Japan's "nuclear allergy," moreover, could be aggravated by such deployments. If so, this would undercut New Delhi's effort to improve relations with this Asian giant, countering Chinese influence and naval power. On the operational side, vessels transiting the Strait of Malacca and patrolling the SCS would be subject to detection, leaving them more vulnerable than they would be in the Indian Ocean. This would permit China to bring substantial ASW (antisubmarine-warfare) and detection assets to bear in what Beijing considers "home" waters. India's second option—to develop and deploy an SLBM with a range on the order of 3,000 km—is more challenging from a technical standpoint. To date, India has yet to successfully test or deploy a land-based ballistic missile with this range, although it is making significant progress on space launch vehicles, which are close cousins to ballistic missiles.

Regardless of which option it picks, India cannot develop a maritime nuclear deterrent force in a vacuum. Other Asian actors will watch, then react politically and militarily. Pakistan can be expected to enhance its ASW capabilities and to patrol Indian Ocean waters more aggressively, signaling that it has the capacity to threaten Indian deterrent forces regardless of how they deploy. China may opt to deploy its own SSBNs to the Indian Ocean and perhaps, over time, begin dispatching ASW-capable units to the region more frequently and more aggressively. Japan must determine whether its concern over nuclear issues outweighs its desire to improve military and security relations with India as a hedge against China's rise. The deployment of an Indian nuclear force to sea will have an impact on the strategic calculations of all Asian maritime powers, even though such a deployment is likely years away.

Economic and Energy Security

Again, the roles India chooses to emphasize for its naval forces and the capabilities the IN develops to fulfill these roles will have profound effects on the other Asian powers—particularly China and Japan, which also worry about the security of their maritime trade and their seaborne energy supplies. Some geographic scoping is required to assess India's economic and energy security and its maritime power with sufficient rigor. Though an operational and tactical publication rather than an effort to define the strategic realm, the 2004 *Indian Maritime Doctrine* statement proclaims that the "Indian maritime vision for the first quarter of the 21st century must look at the arc from the Persian Gulf to the Straits of Malacca as a legitimate area of interest."[33]

This statement is noteworthy for two reasons. First, it acknowledges that India's maritime vision has limits, at least for the short term. (See the discussion of Operation Sukoon, below.) Second, it states a time limit beyond which—presumably—India's legitimate regions of interest may expand. With respect to economic and energy security, India's gaze will indeed remain on the Indian Ocean region for the next decade-plus, ending at the Persian Gulf (or perhaps even the Bab-el-Mandeb) to the west and the Strait of Malacca to the east.

India's Maritime Doctrine notes that maritime power relates more closely than air or land power to the protection of economic interests. It points out that trade is critical to the developing Indian economy, depicting the free flow of commerce through regional SLOCs (sea lines of communication) as of paramount importance. It notes that India is in position to influence the movement and security of shipping through the Indian Ocean SLOCs significantly, provided it has sufficient sea power to do so.[34] This can be read as a statement of defensive potential, a declaration that New Delhi can safeguard shipping bound to and from India. It can also be read as a statement of offensive potential, putting fellow regional powers on notice that New Delhi has the sea power to coerce should it see fit. In fact, the doctrine notes that "control of these choke points could be a useful bargaining chip in the international power game...."[35]

Construing the Maritime Doctrine as narrowly as possible, in both the geographic and the strategic senses, the IN must be able to protect the immediate approaches to Indian seaports; achieve sea denial in India's EEZ; and, ideally, impose sea control as far away as the geographic chokepoints that allow entry into the Indian Ocean. In other words, it must be able to defend Indian home waters while ensuring the safety of merchant traffic in those waters. India's capability to perform these missions is sporadic at present, and it may even decline over the next few years pending new acquisitions.

As noted above, the size of the Indian submarine force is shrinking temporarily and will only rebound after the year 2010, when more of the refitted *Kilos* rejoin the fleet and the newly acquired *Scorpenes* enter service—the latter likely in the 2012–17 time frame.[36] While it is modernizing steadily, the IN surface fleet needs more oceangoing vessels, along with additional patrol craft to monitor and respond to contingencies in the EEZ. To remedy some of these shortfalls, the navy's Project 15A is producing three modern, follow-on destroyers around which surface action groups can be organized to prosecute sea-control missions. These units are slated to join the fleet beginning in 2008.

Vibrant naval aviation will enhance India's ability to conduct sea-denial and sea-control operations, not only in the national EEZ but also along the approaches to the Strait of Malacca and the Strait of Hormuz and elsewhere in the Indian Ocean basin. To bolster its maritime domain awareness, New Delhi recently issued a tender for eight maritime reconnaissance aircraft to replace the navy's aging TU-142s. Indian officials turned down an offer from Washington to lease the IN two P-3Cs as an interim solution.[37] In addition, a recent request from the IN to procure 60 multi-role combat aircraft (over and above a request from the Indian Air Force for 126 such aircraft) would add a new dimension to the navy's land-based air capabilities. While little information is available on this tender, it likely will not be fulfilled until 2010–11.[38]

Aircraft-carrier operations are central to India's ability to control the sea far from Indian shores or deny it to others. New Delhi remains committed to a force of two to three carriers. The navy's current carrier, the *Viraat,* has approximately ten years of service life left. By that point, the IN expects to have INS *Vikramaditya* (the ex-*Admiral Gorshkov*) in service, along with an Indian-built carrier. The *Vikramaditya* is expected to join the fleet in 2008, with an expected service life of twenty-five to thirty years.[39] The indigenous carrier, until recently dubbed an "air-defense ship," should reach its initial operating capability in 2012. Its air wing will include some twenty fixed-wing aircraft and ten helicopters.[40] If the indigenous carrier design proves effective and efficient, India will probably construct a second ship in the class.

India does not anticipate guarding Indian Ocean SLOCs alone. If state or non-state actors posed a substantial threat to shipping, India would work with other sea powers to protect shipping. While India is slowly building up its capacity to conduct such operations, it remains an open question how vigorously Indian naval forces will exercise and train with other navies to support combined operations. This is largely a political issue, and key decisions will be taken at a level well above that of the navy's high command. But the trend appears to be toward close cooperation with local, regional, and great-power navies in anticipation of future combined operations. Indian and U.S. officials point to the escort operations performed by the IN during the run-up to Operation Enduring Freedom, when IN vessels accompanied high-value U.S. vessels through the Strait of Malacca. Washington and New Delhi have discussed renewing this arrangement should circumstances warrant.

Along India's western flank, however, there appears to be a cleavage between aspirations and the combined operational work needed to achieve them. After September 11, the U.S. Central Command organized a combined task force, CTF 150, in the northern Arabian Gulf and Gulf of Oman. CTF 150, whose missions include combating piracy and maritime terrorism, has been a multilateral undertaking since its inception. Naval forces from numerous European countries, Japan, Australia, New Zealand, and Pakistan have taken part in its operations, while officers from various countries—including Pakistan—have commanded it. Interestingly, to date the IN has not participated in this effort, for reasons New Delhi has not made public.[41] Indian naval forces have deployed to CTF 150's area of operations, as well as to the Persian Gulf.

Again, this is more a political than an operational issue. But it does portend some difficulties India could face if it decides to conduct sea-control or sea-denial operations in waters that convey energy supplies to India and indeed to users throughout Asia. The United States and India have been conducting increasingly sophisticated naval exercises—the "Malabar series"—since the mid-1990s. However, multilateral operations under the aegis of CTF 150 are different. They provide participants highly useful experience in operating with multiple sets of rules of engagement, multiple communications capabilities, and multiple operating concepts. It is difficult to envision circumstances in which the flow of Persian Gulf oil and gas came under threat and the United States, Europe, Australia, and Japan stood aside. If India also wants the option of joining a combined maritime security effort, it is losing a valuable training opportunity by remaining aloof from CTF 150.

The reasons behind Indian standoffishness are unclear. They may arise from the U.S. military's bureaucratic divide, which assigns India to the U.S. Pacific Command's area of responsibility and CTF 150 operations to the U.S. Central Command. India understands this issue and is pursuing other opportunities for combined exercises, testing the navy's ability to work with fellow advanced navies to assure free passage through the sea lanes of communication.[42] Regardless, future Indian maritime security operations will likely be multilateral in nature and will almost certainly involve the U.S., Japanese, and European navies.

Naval Diplomacy

The IN has been conducting naval diplomacy almost since its inception. For the most part, naval diplomacy requires no specific capabilities. Instead it requires resources adequate to support highly visible operations, along with the political will and vision to use naval assets to support broad foreign and security policy objectives. Its diplomatic efforts were expansive during the 1980s, supporting New Delhi's assertive foreign policy, but they tapered off in the early 1990s. Since that low point, the IN has again stepped up its exercises with other navies, port calls, operations designed to project a positive image of India, and activities such as the circumnavigation voyage of the INS *Tarangini*. The aircraft carrier *Viraat* visited ports in Southeast Asia for the first time, signaling Indian interest in the region while showing off a capability not possessed by China, the other great power vying for influence in that subregion.[43]

The most recent example of Indian naval diplomacy was Operation Sukoon, which dispatched IN ships to Lebanon to help evacuate Indian, Nepalese, Sri Lankan, and Lebanese nationals. This NEO showcased the IN's increasing capability to operate at significant distances from Indian coasts and to undertake the types of naval-diplomatic operations formerly beyond its capacity (and within the capacity of very few navies). The IN is acquiring capabilities that will further enhance its ability to conduct such operations. Most recently, the U.S. government agreed to sell India the retired amphibious transport USS *Trenton*. Defence Minister Pranab Mukherjee has tied the *Trenton* acquisition directly to naval diplomacy: "The ship would provide the Indian Navy enhanced amphibious capability. In addition, the LPD (landing platform dock) can be deployed for disaster relief operations."[44]

Tsunami relief supplied another recent example of Indian naval diplomacy. Indian naval leaders are rightfully proud of their service's performance off Indonesia, and they call for continuing and expanding such endeavors. The operation represented the largest peacetime mission ever undertaken by the IN, involving thirty-two ships, thirty aircraft, and over 5,500 personnel.[45] The Indian contingent helped locate survivors, evacuate victims, remove salvage and debris, conduct hydrographic surveys prior to reopening ports and harbors, and restore drinking-water and power-generation facilities. These activities supported the governments and residents of Sri Lanka, the Maldives, and Indonesia, as well as those Indian citizens of the Andaman and Nicobar islands who were also affected by the tsunami.

Indian naval diplomacy—in the form of deployments and bilateral exercises—has focused both on navies from states adjacent to key Indian Ocean SLOCs and on navies with the ability to operate in or influence maritime affairs in the Indian Ocean. Over the past year, India deployed its aircraft carrier for exercises with U.S. and French carriers, demonstrating a capability within the reach of only a handful of countries. It also conducted bilateral patrols of the Strait of Malacca in conjunction with the Royal Thai Navy and the Indonesian Navy. (Washington proposed combined patrols of this crucial waterway several years ago. Nearby states turned down the U.S. proposal, deeming it too politically sensitive.) India also set up a joint military cooperation committee with Oman that will lay the groundwork for more extensive military, and particularly maritime, ties.[46] The combination of India's standing in the region, its maritime capabilities, and its renewed willingness to dedicate naval assets to diplomatic initiatives allowed it to make inroads that may make more ambitious operations possible in the future.

Forward Presence

Forward presence is more difficult to define than the three functions discussed above. It is at times difficult to distinguish between forward presence and naval diplomacy. Measuring forward presence is also more problematic, in part because some of the activities undertaken by a navy under the rubric of forward presence may be invisible to the public eye. The ostensible purposes of forward presence are to demonstrate interest in a specific area; demonstrate the ability to deploy and operate in that area, reassuring nearby friends and allies; familiarize forces with the operating environment there; and deter or dissuade potentially hostile powers from operating in that area. In today's security parlance, forward presence is a necessary part of "shaping" the international environment in line with the state's interests. India takes a keen interest in shaping the Indian Ocean region and understands that military forces offer a useful tool for this effort.

In the case of the United States, forward presence has often been used to help justify a large U.S. Navy force structure. Some analysts have argued that the forward-presence mission imposes an undue burden on U.S. forces, driving force-structure decisions and operating tempo to the detriment of other missions and more sensible resource allocations.[47] This is not yet a concern for the IN. In fact, naval leaders may find that adopting an ambitious forward-presence mission may help the service in its budgetary battles with the army and air force. For such a bureaucratic strategy to work, however, the IN must develop a specific plan for forward presence, clearly distinguish forward presence from the navy's other roles, and connect it to force-structure and operational requirements. Some officials have linked the presence mission to counter-piracy efforts and general protection of the sea lanes, but this may prove a thin reed on which to hang significant force-structure requirements. A more robust argument may be the imperative to counter growing Chinese naval power and presence in the Indian Ocean region, and particularly in Southeast Asia.[48]

Conclusions

India's thinking about the place and utility of maritime power ranges throughout Mohan's three concentric circles. The farther India reaches out, however, the more problematic it will become for the IN to realize sustainable capabilities, whether power projection or nuclear deterrence is at issue. This may be difficult to accept for realist strategic thinkers who want their nation to play on the world stage. To the degree that realist-minded leaders persuade New Delhi to deepen relations with the United States, India will need high-end maritime capabilities and the willingness to deploy these capabilities beyond the Indian Ocean region. Otherwise, the Indo-U.S. relationship will remain unbalanced. India's maritime capabilities are growing within Mohan's two inner circles and will—over time—come to satisfy the grand-strategic ambitions of all of India's schools of strategic thought. As noted previously, however, unintended consequences could accrue from potent Indian sea power.

Charles de Gaulle's quip about Brazil—that it is, and will always be, a country of the future—no longer applies to today's nautically minded India. The IN has performed admirably since its birth given stark political, financial, and technological realities. While the IN continues to suffer from the budgetary woes of the 1980s and early 1990s, the quality and number of its platforms and associated capabilities are on the upswing. The navy operates with mounting confidence in a political environment, both domestic and international, that provides it far greater opportunity for maneuver and influence. Indian foreign policy these days is marked by real and growing preparedness to use military power in pursuit of national interests. Given the nation's central geographic location, this allows the navy and coast guard far more latitude for action than the other services.

India is no longer constrained by Cold War politics; nor does New Delhi see any need to carve out a third way between the two former giants. India's relationship with Russia has taken on a businesslike tone, in keeping with Moscow's function as a supplier and recipient of defense technology. Meanwhile, the nation's growing strategic partnership with the United States represents a significant break with past policy. The high-level political impetus behind this new partnership will push it along briskly, and cooperation at sea is one logical way to advance the relationship. As noted above, Indo-U.S. maritime cooperation has been mixed, featuring advanced exercises and operations near Malacca, on the one hand, but distant relations in the northern Persian Gulf, on the other.

The sporadic progress of recent years is likely to continue, with at least two factors holding back full cooperation: reports indicate lingering differences of opinion between military officers and national security officials in Washington and New Delhi,[49] and the ongoing effort on Washington's part to balance its relationships with Pakistan and India remains a complicating factor. While the U.S. relationship with the two South Asian powers is no longer "hyphenated," some tensions will persist in the maritime realm—especially to the degree that the United States continues to provide Pakistan with military technology and work with Pakistani forces at sea.

International political dynamics, however, will likely exert less influence on the direction and pace of India's overall maritime capabilities and strategy than will ongoing domestic tensions between those who favor indigenization and those who espouse using foreign purchases to achieve swifter modernization. Privatization and reform of the Indian defense industry are associated issues.[50] The pace and scope of reform will have a significant impact on India's ability to quickly meet its demand for modern and capable sea services.

Despite questions about the growth of Indian maritime power, it is clear that, for the first time in centuries, India will be a significant player in Asian waters beyond its immediate neighborhood. The nation sits astride key SLOCs for energy security, and it has taken projecting power for purposes as varied as tsunami relief and strategic deterrence. Fellow Asian sea powers will have to take Indian capabilities—not just Indian potential—into account.

CHAPTER 8

JAPANESE MARITIME THOUGHT: IF NOT MAHAN, WHO?

James R. Holmes

The late Colonel John Boyd, who knew a thing or two about strategic thought, was fond of declaring that excellence in warfare and other human endeavors depended on people, ideas, and hardware—in that order.[1] This chapter postulates that Japan has lost sight of this commonsense axiom, allowing strategic thought to atrophy. If so, this decline in strategic thought could impede Tokyo's ability to act outside the confines of the U.S.–Japanese security alliance—as it might need to, given the rise of an increasingly capable, sea-power-minded China and mounting frictions between Beijing and Tokyo. The chapter asks the following questions to assess the state of strategic thinking in Japan's naval forces:

- Why does maritime strategy matter now, in an increasingly interconnected world? Does economic interdependence eliminate the resort to power politics?
- How did Alfred Thayer Mahan view sea power and its uses? How much influence did Mahan exert in Imperial Japan?
- How strictly did the IJN (Imperial Japanese Navy) adhere to Mahan's theories, and, when it departed from Mahanian theory, why, and with what impact?
- How much continuity was there in strategic thinking between the IJN and the MSDF (Maritime Self-Defense Force)? What impact did any shifts in strategic thought have?
- Which strategic theorists do Japanese naval officials consult when they are grappling with vexing issues? If not Mahan, who?
- If indeed strategic thought has languished in postwar Japan's maritime forces, how might political and military leaders revive it? To which strategic theorists should they look?

The chapter closes with a few observations and policy recommendations for Tokyo's naval establishment. Given the preliminary nature of this inquiry, it is somewhat open-ended, in hopes of starting a sorely needed debate in

Japanese and U.S. naval circles rather than supplying answers that are likely to be premature.

Japan, Geography, and Maritime Strategy

While it may no longer be fashionable to equate geography to destiny, Japan's physical position reaffirms this apparently quaint axiom. The concept of maritime power is inseparable from its spatial meaning. Maritime power is at its most basic level concerned with a nation's ability to exploit the sea—a physical, nautical medium. The immutable geographic realities that Japan confronts merit particular attention because they have shaped and will continue to shape Japan's interactions with its neighbors. Japan's maritime posture, then, has always been and will always be intimately linked to geography. The Japanese often describe their key national characteristic in nautical terms, with the familiar notion that "Japan is a small island nation lacking resource endowments and is thus highly dependent upon seaborne commerce for its well being." Clearly, Tokyo must always be mindful of the surrounding oceans.

Yet additional geographic features impinge upon Japan's strategic and maritime postures. It is natural to compare Great Britain and Japan, two insular powers seaward of great continental landmasses.[2] Japan stands considerably off the Asian continent, with nearly one hundred miles separating Honshu Island from the Korean Peninsula. By contrast, only twenty miles separate Britain from continental Europe at the nearest point. Concentrated in a few pockets of flat terrain on the east coast, major Japanese cities face outward toward the Pacific, rather than inward toward the continent. In effect they gaze out at the United States, whereas Britain's major population centers physically tend to direct attention toward their European neighbors. Historically such demographic positioning has reinforced the isolation and insularity of Japan, while Britain has interacted regularly with the rest of Europe. Japan's distinctive geographic and demographic conformation conditions its strategic preferences, pulling Tokyo in divergent directions: geographically, Japan is part of continental Asia, but demographically it inclines toward trans-Pacific ties. Japan has been ambivalent about whether it is (or wants to be) an Asian or a Western power, whereas Britain has managed to craft a special relationship with the United States across the Atlantic while acting as a traditional offshore balancer across the English Channel.[3]

Japanese geography carries strategic implications. The four main home islands stretch 1,200 miles, roughly the entire north-south length of the U.S. eastern seaboard. This archipelago, which extends along the Ryukyu Islands to the south, forms a long crescent that hugs the eastern flanks of Russia and China, Eurasia's greatest land powers. Japan seemingly stands in the way of naval power projection from the mainland.[4] Chinese vessels exiting the East China Sea into the Pacific must contend with the Ryukyus, while the Korean Peninsula, in effect a half-island appended to Eurasia, thrusts out toward the Japanese archipelago like the proverbial "dagger aimed at the heart of Japan." These enduring geographic traits have been arbiters of interstate relations and wars among the four powers for over a century.[5]

Finally, the physical defense of Japan requires credible nautical power projection. Tokyo is saddled with 17,000 miles of coastline to defend. By comparison with the great powers, India's shoreline is 4,600 miles long, while China's extends 11,000 miles, America's 12,000 miles, and Russia's 23,000 miles (primarily facing the empty Arctic). Lacking strategic depth—the widest east-west length of Honshu is a mere 160 miles—Japanese planners must think in terms of defending forward at sea, much as the Israelis do about land warfare.[6] To complicate matters, Tokyo possesses thousands of offshore islands, with the farthest ones located near the Tropic of Cancer. Japan's Maritime Self-Defense Force (JMSDF) describes the nation's defense dilemma in vivid terms: if Wakkanai, the northernmost city of Japan, is Copenhagen, then the Ishigaki, Okinotori, and Minamitori islands are the equivalents of Casablanca, Tripoli, and Alexandria, respectively.[7] In other words, Japan's maritime defense area encompasses an area as large as NATO-Europe, plus the entire Mediterranean.

Several implications flow from this geopolitical analysis. First, whereas continental powers have the option of venturing seaward or retreating from the oceans, Japan enjoys no such luxury. The importance of a coherent strategic framework for Japanese naval planners is hard to overstate. Second, and closely related, Tokyo cannot avoid entanglement with immediate neighbors that harbor maritime ambitions of their own. Japan is located near enough to the Eurasian continent that it must be alert for any realignment or imbalance in regional sea power. Third, if forced to defend its maritime interests by itself, Tokyo would not be able to ignore pressures to build up a maritime force far larger and more capable than its current, world-class if modestly sized fleet. If Tokyo succumbed to these pressures, its actions would almost certainly bring about countervailing actions from its neighbors.

The bottom line: the direction and quality of Japanese strategic thinking about nautical affairs will have ripple effects on the international relations of East Asia and thus bear careful examination. The following thus charts trends in Japanese maritime thinking from the prewar era to the twenty-first century and ventures some policy recommendations.

Mahan's Sea-power Evangelism

A century ago Japanese maritime thinkers, facing similar challenges, looked to America for guidance on sea power. Writing around the turn of the nineteenth century, Alfred Thayer Mahan exhorted an America long disdainful toward foreign political entanglements to amass a kind of "sea power" built on the "three pillars" of overseas commerce, naval and merchant fleets, and naval bases arrayed along the sea lanes to support fuel-thirsty warships.[8] While there was a circular quality to his theorizing—the navy protected a nation's trade, which in turn generated tariff revenue to support the navy—the commercial element of sea power seemed to be uppermost in his thinking. Mahan's self-perpetuating logic beguiled advocates of sea power in his day, and it has a timeless quality.[9] In today's China, which aspires to its own place in the sun, appeals to Mahanian theory are increasingly commonplace.[10]

If there were any geographic bounds to Mahan's vision of sea power, he did not say so. While his writings were appropriate to Great Britain or the United States, consequently, they held only limited relevance for a fledgling regional power such as Imperial Japan. Where should an America rethinking political non-entanglement apply its nautical energies? In East Asia: for Mahan, sea power would assure the United States an equitable share of trade in China, a "carcass" doomed to be devoured by "eagles," namely the great imperial powers.[11] If the United States failed to defend its share of the China trade—Mahanian thought had a strong zero-sum tenor to it—it would lose out, with dire consequences for the nation's prosperity.[12] Although he claimed to deplore the prospect of great-power war, Mahan seemed resigned to it if a rival injected "the alien element of military or political force" into peaceful seagoing commerce.[13]

Both merchant shipping and the U.S. Navy thus needed secure communications with East Asia. Communications, wrote Mahan, was "the most important single element in strategy, political or military."[14] The "eminence of sea power" lay in its ability to control the SLOCs (sea lines of communication), while the power "to insure these communications to one's self, and to interrupt them for an adversary, affects the very root of a nation's vigor...."[15] Perhaps his central precept—and a staple of discourse in contemporary China—was his concept of "command of the sea" as "that overbearing power on the sea which drives the enemy's flag from it, or allows it to appear only as a fugitive; and which, by controlling the great common, closes the highways by which commerce moves to and fro from the enemy's shores."[16] If the United States hoped to assure access to overseas markets, proclaimed Mahan, its navy must construct forces able to "fight, with reasonable chances of success, the largest force likely to be brought against it" in regions vital to U.S. maritime traffic.[17] This ability to impose a local preponderance of naval force was the hub of a prosperity-minded policy of sea power.

To "maximize the power of offensive action," which was "the great end of a war fleet," the United States needed a modest force of twenty armored battleships "capable of taking and giving hard knocks" in a major fleet engagement.[18] Mahan disparaged *guerre de course,* or commerce raiding, as the strategy of the weaker power, hopeless in the face of a navy able to exercise overbearing sea power. His followers instead sought titanic clashes between concentrated fleets of battleships—in other words, a latter-day equivalent to Trafalgar.[19]

The Influence of Mahan upon Japan

Scholars agree that Japanese strategists leapt at Mahan's theories. Mahan recalled that his works had been more widely translated into Japanese than any other language.[20] In 1902, Admiral Yamamoto Gombei paid tribute to Mahan's analytical skills, offering him a teaching post at Japan's Naval Staff College.[21] Declared Captain John Ingles, a British officer who taught at the Naval Staff College for six years, "Japanese naval officers are much impressed with the advantage in a land war of superiority at sea. They have been, I think, faithful students of the American naval historian, Captain Mahan."[22]

But the exact nature of Mahan's influence on the Japanese naval establishment is a matter of some dispute. One view, seemingly predominant among contemporary scholars, draws a straight line between Mahanian precepts and prewar Japanese ideas about sea power. Ronald Spector describes the Japanese as "true disciples of Mahan."[23] Peter Woolley notes that "Japan took Mahan quite seriously. His books were carefully studied. His proclamation that navies were strategically dominant in the modern world was strongly embraced...."[24] Richard Turk affirms that the IJN imbibed Mahanian sea-power theory "in purer form" than did any other navy.[25] Clearly, a sizable body of scholarship accepts the notion that Alfred Thayer Mahan lent Japanese naval strategy its founding precepts and doctrine.[26]

Other scholars take a more skeptical, more variegated view of the Mahan–Japan relationship. While Mahan earned acclaim from powerful naval leaders in Japan, in this view, he was far from the only influence on them. Both Akiyama Saneyuki and Satō Tetsutarō, the former commonly known as the "father of Japanese naval strategy" and the latter as "Japan's Mahan," drew intellectual inspiration from many sources, ranging from ancient Japanese "water force" tactics to the writings of the Chinese theorist Sun Tzu. Satō spent six months studying naval strategy in the United States, but this came on the heels of eighteen months' study in Great Britain, which after all was the world's leading naval power and the model for aspirants to maritime preeminence.[27]

Japanese strategists read Mahan's works selectively, moreover, using his ideas to ratify preconceived ideas about how Japan should configure and use its navy. Even in the United States, some analysts have intimated, in a similar vein, that Mahan was more a propagandist than a perceptive strategic theorist. One, Margaret Tuttle Sprout, dubbed him an "evangelist of sea power."[28] Roger Dingman, a leading skeptic, questions the extent of Mahan's sway over the Japanese naval establishment: "I am skeptical of these claims about Mahan's influence across the Pacific for several reasons. They are, in the first place, little more than claims, unsupported by any substantial body of evidence."[29] Continues Dingman:

> To suggest that Mahan the publicist of seapower was a tool of potentially great power to Japanese naval expansionists...is not to argue that he was in any sense the *cause* of their

actions....While they invoked his ideas and used his language in the wake of the Sino-Japanese War to justify fleet expansion, it was that conflict—and the prospect of another with Imperial Russia—that provided the much more basic sense of threat that yielded affirmative Diet votes for a bigger navy.[30]

Conclude Dingman and like-minded analysts, Mahan was only part of a mélange of influences on Japanese naval thinkers. Japanese officials welcomed his emphasis on command of the sea, which seemed to reaffirm their experiences from wars with China and Russia, but they also used him freely to advance the IJN's parochial aims.

If Mahan was only one among many intellectual influences on the IJN, sea-power theory was only one among many political, bureaucratic, economic, and social factors that shaped the thinking of Japanese naval strategists. Notes one historian, the navy's rise resulted in great part from an "interplay between power, pageantry, politics, propaganda, and nationalism." Naval leaders "significantly altered politics, empire, and society in pursuit of their narrower and more parochial concerns, namely larger budgets." "Politics," he concludes, "was the lifeblood of the Japanese navy, as it was for the navies of Germany, the United States, and Britain in the same historical period."[31] Mahan made a useful ally to IJN leaders, helping them rally public support for an ambitious naval program —just as he made a useful ally to Theodore Roosevelt and his cohort of American navalists or, for that matter, to Admiral Alfred von Tirpitz in his tilts with socialists in the Reichstag.

Since the inception of the IJN, moreover, naval leaders had waged a bitter bureaucratic struggle with the Japanese army for preeminence in the eyes of the government and the populace. Bureaucratic politics tended to deflect Japanese naval strategy from the Mahanian trajectory it would have followed had the IJN abided purely by Mahanian precepts. For the Japanese navy of the mid-1890s, flush with victory over China,

> the problem of grand strategy was more than a topic of theoretical discussion at the Naval Staff College....[T]he navy...pressed for status beyond interservice parity, toward a position of seniority from which it could set the nation's strategic priorities and claim the lion's share of national prestige, public acclaim, and most important, the government's military budget.[32]

To gain this senior position and the funding and prestige it would bring, IJN leaders realized they needed "a carefully elaborated statement of the preeminent importance of sea power, an argument backed by the weight of historical example, taken not just from Japan's own past, but also from the far greater experience of the traditional maritime powers of the West." In short, they set out to propagate a "public credo" as much as a rational maritime strategy.[33] From the Western maritime tradition, the peculiarities of Japan's geopolitical situation, and the IJN's parochial needs, they fashioned a "blue-water" school of strategic thought about the sea.

Imperial Japan's Quasi-Mahanian Naval Strategy

As it took shape, then, Japanese naval strategy bore only partial resemblance to the sea-power-minded strategy Alfred Thayer Mahan espoused. To be sure, leading IJN thinkers such as Akiyama, Suzuki Kantarō, and Satō—who served together at the Naval Staff College in 1910–11, imparting their vision of Japanese sea power to the World War II generation of naval officers—accepted Mahan's general advocacy of dominant sea power.[34] Satō, note David Evans and Mark Peattie, "seems to have fallen under the spell of Mahan's navalism in its most global sense," namely "command of the seas as the projection of naval power abroad and thus the means to national greatness...."[35] Like Mahan, he accentuated the connection among naval strength, maritime trade, and world power, predicating his own sea-power advocacy on *riko o sake, umi o susumu* (avoiding the continent and advancing on the seas). This beckoned naval leaders' attention toward Southeast Asia.[36] This southerly, seafaring outlook on regional strategy stood in stark contrast to the prescriptions issuing forth from the Japanese army, which had cast its gaze westward, on the Asian landmass.

In his treatise *On the History of Imperial Defense* and other works, Satō both confirmed the priorities of the Japanese navy, which had been forged in victories over the Chinese and Russian navies, and sculpted these priorities in line with his own meditations on history and theory. He accepted the Mahanian notion that assured communications was the sine qua non of great maritime power, and that the way to assure communications was to build a battle fleet capable of sweeping the enemy's flag from vital waterways. From the Battle of Tsushima, as well as from his study of Mahan, he concluded that the single, decisive fleet engagement was the arbiter of dominant sea power. And he clearly fell into the "big ship, big gun" camp that represented the mainstream of Japanese naval thought in the decades leading up to the Pacific War.[37] Japan did opt for a Mahanian battle fleet, planning for a climactic fleet engagement with the "hypothetical enemy" Satō Tetsutarō envisioned—the U.S. Navy.[38]

But, as Dingman and other scholars aver, Satō and like-minded Japanese navalists adapted Mahanian sea-power theory to Japan's distinctive geography and political and economic imperatives. How, and why, did they depart from Mahanian precepts? Several factors were in play. First, Mahan had identified six "principal conditions affecting the sea power of nations": (1) geographical position; (2) physical conformation, including climate and "natural productions"; (3) extent of territory; (4) number of population; (5) character of the people; and (6) character of the government and national institutions.[39] These indices of powerful seafaring nations guided Japan in a different direction from that of the United States, or even of Great Britain—to which, by virtue of its insular conformation and its geographic position on the Asian periphery, Japan bore the greatest resemblance.

IJN thinkers recognized that Japan was a regional power with limited resources, whereas Mahan had derived his theories from the example of Britain, the world's leading sea power, which had interests and commitments ringing the world. They also recognized that their government and people saw the nation not as a sea power in the British sense, but as a land power that had wrested away territorial holdings on the nearby Asian landmass and thus had certain interests at sea. Navy leaders were forced to wage a lively debate with their army counterparts, lobbying for a maritime-oriented foreign policy and strategy. Army leaders argued that the IJN should content itself with defending the Japanese homeland against attack. Navy leaders pointed to the importance of the SLOCs connecting Japan to vital foreign resources and markets. They also questioned how the army planned to support expeditionary forces in Asia absent secure communications with the home islands. Secure sea communications, upheld by the IJN, were crucial even to the army's land-oriented vision.[40]

Naval leaders thus crafted a modified Mahanian naval strategy that was local and particularistic. They paid little attention to island bases, one of Mahan's "pillars" of global sea power, accepting the reality of large-scale territorial conquests in nearby Korea, Manchuria, and coastal China. Akiyama, Suzuki, and Satō did turn their attentions toward Southeast Asia as they applied Mahanian precepts to Japanese conditions. But it was not until the 1930s, when the IJN converted its warships from coal- to oil-fired propulsion, that their case for "advancing on the seas" in a southerly direction took on real urgency in terms of the national interest.[41] Japanese thinkers realized that the "southern strategy" they contemplated would likely bring Japan in conflict with the European imperial powers, which held most of Southeast Asia, and ultimately with the United States. In the interwar period, accordingly, the IJN devised a strategy aimed at luring the U.S. Navy across the broad Pacific to a Mahanian fleet engagement, where it would reprise the Battle of Tsushima.[42]

Second, Japanese mariners were a product of their bureaucratic environment and their operational experiences, which primed them to look at sea power differently than did Mahan, the sea-power historian and prophet. Satō and his fellow navalists were practitioners, serving in numerous sea billets, whereas the academically inclined Mahan had seen only scant sea duty and had little taste for more. ("I am the man of thought, not the man of action," confessed Mahan on one occasion, venturing an explanation as to why his perspective differed from that of Theodore Roosevelt, by any definition a man of action.[43]) They also understood that their immediate task was to win ascendancy over the army in the services' perennial turf war. Indeed, Admiral Yamamoto Gombei rushed Satō's *On the History of Imperial Defense* into print to help the navy make its case for bigger budgets and more ships.[44] These priorities help explain why Japanese navalists' ideas diverged from those set forth by Mahan, who, comfortably ensconced in Newport, was largely spared these everyday travails of navy life.

Japanese strategists focused primarily on tactics and operations rather than the more rarefied dimensions of naval warfare, in large part because, in contrast to their American counterparts, they learned about naval strategy more from combat experience than from abstract sea-power theory. Observes Dingman, leading Japanese theorists were combat veterans of the Sino-Japanese and Russo-Japanese wars. Thus "they turned more to their own empire's recent history than to the more distant past as Mahan had," and their "pens were mobilized more to support specific building programs than to elucidate general principles."[45] Their proposals were geared to big ships and big guns. Says Spector, "Japanese admirals were too faithful students of Mahan to put their faith for ultimate victory in any weapon except the battleship."[46]

Tactics and even hardware, then, propelled Japanese naval thought at least as much as the ideal relationship among strategic theory, naval strategy, and force structure. In effect the IJN inverted this relationship, fitting sea-power theory around its immediate needs for ships, budgets, and bureaucratic supremacy.

Japan's Postwar Maritime Posture

"One searches the pages of recent histories of the IJN in vain for any mention of Alfred Thayer Mahan," declares Dingman.[47] Written to commemorate the centennial of the Russo-Japanese War, a recent essay by Admiral Yoji Koda, a senior JSMDF officer, is nearly mute on Mahan.[48] Interviews with retired officers from the JMSDF likewise imply that Mahan is missing from Japanese strategic thought today, and indeed that the MSDF has allowed strategic thought to languish entirely, owing primarily to Japan's close alliance with the United States. Asked to describe the sources of Japanese sea-power thinking, these officers invariably call for reinforcing the alliance with the United States and its navy.[49] While joining in a composite maritime force with the U.S. Navy confers undoubted benefits on the MSDF—giving the MSDF the offensive punch it lacks as a matter of policy—Japan's dependency on its superpower partner clearly has marked drawbacks.

The demise of the IJN in 1945 did not end naval planning for Tokyo, even if it did discredit Alfred Thayer Mahan and other thinkers; it simply starved Japanese naval planning any intellectual sustenance. Former IJN officers soon began rebuilding the nation's maritime forces with full approval and oversight from the U.S. occupation authorities. Indeed, even before the formal surrender ceremonies on board the *Missouri,* the United States ordered Japan to clear heavily mined areas along the Japanese coast.[50] The ad hoc flotilla of minesweepers formed for this purpose, using remnants of the imperial navy, became the nucleus for postwar Japanese naval power.[51]

It quickly became clear that a functioning institution was required to safeguard Japan's basic maritime interests. In 1948, accordingly, the Japanese government established the Maritime Safety Agency, the precursor to the MSDF. The Korean

War induced U.S. defense planners to seek Japanese military assistance. Unbeknownst to the outside world, Japanese minesweepers were deployed to combat zones off the Korean Peninsula under U.S. operational command, performing a critical support function that the U.S. Seventh Fleet lacked.[52] Postwar Japan, then, devised a navy only in response to the demands of its occupiers. Strategic thinking about naval strategy independent of the United States was absent from the start.

Following the full restoration of Japanese sovereignty in 1952, Tokyo rapidly expanded its maritime responsibilities. Strikingly, the 1952 U.S.–Japan defense treaty inked at San Francisco made the security of the Far East—implicitly including Japan's maritime environs—a key area of responsibility for the alliance. The broad geographic scope of the alliance had less to do with Japan's intrinsic needs than with America's emerging containment strategy in Asia.[53]

Four years after the MSDF entered service in 1954, the JDA (Japan Defense Agency) unveiled its first formal defense buildup plan (1958–60), which set forth three central tasks for Japan's maritime defense. First, submarines were deemed the most pressing threat. As such, the MSDF's primary mission was to conduct ASW (antisubmarine-warfare) operations in waters adjacent to the Japanese archipelago.[54] A second, equally urgent mission was to protect the SLOCs. Third, the MSDF needed to defend against a direct invasion from the sea. These three pillars informed subsequent four-year plans and still form the basis for Japan's maritime defense posture. The SLOC defense mission may or may not have reflected thinking inherited from Japan's prewar strategic traditions, but there was little sign that Tokyo thought about sea power in rigorous theoretical terms. Wartime defeat had banished Mahan from the Japanese lexicon, and no one had taken his place.

An intriguing episode during this period illustrates Japan's early naval ambitions in the Cold War.[55] In 1960, as a part of the regular revision and update of the first defense plan, the MSDF floated a proposal to acquire a helicopter carrier for ASW operations. The initial plan for a 6,000-ton vessel was revised upward, calling for an 11,000-ton ship capable of carrying up to eighteen helicopters. Such a project, if executed, would have represented a quantum leap in the tonnage and capability of Japan's nascent postwar fleet. Notably, the Japanese pointed to American requests for sea-based helicopter support during the Korean War as precedent for a carrier acquisition. (In 1953 the United States had offered to lease Tokyo a 7,000-ton escort carrier to track Soviet submarines, while Tokyo considered converting a transport ship into a carrier.)

Japanese aversion to military matters, amplified by bureaucratic politics, ultimately nullified the MSDF's bid for a carrier, but its ambitions along these lines endured. It crafted a fleet centered on helicopter-carrying destroyers, in an effort to sidestep political objections to aircraft carriers. The service eventually got its wish three decades later (discussed below). A carrier of that capacity would have substantially bolstered Japan's ASW capacity, but the MSDF clearly ignored the political climate, budgetary realities, and, most importantly, the proposed vessel's place in Japan's long-term maritime strategy. The MSDF's tendency to covet the latest in naval technology without reference to a broader naval strategy or Japan's political needs persists to this day.

Geopolitical events and domestic debates reinforced the MSDF's central role in securing the nation's welfare. The 1960 revision of the U.S.–Japan security treaty added a "Far East clause" that more explicitly codified the need to protect Japan's nautical environment while widening allied cooperation to the Korean Peninsula, Taiwan, and the northern Philippines. To ease strategic pressures on a nation weary from Vietnam, President Richard Nixon promulgated the "Guam Doctrine," calling on U.S. allies to shoulder responsibilities in proportion to their needs and capabilities. Against this backdrop, Prime Minister Eisaku Sato declared publicly that Korea and Taiwan were areas of security concern for Japan. Response to a cross-strait contingency would have required the MSDF to project forces far beyond the Japanese home islands.[56] Again, both the Far East and Taiwan clauses served America's strategic interests in Asia rhetorically, but they supplied no concrete guidance on how to harness Japan's naval strategy and capabilities for contingencies beyond defense of the home islands.

As Japan agreed in principle to take on greater responsibilities, this mismatch in policy and strategy stood in ever sharper relief, until it became impossible to overlook. As a consequence, genuine debate about the nation's maritime priorities emerged. Despite politicians' declarations that Japan had acquired capabilities adequate to defend its maritime interests by the early 1970s, the force structure continued to exhibit serious deficiencies.[57] Recognizing this misalignment between political ends and naval means, Osamu Kaihara, a secretary general of the National Defense Council, argued that Japan should dramatically scale back its maritime posture, setting limited objectives that the MSDF could realistically achieve. Japan's SLOCs could be cut at countless points on the map, he argued, so protecting far-flung sea lanes exceeded Japan's maritime capacity. Kaihara urged Tokyo to restructure the JMSDF to resemble a coast guard geared exclusively to defending the home islands from a direct invasion.

In contrast, Hideo Sekino, a respected commentator on defense affairs, considered a direct Soviet invasion unlikely. Given Japan's dependence on overseas resources, the nation was most vulnerable to commerce raiding (or *guerre de course* in naval parlance) in a conflict. The 1973 Arab oil embargo lent credence to Sekino's basic premise, and to his recommendation that Tokyo procure the wherewithal to defend sea lanes as far away as northern Indonesia. Sekino insisted that such a posture would be fully compatible with U.S. regional strategy in Asia, enabling Japan to influence events within the alliance.[58] Interestingly, the most persuasive aspect of Sekino's argument was his claim that Japan could best support U.S. strategic interests in Asia by heeding his recommendations.

Broader geopolitical alignments quickly overtook events. U.S.–Soviet détente and Nixon's dramatic opening to China in the early 1970s fed Japanese fears that Washington was preparing to abandon the alliance. In response, the Japanese government issued its first comprehensive report on how the force it envisioned —based on a "standard defense force concept"—would meet Tokyo's national security objectives. Strikingly, it took Japan nearly a quarter of a century to address the most basic responsibility of any nation: matching national policy with a coherent strategy and supporting forces. But little serious thought went into the report. If Japanese officials ever revisited their basic assumptions, the document betrayed little sign of it.

In keeping with the maritime priorities established more than two decades beforehand, the 1976 NDPO (National Defense Program Outline)[59] provided guidelines for the MSDF to (1) defend against a direct invasion of the home islands; (2) provide warning and defense against threats to Japan's coastal areas; (3) protect major ports and straits; and (4) conduct active air reconnaissance and surveillance of the seas adjacent to Japan's Pacific coast (up to 300 miles) and in the Sea of Japan (about 100–200 miles from Japan's west coast).[60] The NDPO's directives envisioned a fleet centering on modern destroyers, submarines, and fixed- and rotary-wing ASW aircraft. Two years later, Tokyo and Washington signed Guidelines for Defense Cooperation that formally committed Japan to maintaining "peace and stability" across the Asia-Pacific region. The expansiveness of the Outline and the Guidelines sealed the ascendancy of Sekino's vision and emphasized the complementary role Japan could play in U.S. security strategy.

By the 1980s, the revival of Cold War competition and a convergence of Japanese and U.S. strategic interests gave rise to unprecedented naval cooperation. In 1981, Prime Minister Zenko Suzuki sketched a Japanese defense perimeter extending one thousand miles from Japanese shores.[61] Two years later a U.S.-Japanese study group examined the potential for combined operations to defend SLOCs against the Soviets. For the rest of the decade, U.S. and Japanese naval forces perfected the art of combined ASW, working to bottle up Soviet submarine forces in the Seas of Okhotsk and Japan. During this period the MSDF matured into a genuine partner of the U.S. Navy in the Pacific theater. By the end of the Cold War, the JMSDF was second only to the United States in Asian waters.

Whatever its benefits, closer allied collaboration held serious risks for Japan. According to one study,

> The SDF's emphasis on the procurement of interceptor aircraft and antisubmarine warfare ships designed to complement and defend U.S. offensive military assets operating from Japan meant that the structure of its defense force became highly skewed, to the point that it lacked the balanced range of capabilities necessary to defend Japan independent of the United States.[62]

Any prudent theorist on naval affairs would have frowned upon this apparent shortsightedness—especially in a nation whose destiny lay on the seas.

Several patterns emerge from this brief survey of MSDF history. First, the Japanese took to heart the bitter lessons of World War II, when the IJN's failure to defend commercial shipping against U.S. submarines led to disaster for the wartime Japanese economy. Tokyo's near-obsessive focus on sea-lane defense during the Cold War stemmed in part from its desire to avoid a replay of these events. Second, major historical events, namely the Korean War and the larger Cold War, seemed to underscore the importance of defending the sea lanes. From the start, Japanese planners focused on ASW and anti-MIW (mine warfare), and subsequent strategy-making deviated little from these central missions. Third, Tokyo's rigid adherence to the ill-defined SLOC defense mission left the MSDF's capabilities lagging far behind its ambitious maritime vision. The ensuing policy–strategy mismatch would not be repaired until the 1980s.

Fourth, preparations for SLOC defense served the allies' needs asymmetrically. The MSDF's primary tasks filled serious gaps in U.S. ASW and MIW capability while dovetailing fully with the U.S. strategy of containing Soviet naval power. Tokyo was able to exercise greater influence within the alliance, as the founders of postwar Japan had hoped, but their grand bargain entailed serious risks that persist today. Japanese naval strategy was always subservient to the U.S. regional posture in Asia. It is no exaggeration to observe that the MSDF lacked an independent identity, becoming a mere appendage of the U.S. military. The American imprint on the Japanese navy is unmistakable. Indeed, Japanese naval officers revere Admiral Arleigh Burke as "the father of the JMSDF."[63] But Japan's heavy reliance on U.S. concepts, doctrine, and equipment amounted to intellectual buck-passing.

Finally, postwar Japan is a case study in the pitfalls of strategy-making without a larger theoretical framework. Policy documents set forth hazily defined notions of regional peace and stability, while service-level directives focus overwhelmingly on operations (sea-lane defense), tactics, and equipment. The tissue binding strategy to national policy is tenuous, if indeed it exists. Imperial Japan's derivative of Mahanian strategic theory clearly did not outlive World War II. Nor do Japanese planners refer explicitly to Sir Julian Corbett's theories, which were predicated almost exclusively on controlling sea communications, even though the menace of *guerre de course* transfixed Japanese naval officials.[64]

The Post–Cold War Era and Beyond: The MSDF Diversifies

The security environment grew more and more complex in the post–Cold War epoch, even as domestic and international constituencies prodded Japan to step up its efforts to maintain peace and stability, commensurate with its economic power. The MSDF saw its roles and missions accordingly, performing tasks well beyond homeland and sea-lane defense.[65] Whether this diversification will impel the MSDF to transform itself into a service with all the trappings of a traditional navy remains to be seen.

Japan got off to a rough start as the superpower rivalry neared its end. During the 1990–91 Gulf War, Tokyo's failure to provide meaningful military assistance provoked accusations of free riding and "checkbook diplomacy," both domestically and abroad. Notably, however, the MSDF ended up playing a critical, path-breaking role, partly reversing the harsh international verdict. The mine-sweeping force Japan deployed to the Persian Gulf after hostilities ceased involved state-of-the-art equipment, and the MSDF discharged its mission. Harking back to the Korean War, Japanese forces again performed functions that outstripped U.S. Navy capabilities.

Determined not to suffer another public-relations disaster, the Japanese Diet passed the International Peace Cooperation Law in 1992, easing restrictions on overseas deployments of Japanese units. The legislation marked the beginning of unprecedented international activism. Starting in 1992, the MSDF took part in numerous relief and peacekeeping operations. Its first such effort involved transporting personnel and equipment to Cambodia for a UN-mandated peace-keeping mission. The carrier-like *Osumi*-class transport vessels (LST or landing ship tank) debuted during the 1999 East Timor crisis, arousing suspicions in some quarters that Japan was taking its first step to enhance power projection. Tokyo's embrace of international operations was only the beginning of the MSDF's expansion in the nautical arena.

Throughout the 1990s, Japan sought to organize regional initiatives to combat piracy in Southeast Asia. As early as 1997, the National Institute for Defense Studies, the JDA's in-house think tank, proposed an ambitious security enterprise dubbed OPK (Ocean Peace Keeping). The OPK concept envisioned a standing maritime security force composed of naval contingents from nearby states. Prime Minister Keizo Obuchi formally proposed a regional coast guard at the 1999 ASEAN+3 Summit. While Obuchi's proposal failed to catch on due to its perceived radical nature, successive prime ministers have lobbied for the OPK initiative in regional forums.[66] When OPK faltered, the Japanese government pressed for bilateral cooperation, including combined exercises and aid. Tokyo achieved considerable success with this more modest approach, forging agreements with littoral states such as Brunei, India, Indonesia, Malaysia, Singapore, and Thailand.[67]

The September 11 terrorist attacks created new incentives for Japan to expand its maritime missions. Prime Minister Junichiro Koizumi pushed legislation through the Diet permitting the Self-Defense Forces to provide rear-area military support to allied forces operating in the Indian Ocean. The MSDF dispatched combat logistics ships, transports, and escorts on a rotating basis. Notably, the MSDF's responsibilities and capabilities gradually grew. Its refueling mission, initially limited to U.S. and British vessels, came to include eight other coalition partners, with Japan meeting some 30 percent of allied fuel demand.[68] As of September 2005, Japanese oilers had dispensed some 410 million liters of fuel, worth $140 million, free of charge.[69] In December 2002, after some prodding from the United States, Japan reluctantly agreed to deploy a frontline Aegis destroyer to the Indian Ocean.[70]

Japan assumed an assertive stance before and after the 2003 Iraq war. While many Japanese politicians and most citizens questioned the legitimacy of the invasion, Koizumi stood firmly behind the Bush administration's claim that Iraq was a central front in the global war on terror. After the Diet enacted the necessary legislation, Tokyo dispatched 600 ground troops to Samawah, a city considered secure, in a noncombat role. The MSDF employed its *Osumi*-class ships to support this mission.

Also in 2003, as part of its broad-based support for the U.S.-led war on terror, Tokyo acceded to the PSI (Proliferation Security Initiative), in an effort to halt the proliferation of weapons technology at sea, aloft, and ashore.[71] A "core" participant in the PSI, Japan has taken part in a series of highly visible exercises held across the globe. Because Japanese law forbade the MSDF to board ships in peacetime, MSDF observers watched the Japanese coast guard during the first round of multinational exercises. To correct this awkward arrangement, one of the "war contingency bills" approved by the Diet in May 2004 loosened restrictions on the MSDF. In October 2004, Japan hosted its first PSI exercise, "Team Samurai," but the MSDF was still limited to patrol and intelligence operations. It dispatched a destroyer, two P-3C surveillance aircraft, and two helicopters to the first PSI drill in Southeast Asia, which Singapore hosted in August 2005.

Humanitarian imperatives also raised the profile of the MSDF. In January 2005, Japan undertook its largest postwar military deployment, sending MSDF units to Indonesia in response to the devastating tsunami. Numbering approximately 1,000 personnel, the relief task force included three ships, five helicopters, and two C-130 transport aircraft. The MSDF dispatched an *Osumi*-class transport ship, along with a refueling vessel and an escort destroyer, to support helicopter operations off the coast of Aceh.[72] Tokyo called on a naval flotilla returning from patrols in the Indian Ocean to furnish additional assistance.[73] The mission, in which Japanese forces worked from an integrated command post in Thailand, represented the first time the three SDF services had operated jointly.

Tokyo's most recent reassessment of its defense policy and military modernization programs conforms to its activism over the past five years. The NDPG (National Defense Program Guidelines) issued in December 2004 reaffirmed Japan's variegated security posture, instructing the SDF to prepare for "new threats and diverse situations" and for any international operations that might arise.[74] The NDPG mandates the capacity to (1) defend against ballistic-missile attacks; (2) respond to incursions by enemy special operations forces; (3) defeat an invasion of Japan's offshore islands; (4) patrol and prevent intrusion into Japan's surrounding seas and airspace; and (5) manage the effects of weapons-of-mass-destruction attacks. The JMSDF has an ambitious slate of missions.

Accordingly, the latest Mid-Term Defense Program, which sets out force-structure priorities to meet the NDPG's directives, forecasts sizable procurements of destroyers, submarines, and fixed- and rotary-wing patrol aircraft during fiscal years 2005–9. Three of Japan's four Aegis destroyers will undergo upgrades to bolster their antiballistic-missile capabilities, while two new Aegis ships will join the fleet over the next decade. These increases will be balanced against efforts to streamline and consolidate the overall fleet, while growth rates in the annual defense budget will be trimmed. The potential disjunction between acquisition plans and resources has raised concerns about feasibility and sustainability.[75]

The planned construction of a new-generation 13,500-ton helicopter destroyer symbolizes the potential new direction of the MSDF, realizing one of the service's decades-long aspirations. The "16DDH"-class ship has attracted significant media and Diet attention owing to its resemblance to an aircraft carrier.[76] The vessel's design features a starboard-side island superstructure and an uninterrupted flight deck, prompting observers to speculate that Japan may be eyeing a carrier capable of handling Harrier-like aircraft. Notes one analyst, "the configuration of the *Osumi* and the DDH-class indicates that Japan is rehearsing carrier-building technology to reserve for itself this potential military option; and thus, that it is considering discarding the constitutional prohibition on the acquisition of power-projection capabilities."[77]

In the meantime, DDH would fulfill many of the peacetime and wartime missions elaborated in the NDPG.[78] As a wartime flagship, the DDH would serve as a command-and-control center, coordinating the activities of other units while its organic helicopters conducted ASW operations. During peacetime operations, or "military operations other than war" (MOOTW), the DDH would join the *Osumi*-class ships for peacekeeping and relief operations, as well as the "diverse situations" Japan foresees confronting on the high seas.

This array of maritime activities clearly reflects greater confidence on the part of Japan's political elite that the MSDF can cope effectively with demanding missions. The new defense plans also suggest that Japanese power-projection capacity will continue to grow. This convergence of intent and capability could very well yield a traditional maritime power along the East Asian littoral.

Such a shift would surely have implications for the regional configuration of power in Northeast Asia and for global security, but several important caveats are in order. First, Japan's activism on the high seas today represents the culmination of gradual, modest steps that took place over fifteen years. This long gestation period permitted decision-makers to ease the prohibitions against overseas deployment without unduly alarming government officials or the Japanese electorate. Second, Tokyo's decisions to employ maritime forces were driven primarily by crisis and, oftentimes, by American pressure to act. The Gulf War fiasco epitomized the highly reactive nature of Japanese decision-making. Third, Japan's ability to respond to crisis beyond the home islands was largely a by-product of enhancements to its alliance with the United States. For instance, Japan's impressive involvement in the war on terror would have been impossible absent the allied renewal process that began in the mid-1990s. Fourth, at a broader level, the MSDF largely remains an appendage of U.S. maritime strategy, bereft of an independent, coherent naval strategy. This situation is acceptable in most contingencies, when Tokyo can count on support from Washington, but it will prove problematic if and when Japan needs to act alone.

Finally, Japan's expansion of the MSDF's roles and missions does entail strategic risks. The looming consolidation and streamlining of frontline forces suggest that Japanese political and military leaders believe the MSDF can do more with less, or at any rate more with the same forces. Such a posture makes eminent sense if future crises take the form of MOOTW, but this planning parameter assumes away the potential for higher-intensity confrontations, including traditional force-on-force engagements on the open seas. This trend is further evidence of Japan's break with Mahanian thought since World War II —and it is occurring at a moment in history when another resurgent military power's seafaring ambitions could usher in a new age of Mahan.

China's Rise: Collision Ahead?

Sino-Japanese relations have seen better days. Some of the problems that have ratcheted the two countries' ambivalence about one other to new highs are perennial features of the relationship, while others are new and possibly more difficult to manage. Among the latter, early signs of maritime competition have appeared in the past two years. Four nautical issues have dogged bilateral ties: (1) China's rapid naval modernization; (2) ongoing cross-strait tensions; (3) boundary and resource disputes in the East China Sea; and (4) incidents at sea. All four problems have followed patterns that spell trouble for future Sino-Japanese maritime interactions.

In November 2004, for instance, a Chinese nuclear attack submarine intruded into Japanese territorial waters, prompting the JMSDF to track the vessel and Koizumi's government to issue a rare public demand for an apology. A newly revised NDPO appeared that same month, declaring that China's naval operations required greater vigilance on the MSDF's part. In February 2005, Tokyo unexpectedly announced that the Japanese Coast Guard would formally take charge of a lighthouse erected by nationalists on the disputed Senkaku/Diaoyutai Island, sparking public protests in China. Beijing has also tabled objections to Tokyo's claims to exclusive economic zones surrounding Japanese-owned atolls in the Pacific.[79] Similarly, a joint U.S.-Japanese declaration that the two countries shared "common strategic objectives" in the Taiwan Strait elicited angry recriminations from Beijing.

Ongoing territorial disputes in the East China Sea resurfaced in the summer and fall of 2005, after the Japanese government announced that it would grant certain companies the right to drill for gas deposits in and near contested areas. When China lodged a protest, Japan accused Beijing of starting extraction operations. In an unprecedented show of force, China deployed a naval flotilla led by fearsome *Sovremenny*-class guided-missile destroyers near the gas field, even as negotiators on both sides sought to defuse the situation. A Chinese ship reportedly trained its guns on a nearby Japanese P-3C patrol aircraft.[80] In August the JDA unveiled its annual defense white paper, specifically declaring China's growing naval power in Asia a matter of concern.[81] Following the release of the white paper, the head of the JDA, Yoshinori Ohno, averred that Chinese maritime activities required attention and called on Beijing to divulge more information about its military expenditures. The Japanese media subsequently leaked a highly classified scenario-planning document outlining a robust military strategy for repelling any Chinese invasion of the Senkaku Islands.

Given this escalating set of events, it has become increasingly urgent to discern how Japanese and Chinese sea power might interact in the future. One useful method for assessing this Sino-Japanese dynamic is to analyze Chinese strategic thinking about naval power and compare it against Japan's approach. Such a comparative analysis will hint at strengths and weaknesses in the MSDF's defense posture, suggesting whether and how Tokyo ought to realign its priorities.

The disparity between Chinese and Japanese strategic thought about maritime affairs could scarcely be sharper. In recent years a vocal school of thought in Beijing has noticed that Alfred Thayer Mahan's works furnish both the logic and the vocabulary to argue for assertive sea power.[82] Proponents of this school of thought write and speak in avowedly Mahanian terms, and in many cases they explicitly cite his works to justify an ambitious maritime strategy. In particular, his portrayal of sea power as "overbearing power" pervades these Chinese thinkers' discourse on maritime affairs. Should the Mahanians win out among the cacophony of voices clamoring for the attention of senior policymakers in Beijing, Chinese strategy will take on distinctly offensive overtones.[83] Japanese strategists and their American partners must remain mindful of this prospect.

Perhaps the most thoughtful spokesman for China's Mahanian school is Professor Ni Lexiong of the Research Institute of War and Culture, Eastern China Science and Engineering University. Professor Ni uses sea-power theory to evaluate the competing claims of advocates of sea power and advocates of globalization. The latter, he contends, believe that

> China should not act by following the traditional sea power theory in pursuing a strong Navy, because today's world situation is different from the time of Mahan...that the globalization of the world's economy has made various countries' interests

interconnected, mutually dependent on each other to a greater degree, and that if a country wants to preserve its life line at sea, the only way to do so is to go through "co-operation" rather than the traditional "solo fight."[84]

Globalization theorists, notes Ni, typically urge Beijing to refrain from a naval arms buildup. To do so would alert "today's naval hegemon," the United States, "making China's naval development a self-destructive play with fire," reminiscent of Imperial Germany's quixotic bid for sea power at the turn of the nineteenth century.[85]

The author hedges by allowing for the possibility that the world is entering a Kantian era of perpetual peace, as many globalization enthusiasts maintain, but he postulates that even a pacific international system will ultimately depend on force. In either case, then, China should build up its naval forces. If the globalization theorists have it right, China will need a muscular navy to play its part in the "world Navy," when one emerges, and to help along the transition to a peaceful international order. Ni clearly believes, however, that the world has not yet evolved beyond its Hobbesian state, in which nations must maintain powerful military forces as a means of self-help. Thus "it is China's necessary choice to build up a strong sea power" to guard against "the threats to our 'outward-leaning economy' by some strong nations"—again, code for the United States—in the lingering "Hobbesian era" he perceives.[86]

Professor Ni reminds his readers of China's humiliation at Japanese hands in 1894–95, when a powerful Japanese battle fleet crushed that of the Qing Dynasty. "The key to winning that war was to gain the command of the sea," he proclaims. Today's China should emulate Imperial Japan's example, keeping in mind that Mahan "believed that whoever could control the sea would win the war and change history; that command of the sea is achieved through decisive naval battles on the seas; that the outcome of decisive naval battles is determined by the strength of fire power on each side of the engagement."[87] This is scarcely the language of someone predisposed to "protracted defensive resistance," the term used by some Western analysts to describe China's naval strategy.[88] If indeed this sort of thinking comes to dominate policy discourse in Beijing, Washington and its Asian partners will be compelled to come to terms with a newly assertive naval strategy on Beijing's part. It behooves Tokyo to relearn its Mahan and to revisit the IJN's history, if for no other reason than to get a glimpse into what a prospective competitor may do in maritime East Asia.

What kinds of problems might these trends in Chinese maritime strategy pose for Japan? Observers in certain quarters of Japan's strategic community have begun to grasp the potential Mahanian challenge that Chinese sea power could present. Studies assessing Chinese maritime intentions and the Sino-Japanese military balance on the high seas have become more and more common.[89] The Japanese worry that China may be eyeing Japan's offshore islands as it extends its naval power eastward. One author cites the creeping expansion of China's naval presence in the SCS (South China Sea) as a worrisome precedent.[90] Indeed, some analysts and authorities in China have hinted subtly at challenging Japan's legal interpretation of its administrative and sovereign prerogatives in the East China Sea, including those pertaining to Okinawa. A Japanese commentator alleges that Beijing harbors hegemonic ambitions to reestablish control over all territories governed by the former Qing Dynasty.[91]

Hideaki Kaneda, a retired JMSDF vice admiral, explicitly links China's emerging maritime strategy to Mahan. Kaneda argues that China meets Mahan's six tests of sea power, including favorable geography, a large population, and the national will to compete on the high seas. He observes that the Chinese are constructing strategic relationships and military bases along the sea lanes stretching from the SCS to the Persian Gulf, which convey the energy resources and other commodities that sustain China's economic well-being. Under Mahanian logic, this emerging diplomatic and defense infrastructure (also known as a "string of pearls"[92]) would permit larger-scale military deployments in the future to protect Chinese commerce. He concludes, "All of Asia must wake up to the arrival of Chinese-style aggressive 'sea power.' Japan, in particular, must reformulate its national maritime strategy with this in mind."[93]

A highly influential journalist, Yoichi Funabashi, implicitly endorses Mahan's view that national will is a key determinant of sea power. Despite the nautical character of Japan's geography, Funabashi bemoans the Japanese people's indifference to maritime matters, imploring Japan "to once again devise a maritime strategy aimed at opening up the four seas that surround it and taking advantage of the blessings of the oceans." As for China, he observes, "China is a major continental power on the rise. By contrast, Japan is expected to show its 'difference' and 'strengths' as a major maritime power more than ever. It should maintain 'free navigation' to build peace and stability in Asia seas and incorporate China in the framework."[94] Despite this somewhat conciliatory tone, Funabashi insists that Japan must nurture a national character that embraces maritime power if it hopes to compete with China on the world stage.

Jun Kitamura, a Japanese consultant to the U.S. Pacific Command, advocates a far more bellicose stance vis-à-vis China. He too complains that "Japan lacks a sense of caution in regard to China's rapid military expansion." Pointing to China's maturing submarine force, he criticizes the Japanese government for failing to "fathom the geopolitical significance of the fighting power of submarines in today's international community." To remedy the apparent shortfall in national maritime consciousness, Kitamura urges the Japanese people to "establish clear national strategies for Japan on their own, and rebuild their military power as effective means to guarantee the strategies as soon as possible." Specifically, he recommends shifting Japan's line of defense seaward, arguing that repulsing a direct invasion would be too late and too costly. To support a forward defense, he says, the JMSDF needs to double in size, acquire a panoply of offensive weaponry, build massive naval bases, and develop its own intelligence infrastructure. Most controversially, he presses for an alliance with Taiwan that keeps the island from falling into Chinese hands, thereby safeguarding Japanese sea lanes adjoining the island.[95]

Whatever the merits of and differences among these analyses, they all concur on one important priority: a fundamental reassessment of Japan's maritime strategy that helps the JMSDF maintain its edge as China's naval power grows. The apparent shift in tone and urgency among these well-respected observers suggests that a spirited debate about Japan's maritime posture, harking back to the Sekino–Kaihara debate, may be in the making. Whether or not Japan's national policy and maritime strategy will veer in the direction these commentators espouse remains to be seen.

In policy terms, the Japanese government has responded concretely to the potential Chinese challenge. Reflecting worries about Beijing's intentions toward the offshore islands, the latest defense white paper sets the capacity to stage an effective response to island invasion as a major priority. Significantly, the report states, "If there is an indication noticed in advance, an operation shall be conducted to prevent invasion by the enemy's unit. If there is no indication in advance and the islands in question were occupied, an operation shall be conducted to defeat the enemy."[96] For the first time, the Ground SDF forces recently joined the U.S. Marine Corps in joint and combined exercises to defend offshore islands.[97] The MSDF would play a central role in carrying ground troops in such a defensive operation. The JMSDF has also engaged in antisubmarine drills with the U.S. Navy near Okinawan waters.[98]

A recent study considers how the SDF's capabilities would measure up against China's military in combat over Japan's offshore islands. The study postulates that if the Chinese side were able to surprise Japan and rapidly occupy the Sakishima Islands, the SDF would find it difficult if not impossible to dislodge enemy forces on its own. Given the short distances involved, land-based Chinese fighter aircraft could easily provide protective cover against Japanese forces, while Japanese aircraft would face much shorter loiter times in the area. The author of the study concludes that a light aircraft carrier capable of handling vertical/short takeoff and landing aircraft would be required to counter such an invasion.[99] Regardless of whether this analysis carries any policy weight, the bluntness with which it discusses a Sino-Japanese confrontation hints at the changing public mood in Japan with regard to a Chinese maritime challenge.

Theoretical and Policy Implications for the JMSDF

From the foregoing analysis of Japanese strategic thought, it is possible to venture a few observations and findings. Specifically,

Applying Strategic Theory Is Tough. Dogmatic adherence to sea-power theory can be harmful if not fatal to maritime nations. So can an indifference to fundamental principles of sea power that unmoors strategy and force planning from any larger sense of national policy and grand strategy. Over the past century, Japan has exhibited extreme tendencies in both directions. In the case of prewar Japan, a variant of Mahanian dogma seeped into the Japanese consciousness about naval power, prodding the IJN leadership into fateful decisions about force structure and operational doctrine. Today, Japan's niche—and therefore highly unbalanced—capabilities and strategy derive from unquestioned assumptions about U.S. security commitments. This could serve Japanese maritime interests ill over the long run.

China's Rise Could Portend Trouble. An area that requires further research is how two differing national approaches to sea power might intersect in practice. Substantial evidence indicates that Beijing is succumbing to Mahan's beguiling logic. If this is so, how will a post-Mahanian JMSDF interact with a Chinese navy fascinated with Mahan? This question has gained substantial policy urgency over the past few years, as naval rivalry between the two powers has taken hold. Is Japan endangering itself by directing the MSDF to keep performing its full array of Cold War–era missions while piling on new international operations, all without boosting defense spending? How might future acquisitions affect Japan's maritime security? Specifically, would ASW and minesweeping prove adequate in a tilt with the PLA Navy?

America Needs a More Coherent Naval Strategy. Assuming the United States wishes to maintain its naval preeminence in Asia indefinitely, it must carefully reexamine its maritime strategy in the region. Tokyo should urge Washington to do so, and it should take an active hand in formulating combined strategy. Key U.S. policy documents such as Seapower 21 and the latest Quadrennial Defense Review represent sorry excuses for strategy, framed in terms too general and abstract to provide meaningful guidance. Many Japanese strategic thinkers, accordingly, have begun reassessing the benefits and costs of a far more independent posture in the maritime realm. How would such an outcome benefit or harm the United States? If U.S. policymakers have thought about this prospect, they give no sign of it. Washington's assumption that Tokyo will automatically follow its lead—or, for that matter, Tokyo's assumption that Washington will furnish military support even in situations that do not engage U.S. interests— could engender mutually unrealistic assumptions about the two partners' will and capability, especially in times of crisis or war. Suppose the United States decided that a Chinese invasion of Japan's offshore islands fell outside of the purview of the defense treaty, what then for the JMSDF?

Japan Needs a Theorist. It behooves the policy community in Tokyo to start thinking ahead now about how Japan should handle contingencies that threaten to strain the security alliance or leave the United States standing on the sidelines.

If Alfred Thayer Mahan is no longer a useful guide to Japanese maritime strategy, who is? Julian Corbett's writings offer a good starting point for this sorely needed debate and for a broader renaissance of strategic thought in Japan. Corbett fits better with contemporary Japanese politics and political culture than does Mahan. He favored big ideas, not technical details or specific weapons systems; he was not a blue-water theorist to the same degree as Mahan; his vision was not universalist like that of Mahan, but admitted of regional strategies such as Japan's; and he was not fixated on absolute victory at sea. Rather, Corbett held out the possibility of limited naval operations aimed at limited political and strategic objectives—a trait which could endear him to a Japanese populace and government still averse to the use of force. And, like today's MSDF leadership, he depicted controlling maritime communications as the foremost challenge facing practitioners of naval operations.[100]

In short, Corbett's works offer a promising platform for strategic discussions. Japan needs to resurrect its tradition of strategic thinking about the sea. Let the debate begin.

CHAPTER 9

CHINA–SOUTHEAST ASIA RELATIONS: PROBLEMS AND PROSPECTS

John Garofano

With its expanding political influence; its increasingly sophisticated nuclear, space, and power-projection capabilities; and an economy poised to overtake those of the United States and European Union in terms of raw purchasing power, the PRC (People's Republic of China) is about to move into a new category of statehood falling somewhere between superpower and mere great-power status. The implications are global, but they will be felt acutely by China's immediate neighbors. The United States, which has long considered itself both a resident Asian power and a force for stability in the region, thus will face a "near peer competitor." Long-standing U.S. allies Japan and the ROK (Republic of Korea) will confront new dilemmas, with Japan having to choose how to make the transition to the status of a "normal" power without sparking a new round of open-ended competition and the ROK considering the effects of any possible resolution of its cross-border issues on future relations with the giant to the north.

Less obvious, and occasioning far less discussion, are the implications of China's rise for security in Southeast Asia. The subregion does not bristle with the same stores of conventional armaments that characterize Northeast Asia, and most of the actors there have sworn off nuclear weapons. Key states are not as wealthy as those of Northeast Asia, and they have not yet focused their energies on the foreign and security policy problems of Northeast Asia. Nor do they have the degree of historical animosity and related baggage toward a rising China that is evidenced in Japan's relations with its neighbors.

Yet in no small part because Southeast Asian states have been focused on domestic economic and social conditions, the rise of China poses a unique set of problems which regional actors may be ill-equipped to manage. While a debate over whether the subregion is ripe for rivalry is premature, one over whether it is ripe for continued peaceful development may be entirely appropriate.

What is the future of China's relations with its neighbors to the south and the east? The answer depends on five sets of considerations that will be examined in turn: China's growing energy demand and the centrality of the SCS (South China Sea) as a potential source of resources, or of myriad problems, for Beijing; the significance of the SCS as a source of both cooperative and conflictual relations among the major actors; China's attitudes and policies toward Southeast Asia, and the larger context of its overall disposition toward territorial disputes/compromise and the use of force; China's growing naval power; and Southeast Asia's responses, political and military, to the rise of China and associated issues. This chapter argues that while just a few years ago most analysts could find little cause for concern, a combination of new factors and complacency makes this subregion an area to watch for potential conflict over the medium term. In particular, a powerful China free of its Taiwan problem will present unique problems for Southeast Asia.

China's Energy Problem and Southeast Asia's Unique Position

China's oil demand doubled between 1995 and 2005 to nearly 7 million barrels per day (bbl/d), making China the world's second largest consumer of oil after the United States (at 21 million bbl/d). This doubling came as a surprise to most analysts, as well as to many Chinese policymakers. Natural gas consumption has increased and is projected to continue increasing at similar rates. China's increased demand for all kinds of energy—the result of dramatic growth in construction and road transport—is responsible for more than half of the world's increase in energy demand from 2000 to 2004 alone. Current Chinese oil imports stand at 4 million bbl/d. Given GDP growth of around 7 percent for the next fifteen years, China's imports are expected to be around 7 million bbl/d by 2020 out of total consumption of 13 million bbl/d. China's share of world oil consumption will rise from 8 percent today to 11 percent in 2030. At between 2.1 and 3 billion tons of oil equivalent (usually expressed as 2,100 million tons of oil equivalent, or Mtoe), its total energy use will exceed that of the European Union; by 2030 it should exceed that of the United States and Canada combined.[1]

The further urbanization of the country; the proliferation of factories, office buildings, and residential construction; and the rise in the number of automobiles from the current 13 million to perhaps 160 million by 2020, all suggest the growing importance of energy security in Beijing's foreign policy. Energy security may be defined as "the security of having an adequate supply of energy, at reasonable and stable prices, aimed at sustaining economic performance and growth," and Chinese leaders are concerned for a number of reasons.[2] Above all, continued economic growth is vital to social peace and the legitimacy of the extant political system. These could be in jeopardy, particularly in the less developed regions, without continued job and wealth creation and distribution.

Two strains of thinking, one economic and one security related, contribute to this sense of insecurity on the part of policymakers in Beijing. The economic issue arises from the lack of appreciation of or understanding of market forces in the energy sector. Energy market analysts are not widespread throughout the bureaucracy, and in general there is a lack of confidence in markets for solving the myriad problems associated with supply. A lack of expertise is compounded by a dearth of low-cost, accurate information, incomplete privatization, limits imposed on foreign participation and ownership, and a decentralized fiscal and political system.[3]

On the more traditional security side, spikes in price and the general political environment following the start of the 2003 Iraq war made perfectly clear, just as the demand issue was exploding, the extent of China's reliance on both a stable political and economic environment in the Middle East and the long transportation lines from there to its major distribution centers. Beijing did not like what it saw as a unilaterally initiated war (despite the UN's long involvement in the problem, right up to the start of the conflict) to secure a U.S. vision of energy security which more likely than not would threaten China's arrangements with Iraq and other countries in the region. The Middle East still holds 60 percent of proven oil reserves and is the source of nearly 40 percent of China's oil imports. Saudi Arabia and others are planning to ramp up production so that the region's share of world production could increase to nearly 50 percent by 2030. Without corrective measures, Middle Eastern oil could increase to 70–80 percent of China's imports by 2015.[4]

Beijing's recent arrangements with Iran, Sudan, Myanmar, Uzbekistan, Russia, Argentina, Canada, Venezuela, and most recently Saudi Arabia flow from these concerns. The "pipeline politics" of the Shanghai Cooperation Organization, which encompasses proposed links from Kazakhstan and Iran, as well as an Asian Free Trade Area proposal intended to promote access to Indonesian and Malaysian oil and gas and to Singapore's refinery capacity, is also part of this post–Iraq war strategy. And China has begun extracting offshore resources from the waters surrounding the Diaoyutai/Senkaku islands, where its territorial claims overlap with those of Japan; from the Xisha/Paracels, where Chinese claims overlap with Vietnam's; and from the Nansha/Spratly area, where several countries assert sovereign rights. Gas pipelines from Irkutsk and Sakhalin and new liquefied natural gas terminals in Guangdong and Fujian contribute to the provision of energy security.

Roughly 75 percent of Chinese oil imports passes through the Malacca Strait. Recent concerns for piracy and terrorist attacks there have been a major impetus to China's creation of a Strategic Petroleum Reserve, as well as its consideration of alternative sea lanes. Four options for alternative sea lanes have been considered: constructing a 250 kilometer oil pipeline or canal across the Kra Peninsula to connect the Andaman Sea to the Gulf of Siam; using the shallow Sunda Strait between Sumatra and Java; using the Lombok Strait east of Java; and laying down a pipeline connecting Gulf of Bengal seaports in Myanmar to Kunming in Yunnan.[5]

Overall, China's growing energy demand has two major implications for the region. First, energy will clearly play a more prominent role in China's grand strategy and in its diplomatic, political, and military relationships with its neighbors. Second, Southeast Asia has a unique role to play here, for several reasons. The region represents a major, nearby source of supply for oil, gas, and other resources. States there are politically stable, particularly relative to the Middle East. They have an interest in economic development—that is, in being a preferred, stable source of supply for Beijing's needs. Finally, China has very recently begun to perceive a vital national interest in ensuring that the sea lines of communication remain open, secure, safe, and peaceful. Southeast Asian states play a major role in contributing to a more or a less safe environment for the massive amounts of energy and other cargo that transit the subregion.

The South China Sea: Peace Now, Conflict Later?

The SCS is the world's fifth largest body of water, covering an area of some 3.5 million square kilometers, stretching from the Singapore and Malacca straits to the Taiwan Strait. It is one of the world's busiest waterways, with some three-quarters of total oil and natural gas shipments transiting the sea annually, forming a lifeline from the Middle East fields to the dynamic economies of East Asia. One-half of the world's annual merchant fleet tonnage sails through the Malacca Strait and the Straits of Sunda and Lombok.[6] The transit of oil through the SCS is three times that through the Suez Canal and fifteen times that which flows through Panama, and the volume is expected to double by 2020. Japan currently receives 75 percent of its oil via the SCS, Taiwan 70 percent, and the ROK 75 percent (figures for China are above). The sea is also one of the world's largest sources of fish production, providing the majority of protein in the diets of much of the Asia-Pacific.

The potential for conflict lies in the competing territorial claims asserted by China, Taiwan, Vietnam, the Philippines, Malaysia, and Brunei. Most of these claims involve the Spratly Islands and the potential resources around them, while Vietnam and Taiwan also claim the Paracel Islands, which have been controlled by China since 1974. The underlying issue is that China claims the entire sea and all of the resources within and beneath it. Beijing bases its territorial claims on occupation for some two thousand years and on the notable absence of competing claims for most of that time. Beijing promulgates its policy using maps first published in 1914 that show Chinese territory as encompassing the entire SCS, up to an unclear but narrow belt of territorial waters held by the other littoral states.[7]

Chiang Kai-shek laid claim to the sea in 1947 using a nine-dashed U-shaped line, a claim formalized by PRC Foreign Minister Zhou En-lai in 1951. Vietnam has claimed both the Spratly and the Paracel groups since 1975, based on history and occupation. Vietnam established a 200-nautical-mile EEZ (exclusive economic zone) in 1977. The Philippines has claimed a large share of the Spratlys, which Filipinos label Kalayaan, since 1971. In 1978, Manila declared these to be part of the sovereign territory. Manila has also established a 200-nautical-mile EEZ. Malaysia extended its continental shelf in 1979 to include some of the Spratlys, while in 1988 Brunei established a 200-nautical-mile EEZ extending just to the south of the group. In 1992 and 1993, Indonesia got involved in these territorial disputes to counter Chinese claims that seemed to encroach upon the productive and profitable Natuna gas fields owned by Indonesia.

And during this spate of activity came one of the more disturbing developments, when in 1992 the Chinese National People's Congress adopted the Law of the Territorial Sea and Contiguous Zone. The law claimed exclusive sovereignty over the Paracel and Spratly islands, asserting a right to evict other national vessels, authorizing pursuit of foreign ships to the high seas, and requiring all foreign warships to notify Beijing of their intent to pass through China's territorial seas and to request permission to do so.

Yet the sources and nature of the legal aspects of the claims are only part of the story, the frequent use or threat to use force is another. Taiwan occupied Itu Aba, the largest of the Spratly Islands, in 1956. China occupied the last of Paracel Islands in 1974, acting militarily as South Vietnam was in its death throes and unable to resist. China occupied nine reefs following a naval confrontation with Vietnam in 1988 in which Vietnamese vessels were sunk with a loss of over 70 sailors. In 1992 Vietnam accused China of drilling in Vietnamese waters and landing troops on Da Luc Reef. From June through September of that year, China seized some twenty Vietnamese cargo vessels carrying goods from Hong Kong. There were further naval confrontations between the two in 1995 over three oil exploration blocks claimed by both countries.

The Chinese then occupied Mischief Reef, an atoll also claimed by Vietnam and the Philippines, sometime prior to February 1995, when Filipino officials discovered Chinese military structures on the reef. Manila tried unsuccessfully to evict the workers and remove the markers they had erected, but China expanded its military structures on the reef and did so again in late 1998. Taiwanese artillery fired on Vietnamese vessels in the disputed area in 1995, and in 1996 three Chinese vessels engaged in a ninety-minute gun battle with a Taiwanese vessel over Campones Island. In 1997 the Philippine Navy ordered a Chinese boat to leave the Scarborough Shoal area and then planted the Philippine flag and markers. China responded by sending ships to survey the Philippine-claimed Panata and Kota islands. The Philippine Navy arrested Chinese sailors near the shoal in January 1998; in the same month, Vietnamese sailors fired on a Philippine fishing boat near Pigeon Reef.[8] In 1999, Malaysia seized Navigator Reef, claimed by the Philippines, and in August 2002 Vietnamese troops based on one rock fired at Philippine military aircraft. Vietnam commenced rebuilding one runway on a disputed Spratly island with the goal of sending tourists there.[9] Currently Vietnam occupies about twenty-two "islands," the Philippines eleven, China fourteen, Malaysia ten, and Taiwan Itu Aba.

Many analysts see a trend, crystallizing in the 1990s and coming to fruition in the past decade, toward less conflict, more joint development, and increased interest on Beijing's part in the peaceful settlement of disputes in the SCS. This may indeed be a recent trend, but the question is how deep are the currents beneath it. Following Beijing's adoption of the 1992 law on territoriality, for example, ASEAN responded with a Declaration on the South China Sea. The declaration was based on the 1976 Treaty of Amity and Cooperation, a foundational ASEAN document enshrining the principles of noninterference and sovereignty. China initially rejected the Declaration, along with its call for multilateral consultations, but Beijing began to reassert its peaceful intentions following a negative reaction from its neighbors. It did so at the first ASEAN Regional Forum meeting in July 1994, and thereafter Foreign Minister Qian Qichen agreed explicitly to some form of multilateral negotiations based on the UNCLOS (UN Convention on the Law of the Sea). Beijing nonetheless repeated its claims to jurisdictions over the entire SCS, asserting that it would negotiate only on conduct—not on sovereignty.

If there was some ASEAN unity on the issue, it fractured in the 1990s, when the Philippines and Vietnam supported a stronger multilateral agreement, as well as provisions for joint exploration. Their proposals were rejected by Malaysia, which moved closer to the Chinese position and began to support bilateralism more strongly. (This move should be seen in the context of Kuala Lumpur's general disenchantment with U.S. foreign policy at this time.) Malaysia proposed its own, nonbinding, weak document, which was in turn rejected by Vietnam and the Philippines, which wanted a binding document. The result was the November 2002 Declaration on the Conduct of Parties in the South China Sea, in which parties agree to resolve territorial disputes without the resort to force, and to exercise self-restraint. The declaration also promotes scientific research, environmental protection, safety at sea, and concerns for transnational crime.

The declaration may be part of ASEAN's search "for explicit confirmation that China's presence in the South China Sea will not jeopardize peaceful coexistence."[10] Yet the declaration does not define the area to which it is supposed to apply, thus leaving it unclear whether it extends to the Spratlys, to the Paracels, or to the SCS as a whole. It does not include many other interested parties, including Singapore, Indonesia, Taiwan, Japan, or the United States; nor does it invite interested parties to join. It does not prohibit the improvement of existing structures or the creation of structures on territory already occupied. And it states that any future modifications to the Code of Conduct shall take place on the basis of consensus.[11]

Several recent agreements have provided cause for hope that further clashes can be avoided. China's October 2003 decision to adhere to the total allowable catch (TAC) agreement made it the first non-ASEAN state to do so. China and the Philippines signed a seismic survey agreement in 2004 and were joined by Vietnam in 2005. Discussions were held in 2006 between China and ASEAN on moving toward a binding code of conduct, and at the East Asian Summit in early 2007, all sixteen states agreed on the importance of energy conservation and security.[12]

On the other hand, Taiwan, increasingly marginalized in discussions on the SCS, announced plans in 2006 to build a 1,150-meter runway on Itu Aba "for humanitarian purposes." Japan, with continuing vital interests in a secure Malacca Strait and its own direct territorial dispute with China, has also been marginalized in discussions.

Pushing the issue of territoriality aside makes sense only until one party feels that the acknowledged intrusion on its sovereignty approaches the level of a vital national interest. The short history above showed that various Asian governments have felt this at various times in the recent past, and so it would be a mistake to attribute the absence of open conflict for a few years to fundamentally altered views of sovereignty. As recently as December 2006, a Foreign Ministry spokesman in Hanoi labeled China's planting of markers a "violation of Vietnam's sovereignty."[13] Furthermore, there has been little to no movement on the nature of the claims, with China relying on history and occupation, Vietnam on historical use (Hanoi recognized China's claims until 1975), the Philippines on proximity and native son Thomas Cloma's 1956 "discovery" of some unoccupied areas in the Spratlys, and Malaysia and Brunei mostly on particular interpretations of UNCLOS.

Indeed, the underlying nature of the claims and the increasing importance of energy may outstrip states' ability to keep territoriality off the table. The 1992 Declaration applies only to ASEAN member states, while the 2002 Declaration relies upon consensually based norms and notably excludes many interested parties. As the Norwegian-Russian experience on sharing resources and settling boundaries demonstrates, if territorial disputes are not settled first, interpretations of resource-sharing agreements can change along with changing power balances.[14] The twin underlying realities of growing power asymmetry and persistent territorial disputes will work in favor of the more powerful actors.

China's Southeast Asia Policy, Foreign Policy, and Use of Force

The extension of China's territoriality another 1,000 nautical miles or so south, together with the establishment of a permanent and strong naval presence, would alter dramatically the balance of power in the region, color the current right of international passage, and potentially pose a direct threat to Vietnam, the Philippines, Malaysia, Brunei, and Indonesia, as well as a direct economic threat to Japan and other states relying on free passage. Thus far ASEAN has not been forced to deal with competing claims due to China's overall foreign policy toward the region, which has taken on a softer tone over the past two decades.

Beijing's overarching policy approach toward Southeast Asia has passed through several phases.[15] During the Cold War, Beijing worked exclusively on a bilateral basis. It was during this period that China's policies created a significant reservoir of distrust, largely through its rhetorical and actual support for local communist and Chinese groups. Indonesia was both ASEAN's leading state and perhaps the strongest opponent of PRC influence in Southeast Asia. From 1978 to 1989, China aligned with Thailand, the United States, and most of ASEAN to oppose the Vietnamese occupation of Cambodia and the Soviet Union's growing influence. As the Cambodian problem approached resolution and the United States withdrew from the Philippines, ASEAN reconsidered its relations with China, but its effort to repair relations foundered somewhat due to Chinese assertiveness in the SCS.[16]

Following Tiananmen, a policy of "good neighborliness" toward China's southern neighbors was initiated roughly at the same time that ASEAN began to tackle, in a general way, security issues and the expansion of its membership. In July 1991, Foreign Minister Qian Qichen attended the opening session of the 24th ASEAN Ministerial Meeting as a guest of Malaysia, and throughout the 1990s China circumspectly embraced an increasingly multilateral approach. In one of the few studies specifically on China's attitudes toward and uses of multilateralism, Kuik Cheng-Chwee finds that for the rest of the decade, China's use of ASEAN institutions passed through three phases. In the first phase of passive involvement, up to 1995, China made a careful calculation that the trend toward multilateralism was unstoppable and that it had to engage if it were to have any control over the process. In the second phase of active participation through 1999, while bilateral diplomacy remained the central feature, Beijing took an active role in cochairing ASEAN Regional Forum meetings, became a full dialogue partner of ASEAN, helped create the ASEAN-China Joint Cooperation Committee, supported the expansion of the APT (ASEAN Plus Three) process to banking and financial cooperation, and expanded its extra-Southeast Asian multilateral initiatives to include the Shanghai Five (later the Shanghai Cooperation Organization). Finally, since 2000, Beijing has been proactive in proposing an ASEAN-China Free Trade Agreement. This major initiative would be a major coup for China, as it would bring participants together to talk about growth and wealth as opposed to problems, and would help guarantee the stable supply of energy and resources so vital to China's economic and political health. Subsequently, China became the first major power to sign the Treaty of Amity and Cooperation as well as a Joint Declaration on Strategic Partnership at the same meeting.[17]

The conceptual backdrops to these multilateral excursions have been the so-called New Security Concept, the Peaceful Rise theory, and the Peaceful Development thesis. The New Security Concept was formulated in the early post–Tiananmen period and introduced at a 1997 ASEAN meeting. It reemphasized cooperative security, multilateral dialogue, confidence-building measures, and peaceful resolution of conflicts. After September 11, 2001 and renewed U.S. expressions of concern for a "China threat," the Peaceful Rise theory consisted of three claims: China seeks development and peace above all, China will never seek hegemony, and a stronger China means more trade and growth for other countries. Most recently the emphasis has been on "peaceful development."[18]

Since September 11, 2001 China has emphasized the noninterference principle so central to ASEAN and the Treaty on Amity and Cooperation. It expresses a strong interest in making the East Asian Summit a success. China has resolved border issues with Russia and is making progress with India. Chinese officials have agreed to joint oil and gas prospecting with the Philippines and Vietnam. In addition to signing the TAC agreement in 2003, China is cooperating on transnational crime and monetary measures. Conscious of the adverse consequences for ASEAN when it entered the World Trade Organization, Beijing proffered the idea of the FTA. ASEAN gained export growth to China—to the tune of about a one-third increase in 2004 alone—making ASEAN China's fourth largest import supplier.[19]

All of this is to emphasize China's increasing attention to the effectiveness of soft power. Helpful actions following the 1997 financial crisis—contributing to the International Monetary Fund-led package for Thailand and Indonesia, pledging not to devalue the renminbi, and pledging to sign the Protocol to the Treaty on the Southeast Asia Nuclear Weapon Free Zone—have contributed to the image of China as a "responsible stakeholder." The Framework Agreement on ASEAN-China Comprehensive Economic Cooperation, negotiated in November 2002, led to the November 2004 agreement to implement an ASEAN-China Free Trade Area by 2010. Further evidence of this approach on the economic side involves a number of currency and loan agreements among the APT.

China's Defense White Papers of 2002, 2004, and 2006 have all stressed cooperative approaches to international problems in order to promote domestic development. According to the latter:

The regional economy maintains an unprecedented strong momentum of growth, and a framework of open and mutually beneficial cooperation based on equality and in diversified forms is taking shape in the region. Multilateral security dialogue and cooperation are being enhanced. The Shanghai Cooperation Organization has entered a new stage of substantive growth, contributing to the establishment of a new mode of state-to-state relations. ASEAN has made steady progress in community-building and in talks on establishing free trade areas with other countries. East Asian cooperation, which is conducted mainly through the ASEAN plus China, Japan and the ROK (10+3) channel, has expanded in scope and its institutional building is improving constantly, continuing to play a major role in promoting peace, stability and prosperity in the Asia-Pacific region. The East Asia Summit has provided a new platform for East Asian cooperation.[20]

Denny Roy concludes that "Chinese diplomacy has succeeded to the point where most Southeast Asians seem persuaded that China does not pose an immediate security threat."[21] Yet China clearly uses multilateralism, as Christopher Hughes writes, to protect core national interests by preventing the rise of a regional hegemon. In addition, China is gaining a great deal of control over its relationship with Southeast Asia through its desire for a China-ASEAN Free Trade Area by 2015, as demonstrated by the November 2002 Framework Agreement. Hughes sees evidence of increasing Chinese power exertion in the 2004 agreement for PRC and ASEAN representatives to the UN to engage in regular consultations, in the joint PRC-ASEAN position that the UN should play a leading role in the reconstruction of Iraq, and in ASEAN's statement of support for China's role on the North Korea problem.[22] The 2003 Joint Declaration on the ASEAN-China Strategic Partnership, expressing a hope that APT would lead to the development of an "East Asian community," can be seen as further evidence given the preponderant role China would play in setting the norms and rules of such a community. Furthermore, little progress has been made on the central maritime border issues. There has been no progress toward settlements with Japan or, in the SCS, with Vietnam over the Paracels.

Chinese leaders may also be intellectually predisposed against fully acknowledging the role of international agreements and regimes. As Peter Kien-Hong Yu writes, mainland Chinese leaders do not distinguish between the many kinds of international regimes, mechanisms, and systems, and in fact have no standard way to translate or transliterate the phrase "international regime." Neither U.S. nor Southeast Asian leaders have sought to present overarching settlements in a dialectical way that is acceptable to Beijing. Nor have Southeast Asian claimants convinced Beijing that there is a good reason to accept a constraining, multilateral settlement.[23] Kuik Cheng-Chwee notes that Beijing is much more comfortable with economic institutions than with security institutions due to the inherent requirement that a degree of sovereignty be surrendered in the latter.

As Yu also notes, the nature of the sovereignty disputes allows for no obvious solution or settlement; nor does UNCLOS, as is evidenced by the parties' various interpretations of it to support their claims. In one exhaustive study,

Mark Valencia, Jon M. Van Dyke, and Noel A. Ludwig have proposed several schemes for dividing up the territory and resources of the SCS, but they acknowledge that no one scheme is likely to be satisfactory to all or even most of the claimants.[24]

A skeptical member of the Southeast Asian political community might conclude that power, in the end, will determine how competing sovereignty claims are settled. Such sentiments are not, however, revealed in the behavior of Southeast Asian governments.

Southeast Asia's Response to the Rise of China

China's primary goal with respect to ASEAN is to prevent bandwagoning with the United States, which may be said to have characterized ASEAN policy during the Cold War. This now appears less likely and is critical given the borders with Laos, Cambodia, and Vietnam. How has Southeast Asia responded to the rise of China? Regional and individual state behavior are most often described using a mix of the political science and policy prescriptive terms of balancing, bandwagoning, engagement, and hedging. Where one falls on this spectrum is often determined by the lenses one brings to the study. David Kang finds predominant bandwagoning, Yuen Foong Khong finds "soft balancing" amid a constructed discourse of uncertainty, and Amitav Acharya and See Seng Tan find predominant balancing amid institution-building and norm construction.[25]

If we use a strict neorealist definition of balancing, no states in the region are doing so. That is, states are not concertedly building up militarily or forming strong military alliances in order to confront a perceived near-term threat.[26] This excludes a great deal of behavior that is directed against a potential long-term threat, however, including the maintenance of good defense relationships with the United States and the execution of some military modernization. Thus, if we lower the bars regarding intent, time horizon, and actions taken, we can see that many states are pursuing a mix of strategies.

Indonesian military leaders privately label China the country's greatest military threat, with a major challenge being Chinese claims to the Natuna Islands and their possible energy reserves. Yet Indonesia realizes that China is a major buyer of its bulk commodities and may be a more dependable supplier of weapons than the United States, and so it balances less than do Singapore, Thailand, and perhaps the Philippines.

The Singapore–Washington relationship is something between an alliance and a strong friendship. Singapore hosts the U.S. Navy's western logistics base and has built a pier at Changi Naval Base for U.S. aircraft carriers. For its part, Thailand remains a "major non-NATO ally" and yet engages with China on economic growth, criticizes Taiwan and Falun Gong, and has offered lukewarm support to the United States concerning Iraq. The Philippines clearly perceives an external threat and realizes that it has been too weak since 1995 to defend its claims in the Spratlys. The 1997 Visiting Forces Agreement and the 2003 Mutual Logistics Support Agreement led to the Philippines being labeled, along with Singapore and Thailand, a "major non-NATO ally" in 2003. Major joint exercises and a U.S. role in fighting Abu Sayyaf have solidified the balancing nature of the Philippines' approach.

Vietnam and the United States have gone further down the road of full diplomatic normalization. The Bilateral Trade Agreement has increased trade dramatically, U.S. naval ships are making port visits, the two states are cooperating on AIDS, and high-level political visits have occurred. Vietnam continues to push its claims in the SCS by pursuing deals on exploration and prospecting, and violence continues to flare, as in 2005 when Vietnamese fishermen strayed into Chinese waters. Vietnam supports a U.S. military presence and cooperates on counterterrorism, drugs, demining, search and rescue, and disaster relief. Vietnamese observers attend Cobra Gold, U.S. naval vessels now visit Vietnam, and the 2005 visit of the Vietnamese prime minister to Washington promised further cooperation.[27]

Malaysia and the United States have increasingly cooperated since 2001, with defense ties also growing, including a rapidly growing number of U.S. ship visits (e.g., that of the carrier USS *John C. Stennis* in 2004), and providing jungle training for U.S. troops. The former Malaysian prime minister has said publicly he does not consider the PRC a threat and that China should remain a constructive player.

The one unifying theme to ASEAN state responses is the attempt to use economic cooperation and engagement to manage security relations with China. This is not a new strategic innovation. It derives from a set of ideas about how states may use trade and other economic flows to structure anarchy in ways that create common interests among states, dampen security competition, and support an ordered international system in which the "expectation of war disappears" as states resolve conflicts through "judicial processes, not coercive bargaining."[28] In fact, these ideas have had a powerful impact in shaping the present world. According to Richard Rosecrance in *The Rise of the Virtual State,* growing international economic integration is held to render societies increasingly dependent upon others for their prosperity, to make war more costly, and to create strong mutual interests in peace.[29] In a related thesis, Thomas Friedman holds that deepening integration convinces individuals to seek personal prosperity rather than national glory, thereby weakening the status and influence of the military within society and politics. "People in McDonald's countries," writes Friedman, "prefer to wait in line for burgers" than to fight.[30]

While conflict may not occur over the SCS, the Southeast Asian policy response is unlikely to prevent it, as it rests of mistaken assumptions. In a recent study of European security politics in pre–World War I Europe, David Rowe has shown how the political and economic constraints brought about by increased interdependence led to less and less credible threats, weakening deterrence and leading to a spiral of conflict.[31] As states pursue strategies that tie China into the global economy, the resulting constraints against military force may emerge systemically, limiting the deterrent and enforcement ability of all states.

Alternatively, the effects of increased interdependence may constrain smaller states more than larger ones. If we examine cases of foreign policy conflicts that are of critical importance to both China and its neighbors, Beijing foregoes cooperation and acts as a rational self-interested power with a focus on its own power and wealth. On the Mekong River system, for example, Beijing has forged ahead on dam-building, to the economic, physical, and long-term detriment of downstream neighbors.[32]

Rather than a more robust and stable Asia, deep economic integration may create a less-stable order at greater risk of collapse. The longevity of America's role in Asia has already been questioned. Beijing, Taiwan, or any of the parties to the SCS claims could come to believe that wealth is so important for states against which they lay claims that those states might not be willing or able to defend their interests. In addition, China may yet emerge as an economic threat to the Southeast Asian states. Specifically, the interdependent relationship will cause pain in certain sectors of some states, which in turn could cause social and political problems. China is attracting huge sums of FDI (foreign direct investment), much of which went to Southeast Asia before the mid-1990s. Much more deleterious for Southeast Asian economies, however, is the impact of more competitive manufactured goods from China on such major markets as the United States and Japan. ASEAN has lost market share in telecommunications, clothing, and office and electrical machinery.[33]

There is little evidence that ASEAN as a whole recognizes or challenges the assumptions—assumptions I would argue are faulty—about the possible implications of greater economic interdependence on political stability. If they did recognize the dangers, it is likely they would be more forceful in demanding agreement on actual conduct in areas such as the SCS, and that ASEAN as a whole would consider the potential for balancing against Chinese power.

China's Looming Naval and Military Presence

China's rising power has been well documented and will not be revisited here in detail.[34] What is clear is that Beijing is acquiring an ever-increasing ability to shape the security environment of Southeast Asia, as well as the perceptions and policies of individual states. This section examines China's growing military presence before turning to recent policies and long-term intentions.

China's defense budget continues to experience a fifteen-year trend of double-digit increases, with current spending at between $35 billion and $105 billion and the 2007 budget slated to receive a nearly 18 percent increase in this, the second year of the current five-year spending plan. Spending is focused on engendering a revolution in military affairs, to include "informationalization" and communications; on force projection; and on the ability to conduct precision strikes to defeat enemy command, control, communications, and computer capabilities in short order. These military modernization programs were prompted and reinforced by a sequence of international developments, including the rapid U.S. victory in the first Gulf War, the 1996 Taiwan Strait crisis, during which the PRC realized it could not compete with the United States in an operational sense, and the errant U.S. bombing of the Chinese embassy in Belgrade in 1999.[35] The impact on procurement has been dramatic. To highlight only some of the naval and related purchases, Beijing has invested in second-generation nuclear and conventional submarines, frigates, destroyers with deadly antiship missiles, various platforms for amphibious force projection, army attack helicopters, and even aircraft carriers. By 2010 the naval inventory will total up to forty-three destroyers, fifty-five frigates, and sixty-two submarines. Fourth- and fifth-generation strike fighters, fighter bombers, AWACS-like early-warning aircraft, close air support, and critical support aircraft are being developed, purchased, or upgraded.[36]

The transformation of the PLAN (People's Liberation Army Navy) is aimed at exerting greater control over contiguous waters while deterring larger foes in conflict scenarios. Operationally, the 2006 Defense White Paper claims the navy's strategy is to attain "gradual extension of strategic depth for offshore defensive operations and enhancing its capabilities in integrated maritime operations and nuclear counterattacks." According to Timothy Hu, central to this is "the establishment of a sea denial capability to prevent the U.S. Navy from being able to deploy into waters that cover what Chinese naval strategists call the Second Island Chain," stretching from the Japanese islands to Guam and the Marshall Islands. The PLAN's ambitious program of acquiring new classes of submarines will go far toward accomplishing these goals.[37]

While the motivations are many, conflict scenarios over Taiwan and North Korea must be foremost in the minds of those responsible for the modernization program. However, much of the new weaponry provides capabilities and presence that will be relevant to a "post-Korea" and "post-Taiwan" world. The planned development and purchase of tanker aircraft, for example, will afford a new PLA Air Force presence over the SCS. Put another way, if the central goal of the buildup has been to defeat Taiwan and deter the United States in a Taiwan conflict scenario, the effect is that by the end of this decade the PRC will have the ability, in the words of the U.S. Department of Defense, to defeat "a moderate-size adversary." These contradict such theses as David Shambaugh's that "there is scant evidence of the PLA developing capabilities to project power beyond China's immediate periphery."[38]

Indeed, once those conflicts are settled, it is likely Beijing will turn to securing its southern flank, where, as with Taiwan, it has what it considers to be unsettled borders, with adversaries that, generally speaking, would rank as smaller than moderate sized. Coterminous with this shift would be the development, as stated in current plans for the second long-term phase of defense development strategy, covering 2011 to 2020, of a military that is the equal of the military of any second-tier nation, including Japan, Russia, or the western European powers. Thus both near- and medium-term plans and acquisitions will provide China with a preponderant naval and air presence, particularly in the SCS area.

What Drives China's Policies?

It is worth attempting to tease out the various possible motivations in Chinese policy toward the SCS in order to hypothesize on the extent to which compromise or new solutions are possible. One line of thought might fall roughly into the category of "defensive realism." Peter Kien-Hong Yu emphasizes the role of walls in Chinese history and culture and sees the U-shaped line as a southern, maritime counterpart to the Great Wall in the north, with James Shoal as the perceived southernmost territory of China. In this view, the late addition of this maritime wall to China's strategic thinking reflects the historic lack of threats from the south and the emergence of Western industrialization and imperialism. It also reflects Beijing's desire, which originated during the 1950s and 1960s, to assert exclusive claims over portions of the territory and resources of the sea. China views the SCS as akin to internal waters. Since its first use in 1914, the line has always had notable "breaks" in it (Taiwan's version is dotted) signaling the rights of passage and international use.[39]

On the other hand, James Holmes and Toshi Yoshihara describe what could be a trend that could be away from defensive realism. They note that Chinese planners look to the nineteenth-century navalist Alfred Thayer Mahan, who instructs them that their contiguous waters are their domain and that dominant sea power is essential. This is in keeping with tradition as well, since China has long considered the SCS a national preserve. Mahan's formula of "commerce, bases and shipping" means, among other things, that China needs bases such as Itu Aba, one of the largest in the Spratlys, as well as adjacent cays. Together, the authors note, these would constitute a presence superior to that of Mischief Reef. Beijing will also need, they argue, seagoing communications along the coasts and northern edge of the SCS, where opponents could potentially foil operations against Taiwan. The drive for energy security only reinforces these needs. Yu, too, acknowledges that domestic politics and nationalism may also play an increasing role in Chinese claims concerning the SCS, as well as in the other interested states.

Economic development and energy security comprise a third set of possible motivations. As described above, economic modernization has been the overriding goal of Chinese policy since 1978 and is a foundation stone for social harmony and political stability. Central to economic development, of course, is an available, secure, and affordable supply of resources and energy. Regarding energy, China has been a net importer of oil since 1993, with near-double-digit economic growth and nearly a quarter of the world's population in a country with about 2.3 percent of proven oil reserves. Oil consumption is expected to reach 10.5 billion bbl/d by 2020. China will need to import up to 60 percent of its total by 2020. Also, Chinese oil policy thus far conforms well to either a mercantilist or a Maoist doctrine of self-reliance.

Conclusions

Most likely China, like every country (and individual), is motivated by a variety of causes, some of which may even be contradictory. What seems clear is that the trend toward overwhelming power and presence to the nation's south will continue, as none of the defensive-minded motivations are sufficiently strong to override trends in the growth of wealth and the natural expansion of military power. Nor is there evidence of change regarding long-standing views about the place of the southern waters in China's territorial integrity.

On the Southeast Asian side, there are economic growth, minimal military modernization, and laudable institutional activities that continue to tout the possibility of moving toward a full-fledged security community. But there is little recognition of the dangers of economic integration and concomitant "security complacency," the widespread belief that diplomatic interaction will settle what have been in the past and could again become zero-sum territorial and resource competitions. Southeast Asian states neither hedge fully nor balance effectively against the rising influence of China. Nor has ASEAN or any other institution stepped in to become an institutional midwife to the settlement of what are real, if suppressed, disputes. ASEAN "has no power to deploy because it is neither a defence community nor a party to a countervailing structure of alignments,"[40] as Michael Leifer writes.

Such are some of the major trends and currents of thought. Practically speaking, the next major watershed in China's foreign policy is likely to follow some kind of a settlement of the Taiwan issue. Once this issue, which has been at the heart of great-power politics and to some extent regional politics for more than half a century, is concluded, Beijing will either lose a major source of nationalism and unity, or turn to other foreign policy concerns. If the 1992 Law of the Territorial Sea and Contiguous Zone has meaning, it could become the basis for a much more assertive policy, backed by the much greater military presence afforded by what will be a military with serious power-projection capabilities.

NOTES

Chapter 1

1. Paul Kennedy, "The Rise and Fall of Navies," *International Herald Tribune,* April 5, 2007.

2. Center for Naval Analyses, *National Security and the Threat of Climate Change* (Alexandria, VA: Center for Naval Analysis, 2007), 24. The Center for Naval Analysis formed a Military Advisory Board involving a highly distinguished group of retired generals and admirals to assess the impact of climate change on national security.

3. Don Hinrichsen, "Ocean Planet in Decline," Peopleandplanet.net, January 25, 2007, http://www.peopleandplanet.net/doc.php?id=429&section=6.

4. James R. Holmes and Toshi Yoshihara, "Soft Power at Sea: Zheng He and Chinese Maritime Strategy," *U.S. Naval Institute Proceedings* (October 2006): 34–38.

5. UN Conference on Trade and Development, *Review of Maritime Transport, 2004* (Geneva: United Nations, 2004), 99.

6. UN Conference on Trade and Development, *Review of Maritime Transport, 2006* (Geneva: United Nations, 2006), 133–35.

7. "Shipbuilding Surges in China," *Journal of Commerce Online,* September 29, 2006.

8. Donald Urquhart, "China's Cosco Shipyard in US$113m Expansion Drive," *Business Times* (Singapore), August 1, 2006.

9. Conrad Raj, "Cosco Shipyards Wow the World," *Business Times* (Singapore), May 23, 2006.

10. See U.S. Energy Information Administration, "China," EIA Country Analysis Briefs, July 2004, http://www.eia.doe.gov/emeu/cabs/china.html.

11. U.S. National Intelligence Council, *Report of the National Intelligence Council's 2020 Project: Mapping the Global Future* (Washington, DC: Government Printing Office, December 2004), 50, 62.

12. Holger H. Herwig, *"Luxury" Fleet: The Imperial German Navy, 1888–1918* (Atlantic Highlands, NJ: Ashfield, 1987).

13. Alfred Thayer Mahan, *The Influence of Sea Power upon History, 1660–1783* (Boston: Little, Brown, and Company, 1890; reprint, New York: Dover Publications, 1987), 71.

14. Eric J. Grove, "Introduction," in *Some Principles of Maritime Strategy*, ed. Julian S. Corbett (London: Longmans, Green, 1911; reprint, intro. Eric J. Grove, Annapolis: Naval Institute Press, 1988), xxx. Another good reference by an early-twentieth-century British theorist is C. E. Callwell, *Military Operations and Maritime Preponderance: Their Relations and Interdependence* (Edinburgh: William Blackwood and Sons, 1905; reprint, Annapolis: Naval Institute Press, 1996).

15. Alfred Thayer Mahan, "Discussion of the Elements of Sea Power," in *Mahan on Naval Strategy*, ed. John B. Hattendorf intro (Annapolis, MD: Naval Institute Press, 1991), 31–96.

16. Ibid., 53–62.

17. Peter Padfield, *Maritime Supremacy and the Opening of the Western Mind* (Woodstock, NY: Overlook, 2002), 1–19.

18. Geoffrey Till, *Seapower: A Guide for the Twenty-first Century* (London: Frank Cass, 2004), 76–110.

19. Mahan, *Influence of Sea Power*, 138.

20. Corbett, *Some Principles of Maritime Strategy*, 91–94; Charles E. Callwell, *Military Operations and Maritime Preponderance: Their Relations and Interdependence* (Edinburgh: William Blackwood and Sons, 1905; reprint, Annapolis: Naval Institute Press, 1996).

Chapter 3

1. Ian Nish, *Alliance in Decline: A Study in Anglo-Japanese Relations* (London: The Athlone Press, 1972), 18.

2. Ibid., 60, 61, 71.

3. Ibid., 83.

4. Arthur J. Marder, *Old Enemies, New Friends: The Royal Navy and the Imperial Japanese Navy*, vol. 1, *Strategic Illusions* (New York: Clarendon Press, 1981), 5; Peter Lowe, *Great Britain and Japan, 1911–15* (London: Macmillan, 1969); Nish, *Alliance in Decline*, 131.

5. Timothy D. Saxon, "Anglo-Japanese Naval Cooperation, 1914–1918," *Naval War College Review* 53, no. 1 (winter 2000): 62–92; Martin Gilbert, ed., *Winston S. Churchill*, vol. 3, *1914–1916*, companion vol. 3, pt. 1 (Boston: Houghton Mifflin, 1973), 65; Churchill to Grey, August 11, 1914, CHAR 13/43, Churchill Archives Centre, Churchill College, University of Cambridge, Cambridge, Cambridgeshire.

6. Frederick R. Dickinson, *War and National Reinvention: Japan in the Great War, 1914–1919* (Cambridge: Harvard University Press, 1999), 34–77, 138–48; J. Charles Schencking, *Making Waves: Politics, Propaganda, and the Emergence of the Imperial Japanese Navy, 1868–1922* (Stanford: Stanford University Press, 2005), 201–22.

7. The British briefly considered some sort of intervention in this war following the Battle of Antietam and the Emancipation Proclamation. Howard Jones, *Union in Peril: The Crisis over British Intervention in the Civil War* (Chapel Hill: University of North Carolina Press, 1992). On the British strategic retreat from North America, see: Kenneth Bourne, *Britain and the Balance of Power in North America, 1815–1908* (Berkeley: University of California Press, 1967).

8. Plans for war against Japan predated World War I, but after that conflict, they became much more serious in purpose. Edward S. Miller, *War Plan Orange: The U.S. Strategy to Defeat Japan, 1897–1945* (Annapolis: U.S. Naval Institute Press, 1991).

9. Foreign Office Memorandum on Effect of Anglo-Japanese Alliance upon Foreign Relationships, February 28, 1920, F 199/199/23, The British National Archives, Richmond, Surrey.

10. Foreign Office Memorandum on Effect of Anglo-Japanese Alliance upon Foreign Relationships, February 28, 1920, F 199/199/23, The British National Archives, Richmond, Surrey.

11. Foreign Office Memorandum on Effect of Anglo-Japanese Alliance upon Foreign Relationships, February 28, 1920, F 199/199/23, The British National Archives, Richmond, Surrey.

12. Foreign Office Memorandum on Effect of Anglo-Japanese Alliance upon Foreign Relationships, February 28, 1920, F 199/199/23, The British National Archives, Richmond, Surrey.

13. Curzon to Geddes, June 29, 1921, in *Documents on British Foreign Policy, 1919–1939,* eds. Rohan Butler, J. P. T. Bury, and M. E. Lambert, 1st ser., vol. 14 (London: Her Majesty's Stationery Office, 1966), 316.

14. E. M. Hobart Hampden, "The Alliance and Internal Conditions in Japan," March 28, 1920, in *Documents on British Foreign Policy, 1919–1939,* eds. E. L. Woodward, and Rohan Butler, 1st ser. vol. 6 (London: Her Majesty's Stationery Office, 1956), 1052.

15. Cabinet Memorandum, "The Anglo-Japanese Alliance," June 17, 1921, and Cabinet Memorandum, July 4, 1921, in *Winston S. Churchill,* ed. Gilbert, vol. 4, *April 1921–November 1922,* companion vol. 4, pt. 3, 1513, 1541.

16. H. G. Parlett, Minute, March 27, 1920, and Murray to Foreign Office, February 12, 1920, in *Documents on British Foreign Policy, 1919–1939,* eds. E. L. Woodward and Rohan Butler, 1st ser., vol. 6 (London: Her Majesty's Stationery Office, 1956), 1051–2, 1054.

17. Geddes to Curzon, June 24, 1921, *Documents on British Foreign Policy,* 1st ser., vol. 14, 311; "Memorandum of a Conversation between the Secretary of State and the British Ambassador," June 23, 1931, U.S. Department of State, *Foreign Relations of the United States, 1921,* vol. 2 (Washington, DC: U.S. Government Printing Office, 1936), 314–16.

18. Hosoya Chihiro, "Britain and the United States in Japan's View of the International System, 1919–37," in *Anglo-Japanese Alienation, 1919–1952: Papers of the Anglo-Japanese Conference on the History of the Second World War,* ed. Ian Nish (Cambridge: Cambridge University Press, 1982), 8.

19. Andrew Field, *Royal Navy Strategy in the Far East, 1919–1939: Preparing for War against Japan* (London: Frank Cass, 2004), 19–64; Stephen E. Pelz, *Race to Pearl Harbor: The Failure of the Second London Naval Conference and the Onset of World War II* (Cambridge: Harvard University Press, 1974), 111.

20. Emphasis in the original. Field, *Royal Navy Strategy,* 64.

21. Field, *Royal Navy Strategy,* 74–78, 92.

22. Churchill to Baldwin, December 15, 1924, in *Winston S. Churchill,* ed. Gilbert, vol. 5, *The Exchequer Years, 1922–1929,* companion vol. 5, pt. 1, 304.

23. Churchill to Baldwin, December 15, 1924, in *Winston S. Churchill,* ed. Gilbert, companion vol. 5, pt. 1, 304.

24. Cabinet Memorandum: "Navy Estimates," January 29, 1925, in *Winston S. Churchill,* ed. Gilbert, companion vol. 5, pt. 1, 364.

25. Lord Beatty to Lady Beatty, January 26, 1925, in *Winston S. Churchill,* ed. Gilbert, companion vol. 5, pt. 1, 356.

26. Paul Haggie, *Britannia at Bay: The Defence of the British Empire against Japan, 1931–1941* (New York: Oxford University Press, 1981), 11; Pelz, *Race to Pearl Harbor,* 105–6, 116; W. David McIntyre, *The Rise and Fall of the Singapore Naval Base, 1919–1942* (London: Archon Books, 1979), 111.

27. McIntyre, *Rise and Fall of the Singapore Naval Base,* 19–85, 106.

28. Field, *Royal Navy Strategy,* 99–100.

29. Haggie, *Britannia at Bay,* 59.

30. Haggie, *Britannia at Bay,* 11; Pelz, *Race to Pearl Harbor,* 105–6, 116.

31. Ian Nish, "Japan in Britain's View of the International System, 1919–37," in *Anglo-Japanese Alienation, 1919–1952: Papers of the Anglo-Japanese Conference on the History of the Second World War,* ed. Ian Nish, (Cambridge: Cambridge University Press, 1982), 39–40.

32. Geoffrey Till, "Adopting the Aircraft Carrier: The British, American, and Japanese Case Studies," in *Innovation in the Interwar Period,* eds. Williamson R. Murray and Allan R. Millett (New York: Cambridge University Press, 1998), 301–65.

33. Roy Jenkins, *Churchill: A Biography* (New York: Plume, 2002), 498–503; Martin Gilbert, *Churchill: A Life* (New York: Henry Holt and Company, 1991), 568–70.

34. Pelz, *Race to Pearl Harbor,* 180, 184, 193.

35. Haggie, *Britannia at Bay,* 118.

36. Ibid., 107.

37. Ibid., 97.

38. Ibid., 118.

39. Waldo Heinrichs, *Threshold of War: Franklin D. Roosevelt & American Entry into World War II* (New York: Oxford University Press, 1988), 129–30, 135–36, 215–20.

40. Cabinet Memorandum, "The Anglo-Japanese Alliance," June 17, 1981, in *Winston S. Churchill,* ed. Gilbert, companion vol. 4, pt. 3, 1512–13; G.R. Storry, notes of Oxford University Conservative Association: "Questions to Mr. Winston Churchill," February 23, 1934, in Gilbert, ed., *Winston S. Churchill,* vol. 5, *The Wilderness Years, 1929–1935,* companion vol. 5, pt. 2, 726; War Cabinet Paper, November 21, 1939, and Winston S. Churchill broadcast, March 30, 1940, in *The Churchill War Papers,* ed. Martin Gilbert, vol. 1, *At the Admiralty, September 1939–May 1940* (New York: W.W. Norton and Company, 1993), 401–3, 938.

41. John G. Winant Recollections and Churchill to Auchinleck, December 7, 1941, in *Churchill War Papers,* ed. Gilbert, vol. 3, *The Ever-Widening War, 1941,* 1574–75.

42. Hosoya Chihiro, "Britain and the United States in Japan's View of the International System, 1937–41," in *Anglo-Japanese Alienation, 1919–1952: Papers of the Anglo-Japanese Conference on the History of the Second World War,* ed. Ian Nish (Cambridge: Cambridge University Press, 1982), 58–66.

Chapter 4

1. This episode is described at http://www.sabrizain.demon.co.uk/malaya/potomac.htm.

2. It was not until the reorganization of the modern Foreign Service in 1924, with the passage of the Rogers Act, that uniform standards among U.S. consular and diplomatic representatives were established. See the Department of State Historian's Web site, http://www.state.gov/r/pa/ho/faq.

3. Early U.S. Navy operations in Asia are discussed in Charles Oscar Paullin, *American Voyages to the Orient, 1690–1865; An Account of Merchant and Naval Activities in China, Japan and the Various Pacific Islands,* 2nd ed. (Annapolis, MD: Naval Institute Press, 1971).

John King Fairbank, *Trade and Diplomacy on the China Coast: The Opening of the Treaty Ports, 1842–1854* (Cambridge, MA: Harvard University Press, 1953) also remains useful.

4. Norman Graebner, *Manifest Destiny* (Indianapolis: Bobbs-Merrill, 1968) remains the classic history of this subject; also see Anders Stephanson, *Manifest Destiny: American Expansion and the Empire of Right* (New York: Hill & Wang, 1995).

5. This incident occurred in 1859, off the northern Chinese forts at the mouth of the Taku River; see Robert W. Love Jr., *History of the U.S. Navy Volume I: 1775–1941,* (Harrisburg, PA: Stackpole Books, 1992), 238–39.

6. See Bernard D. Cole, *Gunboats and Marines: The U.S. Navy in China* (Wilmington, DE: University of Delaware Press, 1982). *Ashuelot* had a memorable career: a double-ended paddlewheeler built for service in the American Civil War, this gunboat served for almost twenty years in Asian waters, from 1867–1883, most of it on China's coast and rivers. See http://en.wikipedia.org/wiki/USS_Ashuelot_(1865).

7. Mahan's magnum opus, *Influence of Sea Power,* was originally published in 1890. He lived from 1840 to 1914, thus dying at the onset of the war many expected to validate his theories. Japan's views on Mahan are described in Sadao Asada, *From Mahan to Pearl Harbor: American Strategic Theory and the Rise of the Imperial Japanese Navy* (Annapolis, MD: Naval Institute Press, 2006).

8. See James R. Reckner, *Teddy Roosevelt's Great White Fleet* (Annapolis, MD: Naval Institute Press, 1989). The battleships were accompanied by six destroyers and four supply ships.

9. Text is at http://www.usd.edu/~sbucklin/primary/taftkatsura.htm.

10. Text is in Ruhl J. Bartlett, *The Record of American Diplomacy,* 4th ed. (New York: Alfred A. Knopf, 1964), 415.

11. Text is at http://www.firstworldwar.com/source/21demands.htm.

12. Text is at http://www.ibiblio.org/pha/policy/pre-war/9_power.html.

13. The text of the Nine-Power Treaty may be found at http://www.ibiblio.org/pha/policy/pre-war/9_power.html.

14. China rightfully felt betrayed by the Allies, especially by President Woodrow Wilson, who transferred German possessions in China to Japan despite China's contribution of hundreds of thousands of laborers to World War I's Western Front. This continued colonial treatment gave rise to the student-led riots across China known as the May 4th incident. See Chow Tse-tsung, *The May Fourth Movement: Intellectual Revolution in Modern China* (Stanford, CA: Stanford University Press, 1960), or Jonathan Spence, *The Search for Modern China,* 2nd ed. (Boston: W.W. Norton & Co., 2001), sec. III.

15. Article XIX of the Five-Power Treaty, the full text of which is at http://www.microworks.net/pacific/road_to_war/washington_treaty.htm.

16. Text is at http://www.yale.edu/lawweb/avalon/diplomacy/forrel/1922v1/tr1921.htm.

17. The best description of this phenomenon remains Richard Storry, *The Double Patriots: A Study of Japanese Nationalism* (Boston: Houghton Mifflin, 1957).

18. Text is at http:www.firstworldwar.com/source/anglojapanesealliance1902.htm.

19. See Cole, *Gunboats and Marines.*

20. The best work on Army planning during this period is Brian Linn, *Guardians of Empire: The U.S. Army and the Pacific, 1902–1942*(Chapel Hill, NC: University of North Carolina Press, 1997), and Henry G. Cole, *The Road to Rainbow: Army Planning for Global War, 1934–1940* (Annapolis, MD: Naval Institute Press, 2002). For U.S. Navy planning, see Edward S. Miller, *War Plan Orange: The U.S. Strategy to Defeat Japan, 1897–1945* (Annapolis, MD: Naval Institute Press, 1991).

21. Although it must be noted that, beginning in 1929, Depression-era concerns and other U.S. Navy priorities would have severely restricted the amount of resources available for building fortifications on far-flung islands.

22. See the seminal and still important article by Samuel P. Huntington, "National Policy and the Transoceanic Navy," *U.S. Naval Institute Proceedings* 80, no. 5 (May 1954): 483–93.

23. Formally issued in 1986; see John B. Hattendorf, *The Evolution of the U.S. Navy's Maritime Strategy, 1977–1986* (Newport, RI: Naval War College Press, 1986), http://www.nwc.navy.mil/press/newportpapers/documents/19.pdf.

24. To little effect. The author was a firsthand witness to and participant in these bureaucratic battles during the 1980s.

25. Text is at http://www.navy.mil/navydata/policy/fromsea/fromsea.txt.

26. Text is at http://www.navy.mil/navydata/policy/fromsea/ffseanoc.html.

27. Ibid.

28. This discussion includes reference to Sam Bateman, "Navies of the World Unite: Will the New U.S. Maritime Strategy Work?" *IDSS Commentaries* 79 (2006), August 11, 2006, http://www.ntu.edu.sg/RSIS/publications/Perspective/IDSS0792006.pdf. For the text of *Sea Power 21,* see Vern Clark, "Sea Power 21," *U.S. Naval Institute Proceedings* (October 2002), http://www.usni.org/PROCEEDINGS/ARTICLES02/PROCNO10.HTM.

29. White House, *The National Strategy for Maritime Security* (Washington, DC: Government Printing Office, September 2005), http://www.whitehouse.gov/homeland/maritime-security.html.

30. White House, *National Strategy for Maritime Security,* 4.

31. Chief of naval operations directed meeting at the Naval War College, August 2006, in which the author participated.

32. Bateman, "Navies of the World Unite," 1.

33. John G. Morgan Jr. and Charles W. Martoglio, "The 1,000-Ship Navy Global Maritime Network," *U.S. Naval Institute Proceedings* (November 2005): 14–17.

34. Sam Bateman, "Regional Responses to Enhance Maritime Security in East Asia," *Korean Journal of Defense Analysis* 93, no. 2 (summer 2006): 26.

35. William F. Fallon, testimony before the Senate Armed Services Committee Hearing on Military Strategy and Operational Requirements in the FY 2007 Defense Budget, March 7, 2006.

36. There are two other forward-deployed U.S. fleets: the Sixth, in the Mediterranean, and the Fifth, in its Southwest Asian area of responsibility.

37. See "PRC FM Spokesman Protests Collision of US Navy Ship, Chinese Fishing Boat," Agence France Presse, September 26, 2002, in FBIS-CPP20020926000105.

38. See for instance Chris Cockrell, "PRC Seeks Control over Coastal Exclusion Zone," *China Post,* January 29, 2003, http://www.chinapost.com.tw.

Chapter 5

1. The author thanks Profs. Lyle Goldstein, William Murray, and Andrew Wilson for their invaluable guidance and support in the development of this chapter, which draws extensively on a variety of articles that he has previously coauthored with them. This chapter is solely based on the author's personal opinions, and in no way reflects the policies or analyses of the Naval War College, the Navy, or any other element of the U.S. government.

2. Liu Yijian, "Theory of the Command of the Sea and its Development," *China Military Science,* January 2005, 42–46, OSC-CPP20050427000217.

3. Unless otherwise indicated, quotations in this paragraph are from Xu Qi, "Maritime Geostrategy and the Development of the Chinese Navy in the Early 21st Century," *China Military Science* 17, no. 4 (2004): 75–81. [Translated by Andrew Erickson and Lyle Goldstein and published in *Naval War College Review* 59, no. 4 (autumn 2006).]

4. Ye Zicheng, "China's Sea Power Must Be Subordinate to its Land Power," *International Herald Leader,* March 2, 2007, OSC-CPP20070302455003.

5. Peng Guangqian and Yao Youzhi, eds., *The Science of Military Strategy* (Beijing: Military Science Publishing House, 2005), 449.

6. "World Briefing/Asia: China: Hu Calls for Strong Navy," *New York Times,* December 29, 2006, http://query.nytimes.com/gst/fullpage.html?res=9C0CE3D71F31F93AA15751C 1A9609C8B63.

7. David Lague, "China Airs Ambitions to Beef Up Naval Power," *International Herald Tribune,* December 28, 2006, http://www.iht.com/articles/2006/12/28/news/china.php.

8. "Chinese President Calls for Strengthened, Modernized Navy," *People's Daily,* December 27, 2006.

9. "Chinese President Calls for Strong Navy," VOA News, December 28, 2006, http:// voanews.com/english/2006-12-28-voa41.cfm.

10. "U.S. Confirms Aircraft Carrier Had Close Brush with Chinese Submarine," *Japan Today,* November 14, 2006, http://www.japantoday.com/jp/news/390343.

11. Caitlin Harrington, "Chinese ASAT Test Rekindles Weapons Debate," *Jane's Missiles and Rockets,* March 1, 2007, Jane's Information Group, http://www.janes.com.

12. "Concern over China's Suspected Weapon Test," *Jane's Intelligence Watch Report— Daily Update,* January 19, 2007, http://www.janes.com.

13. James Holmes, "'Assassin's Mace' Is the PRC's Key in New Race," *Taipei Times,* February 17, 2007.

14. Xu, "Maritime Geostrategy."

15. Liu, "Theory of the Command of the Sea."

16. See Information Office of the State Council, People's Republic of China, *China's National Defense in 2006,* December 29, 2006, http://www.fas.org/nuke/guide/china/ doctrine/wp2006.html.

17. Pentagon, *Military Power of the People's Republic of China, 2006,* 1.

18. State Council, *China's National Defense in 2006.*

19. Richard A. Bitzinger, "Is What You See Really What You Get? A Different Take on China's Defence Budget," *RSIS Commentaries* 14, February 27, 2007, 1.

20. Ibid.

21. "A Fair Exposition of China's Defense Budget (Opinion)," *People's Daily,* March 6, 2007, http://english.people.com.cn/200703/06/eng20070306_354817.html.

22. Jim Yardley and David Lague, "Beijing Accelerates its Military Spending," *New York Times,* March 5, 2007, http://www.nytimes.com/2007/03/05/world/asia/05military.html? _r=1&ref=world&.

23. Jim Yardley and Thom Shanker, "Chinese Navy Buildup Gives Pentagon New Worries," *New York Times,* April 8, 2005.

24. See for example Bill Gertz, "Chinese Produce New Type of Sub," *Washington Times,* July 16, 2004, 1.

25. Pentagon, *Military Power of the People's Republic of China,* 4.

26. Ibid.

27. Unless otherwise specified, data for this paragraph are derived from "Shang class (Type 093) (SSN)," Submarines—Attack Submarines (SSN), China, *Jane's Fighting Ships,* January 29, 2007, http://www.janes.com.

28. Richard D. Fisher, Jr., "Trouble Below: China's Submarines Pose Regional, Strategic Challenges," *Armed Forces Journal,* March 2006, 34.

29. "Defense Production and R&D, China," *Jane's Sentinel Security Assessment—China and Northeast Asia,* December 13, 2006, http://www.janes.com.

30. Unless otherwise specified, data for this paragraph are derived from "Jin class (Type 094) (SSBN)," Submarines—Strategic Missile Submarines, China, *Jane's Fighting Ships,* January 29, 2007, http://www.janes.com.

31. Scott Bray, "Seapower Questions on the Chinese Submarine Force," Federation of American Scientists Web site, December 20, 2006, http://www.fas.org/nuke/guide/china/ONI2006.pdf.

32. Ibid.

33. Zhao Daxun and Li Guoxing, *USN Submarines' Design Characteristics and Quality Control* (Harbin: Harbin Engineering University Press, 2000), 2.

34. He Shan, "Can the 'Virginia' Class Become the New Century's Maritime Hegemon?" *Modern Navy* 10 (2004): 18–21.

35. Yang Yi, "Who Can Estimate the Future Number of Submarines?" *Naval and Merchant Ships,* July 2006, 28.

36. See, for example, Wang Hui, "Weaponry and Equipment for Attacking Carriers," *Modern Navy* 10 (2004): 34.

37. Ying Nan, "The Military Employment and Characteristics of Offensive Mine Warfare," *Naval & Merchant Ships* 40 (September 1999): 10.

38. Wang Wei, "Enduring and Yet Fully Relevant: A Discussion of Sea Mines," *National Defense,* November 2002, 58.

39. Hou Jianjun, "U.S. Navy Mine Warfare Equipment," *Modern Navy* 6 (2003): 27.

40. "Three Assassin's Maces for an Aircraft Carrier: Submarines, Mines, and Anti-ship Missiles," *Ship Electronic Engineering* 5 (May 2001): 80.

41. Hai Lin, "An Evaluation of the People's Liberation Army's Sea Mine Warfare Combat Strength," *World Outlook* 9 (May 2005): 16.

42. Bray, "Seapower Questions."

43. Pentagon, *Military Power of the People's Republic of China,* 5.

44. Bray, "Seapower Questions."

45. Zhang Shen, "The Chinese Navy's New Amphibious Transport Dock Ship Revealed," *China Advanced Military Power* 64 (July 2006), 57.

46. Pentagon, *Military Power of the People's Republic of China,* 3.

47. Ibid., 4.

48. Unless otherwise indicated, this paragraph is derived from "Procurement—China."

49. For this quote and additional background on the Type 071, see Richard Fisher, "China's New Large Amphibious Assault Ship," International Assessment & Strategy Center, January 8, 2007, http://www.strategycenter.net/research/pubID.136/pub_detail.asp.

50. Pentagon, *Military Power of the People's Republic of China,* 46.

51. "Air Force—China," *Jane's Sentinel Security Assessment—China and Northeast Asia,* January 5, 2007, http://www.janes.com.

52. Ibid.

53. Pentagon, *Military Power of the People's Republic of China*, 6.

54. Ibid.

55. "Procurement—China."

56. "Defense Production and R&D, China."

57. "Air Force—China."

58. Ibid.

59. "Procurement—China."

60. "Air Force—China."

61. "Fighter Aircraft," *China Defence Today*, http://www.sinodefence.com/airforce/fighter/default.asp.

62. Evan Medeiros and others, *A New Direction for China's Defense Industry* (Santa Monica, CA: RAND, 2005), 199.

63. For detailed explanations of the J-10 estimates, see Richard Fisher, "China's J-10 Jet Fighter: How Much Do We Know?" International Assessment & Strategy Center, January 16, 2007, http://www.strategycenter.net/research/pubID.140/pub_detail.asp.

64. "Air Force—China."

65. Dong Ruifeng, "J10 Fighter Research and Development Team Makes First Public Appearance," *Liaowang* 2 (January 8, 2007): 35–37, OSC-CPP20070111710011.

66. "LM WS10A Tai Hang," *Jane's Aero-Engines*, Jane's Information Group 2006, http://www.janes.com.

67. See, for example, Sergio Coniglio, "China Develops Stealth Fighter," *Military Technology*, February 2006, 44.

68. "Air Force—China."

69. "Shaanxi Aircraft Company SAC Y-8/Y-9 (Special Mission Versions)," *Jane's All the World's Aircraft*, December 7, 2006, http://www.janes.com.

70. "Air Force—China."

71. "KJ-2000 Airborne Warning & Control System," *China Defence Today*, http://www.sinodefence.com/airforce/specialaircraft/kj2000.asp.

72. "Y-8 'Balance Beam' Airborne Early Warning Aircraft," *China Defence Today*, http://www.sinodefence.com/airforce/specialaircraft/y8balancebeam.asp.

73. See, for example, "Observation Post of Military Situation," HK Phoenix TV, *Military News*, June 21, 2006, OSC-CPP20060626715001.

74. "WZ-10 Attack Helicopter," *China Defense Today*, http://www.sinodefence.com/airforce/helicopter/wz10.asp.

75. Unless otherwise indicated, this paragraph derived from "Procurement—China."

76. Unless otherwise indicated, this paragraph derived from "Unmanned Aerial Vehicles," *China Defence Today*, http://www.sinodefence.com/airforce/uav/default.asp.

77. Yitzhak Shichor, "The U.S. Factor in Israel's Military Relations with China," *China Brief* 5, no. 12 (May 24, 2005), http://www.jamestown.org/publications.

78. "China is No Exception to the Aerospace Fervor," *Aviation Week & Space Technology* 165, no. 19 (November 13, 2006): 20.

79. "Procurement—China."

80. Pentagon, *Military Power of the People's Republic of China*, 3, 11.

81. "CSS-4 (DF-5)," *Jane's Strategic Weapon Systems*, May 3, 2006, http://www.janes.com.

82. "CSS-5 (DF-21)," *Jane's Strategic Weapon Systems*, May 3, 2006, http://www.janes.com.

83. Pentagon, *Military Power of the People's Republic of China*, 27.

84. Robert Hewson, "Dragon's Teeth—Chinese Missiles Raise Their Game," *Jane's Navy International*, January 1, 2007, http://www.janes.com.

85. Richard R. Burgess, "Sub Reliance—China's Advancing Undersea Force Reflects the Increasing Boldness of its Maritime Strategy," *SeaPower*, February 2007, 21.

86. See, for example, Eric A. McVadon, "China's Maturing Navy," *Naval War College Review* 59, no. 2 (spring 2006), http://findarticles.com/p/articles/mi_m0JIW/is_2_59/ai_n16689839/pg_1.

87. Unless otherwise indicated, data in this paragraph are derived from "Air Force—China."

88. Pentagon, *Military Power of the People's Republic of China*, 5.

89. Ibid.

90. "Land-Attack Cruise Missile (LACM)," *China Defence Today*, http://www.sinodefence.com/strategic/missile/cruisemissile.asp.

91. For claims concerning the Yingji-63 and the Donghai-10, see "China Tests New Land Attack Cruise Missile," *Jane's Missiles and Rockets*, October 1, 2004, http://www.janes.com.

92. Unless otherwise specified, this paragraph is based on the information from Hewson, "Dragon's Teeth."

93. "SS-N-22 'Sunburn' (Fu-Feng-1/JL-9)," *Jane's Strategic Weapon Systems*, June 23, 2006, http://www.janes.com.

94. "KR-1/AS-17 'Krypton'/Kh-31," *Jane's Strategic Weapon Systems*, June 23, 2006, http://www.janes.com.

95. See also Miroslav Gyürösi, "Kh-59MK Refined to Meet Chinese Requirements," *Jane's Missiles & Rockets*, October 1, 2003, http://www.janes.com.

96. See "Small Satellite Development Attains Breakthroughs," *Spaceflight & Aviation, Armed Forces Dual Use Technology and Products* 5 (2004), http://www.space.cetin.net.cn/docs/mp0405/mp0405hthk.htm.

97. See, for example, Zuo Saiqun, "'Sea Eye' Looks Down on 10,000 Miles of Sea Dominion—Recording Our Country's First Ocean Satellite," *People's Net*, May 16, 2002, http://www.people.com.cn/GB/kejiao/42/155/20020516/729817.html.

98. Sun Zhihui, ed., *China Ocean Yearbook 2004* (Beijing: Ocean Press, 2005), 569.

99. "China to Launch 'Haiyang-1B' (Ocean 1B) in April," *People's Daily Online*, February 2, 2007, http://english.people.com.cn/200702/02/eng20070202_347051.html.

100. Yao Runping, "China to Launch 2nd Series of Oceanic Survey Satellites," Xinhua, February 1, 2007, http://news.xinhuanet.com/english/2007-02/01/content_5683132.htm.

101. Roger Cliff, *The Military Potential of China's Commercial Technology* (Arlington, VA: RAND, 2001), 29.

102. "From 100 to 1000 Kilograms, Our Country Is Moving Toward Small Satellite Manufacturing Seriation," *SpaceChina.com*, November 24, 2003, http://www.spacechina.com/index.asp?modelname=nr&recno=6574.

103. Hu Zhang, "The 'Long March 2-C' Takes Flight from Three Locations within One Year—A New Benchmark in the Progress of Satellite Construction Technology," Chinese Aerospace Project Consultation Center, November 24, 2004, http://www.spacechina.com/index.asp?modelname=nr&recno=14842.

104. Reserve Colonel Ying Shaoji, "A Discussion of Communist China's Small Satellite Science and Technology Trends," *Air Force Science Monthly*, http://www.mnd.gov.tw.

105. Geoffrey Forden, "Strategic Uses for China's Bei Dou Satellite System," *Jane's Intelligence Review,* October 1, 2003, www.janes.com.

106. Luan Shanglin, "China Puts New Navigation Satellite into Orbit," Xinhua, February 3, 2007, http://news.xinhuanet.com/english/2007-02/03/content_5689019.htm.

107. "China to Launch 2 Satellites for Compass Navigation System," *China Daily,* November 14, 2006, http://english.peopledaily.com.cn/200611/14/eng20061114_321287.html.

108. See "There Is a GPS System with 'Chinese Characteristics'—The Beidou Satellite System's Strategic Use," *World Outlook* 8 (2004).

109. Gustav Lindstrom and Giovanni Gasparini, *The Galileo Satellite System and its Security Implications,* Occasional Paper no. 44 (Paris: European Union Institute for Security Studies, 2003), 29, http://www.iss-eu.org/occasion/occ44.pdf.

110. See, for example, Yu Xiang, "Implementation of the EU's 'Galileo' Project Enters the Next Stage," *Aerospace Electronic Warfare* 2 (2005).

111. Lindstrom and Gasparini, *Galileo Satellite System.*

112. Peter B. de Selding, "Europeans Raise Red Flags over Chinese Satellite Navigation Plan," *Space News,* June 12, 2006, http://www.space.com/spacenews/archive06/China_061206.html.

113. Forden, "Strategic Uses."

114. "China Starts to Build Own Satellite Navigation System," *Space Daily,* November 3, 2006, http://www.spacedaily.com/reports/China_Starts_To_Build_Own_Satellite_Navigation_System_999.html.

115. Ling Zhu, "China Starts to Build Own Satellite Navigation System," Xinhua, November 2, 2006, http://news.xinhuanet.com/english/2006-11/02/content_5280896.htm.

116. Li Xinran, "China Capable of Building Aircraft Carrier," *Shanghai Daily,* January 2007, http://www.shanghaidaily.com/article/?id=302268&type=National.

117. "China Says Aircraft Carrier Possible by 2010: Paper," *Muzi,* March 7, 2007, http://dailynews.muzi.com/news/ll/english/10038207.shtml.

118. Author's interview with Chinese official, Beijing, June 2006.

119. Bray, "Seapower Questions."

120. *Observation Post of the Military Situation,* Phoenix Television, March 15, 2006, OSC-CPP20060317515025.

121. Author's interview, Beijing, June 2006.

122. "Senior Military Officer: China to Develop its Own Aircraft Carrier Fleet," *Wen Wei Po,* March 10, 2006, OSC-CPP20060310508004.

123. Author's interview, Beijing, June 2006.

124. Author's interviews, Beijing, December 2005.

125. Office of Naval Intelligence (ONI), *Handbook on China's Navy 2007* (Washington, DC: Office of Naval Intelligence, 2007), 58.

126. Ibid., 46.

127. Unless otherwise specified, data in this section are derived from "People's Liberation Army Navy (PLAN)," Administration, China, *Jane's Fighting Ships,* January 29, 2007, http://www.janes.com.

128. ONI, *Handbook,* 61–62.

129. Ibid., 6.

130. See State Council, *China's National Defense in 2006.*

131. Fisher, "Trouble Below," 34.

132. ONI, *Handbook,* 55.

133. Author's interview with Chinese scholar, Newport, RI, January 2007.

134. ONI, *Handbook,* 30.

135. Li Dajun, "Commander of Mine-Warfare Vessels," *Modern Ships* 129 (September 1996): 18.

136. See State Council, *China's National Defense in 2006.*

137. Liu Feng'an and others, "Basic Project Promoting Changes in Military Training—A Summary of Reform in the Content of All-Military and Armed Police Force Training and Outline Compilation and Revision Work," *PLA Daily,* December 28, 2006, 1, OSC-CPP20061228710014.

138. "Make Changes to the Training Mechanisms, Contents, and Methods—Second on Promoting the Innovation and Development of Military Training in the Navy in the New Stage of the New Century, " *People's Navy,* July 28, 2006, 1, OSC-CPP20060906318003.

139. "Act Pragmatically, Be Committed to Implementation—Third on Promoting the Innovation and Development of Military Training in the Navy in the New Stage of the New Century," *People's Navy,* July 31, 2006, 1, OSC-CPP20060906318002.

140. ONI, *Handbook,* 88.

141. Ibid., 56.

142. Ibid., 89.

143. Wang Hai and Zhang Xiaoqi, "Digital Sea Chart Ushers in New Era of Navigation," *PLA Daily,* January 23, 2007, OSC-CPP20070124715005.

144. ONI, *Handbook,* 67–72.

145. "Act Pragmatically, Be Committed to Implementation."

146. ONI, *Handbook,* 73–77.

147. Ibid., 86.

148. Liu Beizhan and others, "Brave Sword—Recording a Certain Frigate Unit's Commander Wang Bin," *People's Navy,* March 28, 2002, 1.

149. Lin Zailian and others, "Put the Vanguard Status into Practice and Raise High the Banner of the Pioneer—A First Hand Report on How the Boat 814 Party Branch Fulfilled its Duty as a Combat Stronghold," *People's Navy,* March 30, 2002, 3.

150. Jiang Minjun and others, "Take Advantage of the East Wind to Navigate Well—A First-Hand Record of New Outline Test Exercises by a Destroyer Detachment from the South Sea Fleet," *People's Navy,* March 5, 2002, 1–2.

151. Zailian and others, "Put the Vanguard Status into Practice."

152. Wen Shangjing and others, "Warship 852 Obtains Substantial Results in Innovating Training Methods," *People's Navy,* May 11, 2002, 2.

153. Zhang Zuowei and others, "'Sea Engineers' Temper Themselves Through Meritorious Service," *Naval & Merchant Ships* 310 (July 2005): 3.

154. Liu Ronghua and others, "China's First Petty Officers Take Position," *People's Navy,* April 9, 2002, 2.

155. Chen Qizheng and others, "Locking in on the Battlefield of the Future—Recording a Certain Minesweeper Brigade from Unit 9108's Heroic Efforts at Difficult Mine Sweeping Exercises," *People's Navy,* March 21, 2002, 1–2.

156. "Conscientiously Put Military Training in a Strategic Position—First on Promoting the Innovation and Development of Military Training in the Navy in the New Stage of the New Century," *People's Navy,* July 26, 2006, 1, OSC-CPP20060906318001.

157. ONI, *Handbook,* 34.

158. Ibid., 37.

159. Xu Hongming and others, "Train in Both 'Attack Techniques' and 'Concealment Methods': A Certain East Fleet Submarine Detachment Can Attack and Hide Without 'Weak Spots,'" *People's Navy*, November 9, 2002, 3.

160. Liu Xianglin and others, "Reporting on a Certain North Sea Fleet Submarine Base's 'Underwater Vanguard Boat' (Part 2)," *People's Navy*, October 14, 2004, 2.

161. Jia Fenghua and others, "Greeting the 16th Party Congress with Excellent Performance Records: A Certain Submarine Detachment from the North Sea Fleet Trains Hard to Improve Survivability Through Self-Designed Exigencies," *People's Navy*, August 31, 2002, 2.

162. Srikanth Kondapalli, *China's Naval Power* (New Delhi: Institute for Defence Studies and Analyses, 2001), 142.

163. Liu and others, "China's First Petty Officers."

164. Zou Qinjing and others, "Ma Lixin: The Dragon Cruises the Ocean Depths," *People's Navy*, February 5, 2005, 1, 3.

165. Lu Yongzheng, "A Certain Submarine Detachment Makes a Great Leap in War Management Capability," *People's Navy*, October 31, 2002, 2.

166. Zhang Luocan, "Littoral Port Training Room Attacks Difficulty: A Certain Submarine Detachment Exercises," *People's Navy*, March 23, 2002, 1.

167. Gui Pingdian and others, "Navy Airmen: High, Difficult Subjects Sharpen New Recruits," *People's Navy*, August 8, 2002, 2.

168. Sun Shiwei and others, "Can Already Both 'Seal the Throat with One Sword' and 'Escape by Cunning Maneuvering': A Certain Submarine Unit's Training Stressing Both Attack and Defense," *People's Navy*, July 20, 2002, 1.

169. Xu Hongming and others, "Lay Mines 'in the Enemy's Rear Area'—An Eyewitness Account of a Certain PLAN Submarine Exercise Involving Breaking Through Anti-Submarine Formations," *Modern Navy* 4 (2003): 38.

170. Zhang, "Littoral Port Training Room."

171. Kondapalli, *China's Naval Power*, 143.

172. "PLA Navy Captain Ma Lixin Leads Drill Using New-Type Submarine," CCTV-1, February 27, 2005, OSC-CPP20050302000014.

173. Zou and others, "Ma Lixin."

174. Zhang Shoujun and others, "Ocean Depths Sharpen Crack Troops," *People's Navy*, December 27, 2005, 3.

175. Liu Huaqing, *The Memoirs of Liu Huaqing* (Beijing: People's Liberation Army Press, 2004), 474–77, 494.

176. Peng Ziqiang, *The Research and Development of Chinese Nuclear Submarines* (Beijing: Central Party School Press, 2005), 286.

177. Huang Caihong and others, *Nuclear Submarines* (Beijing: People's Press, 1996), 91.

178. See, for example, Fang Fang and others, "The Effects of Long-Term Voyages on the Blood Cell Components and Rheology of Sailors on Naval Ships and Nuclear-Powered Submarines," *Chinese People's Liberation Army Journal of Preventive Medicine* 4 (2004): 261–64.

179. Bray, "Seapower Questions."

180. Unless otherwise specified, this paragraph derives from ONI, *Handbook*, 43–44.

181. Wang Zufeng and others, "A Certain South Sea Fleet Mobile Sea Mine Warehouse Guides Officers: Receive New Mission Assignment Requiring Independent Initiative," *People's Navy*, October 8, 2005, 1.

182. Gao Erjian and others, "A Certain East Sea Fleet Sea Mine Warehouse Has a Foothold in Actual Combat: Training in All Weather Field [with] Independent Safeguards," *People's Navy*, October 8, 2005, 1.

183. Kondapalli, *China's Naval Power*, 141.

184. "Outstanding XO Exercise Improves Complex Training Quality: Some North Sea Fleet Frigates Let XOs Lead Training 'Big Bridge,'" *People's Navy*, February 23, 2002, 2.

185. Du Xier and others, "Passing Through 'Deadly Seas,'" *People's Navy*, January 25, 2005, 2.

186. Ibid.

187. Information in this paragraph derives from Cao Ming and others, "Following South China Sea Fleet Unit '809' Ship Sweeping Mines at Sea," *Modern Navy* 4 (2003): 18–19.

188. The last three sentences derive from Cao Ming and others, "Ship 809: Clearing the Way for the Battlefield," *People's Navy*, February 22, 2003, 1–2.

189. "On the Scene in the East China Sea: A Joint Military-Civilian Mine Sweeping Exercise," *Naval & Merchant Ships*, January 4, 2001, 5–6.

190. Unless otherwise specified, information for this paragraph derived from Zha Chunming and others, "An On-the-Spot Report of a People's Militia Sea Drill at a Certain Navy Base," *Naval & Merchant Ships* 3 (February 2005): 4.

191. Niu Rong and others, "The Chinese Navy's Type 918 Minelaying Ship," *Naval & Merchant Ships* 7, no. 310 (2005): 11.

192. ONI, *Handbook*, 49–50.

193. Gui and others, "Navy Airmen."

194. He Yuemin and Xie Xi, "A Unit Organizes Sea-Air 3D Confrontational Exercise to Improve its Emergency Maneuvering Capability," *PLA Daily*, August 30, 2002, 1, OSC-CPP20020830000027.

195. "Air Force—China."

196. ONI, *Handbook*, 49.

197. M. Taylor Fravel, "The Evolution of China's Military Strategy: Comparing the 1987 and 1999 Editions of Zhanlüexue," in *China's Revolution in Doctrinal Affairs: Emerging Trends in the Operational Art of the Chinese People's Liberation Army*, ed. James Mulvenon and David Finkelstein (Alexandria, VA: CNA Corporation, 2005), 82.

198. This paragraph derived from ONI, *Handbook*, 24, 27.

199. For quotation, see Liu, *Memoirs of Liu Huaqing*, 434; for other data, see Shi Yunsheng, "Introduction," in *China Navy Encyclopedia*, vol. 1 (Beijing: Sea Tide Press, 1998), 16–31; Huang and others, *Nuclear Submarines*, 16–19. Shi is a former PLA Navy commander (1996–2003).

200. Peng and Yao, *The Science of Military Strategy*, 441.

201. Ibid., 446.

202. Ibid., 449.

203. Ibid., 456–57.

204. Ibid., 472.

205. ONI, *Handbook*, 33.

206. Ibid., 24.

207. Ibid., 26.

208. Xu, "Maritime Geostrategy."

209. Peng and Yao, *The Science of Military Strategy*, 443.

210. See Liu, *Memoirs of Liu Huaqing*, 437.

211. ONI, *Handbook,* 26.

212. See "U.S. Navy Preoccupied with Major Adjustment," *People's Daily,* July 9, 2004.

213. See Zu Ming, "A Schematic Diagram of the U.S. Naval Forces Deployed and System of Bases in the Western Pacific," *Naval & Merchant Ships* 2 (January 2006): 24.

214. John Wilson Lewis and Xue Litai, *Imagined Enemies: China Prepares for Uncertain War* (Stanford, CA: Stanford University Press, 2006), 120.

215. Liu, *Memoirs of Liu Huaqing,* 501–2.

216. See, for example, "Underwater Communications—Submarine Communications Systems, China," *Jane's Underwater Warfare Systems,* March 21, 2006, http://www.janes.com.

217. Garth Hekler, Ed Francis, and James Mulvenon, "Command, Control, and Communications in the Chinese Submarine Fleet," in *China's Future Nuclear Submarine Force,* ed. Andrew S. Erickson, Lyle J. Goldstein, William S. Murray, and Andrew R. Wilson (Annapolis, MD: U.S. Naval Institute Press, 2007), 212–28.

218. ONI, *Handbook,* 27.

219. The author thanks Lt. Michael Grubb, USN, for the substantial insights he contributed to this section.

220. Wang and Zhang, "Digital Sea Chart Ushers in New Era of Navigation," 320.

221. Ibid., 330.

222. Ibid., 324–25.

223. Ibid., 325.

224. For detailed paragraphs on defensive sea-mine barriers and using sea mines to "Resist Enemy Blockade of [PLAN] Bases," see Wang and Zhang, "Digital Sea Chart Ushers in New Era of Navigation," 341, 344.

225. Wang and Zhang, "Digital Sea Chart Ushers in New Era of Navigation," 327.

226. Ibid., 336.

227. Ibid., 334.

228. Ibid., 336–37.

229. Ibid., 318–19.

230. Ibid., 334–35.

231. Ibid., 336.

232. Ibid., 327–28.

233. Ibid., 337.

234. Bray, "Seapower Questions."

235. "Senior Military Officer."

236. Thomas G. Mahnken, *Uncovering Ways of War: U.S. Intelligence and Foreign Military Innovation, 1918–1941* (Ithaca, NY: Cornell University Press, 2002), 44.

237. Ibid., 84.

238. Ibid., 64.

239. Du Gang, "A Discussion of Military Force Requirements during China's Peaceful Development," *Strategy & Management* 3 (2004): 55.

240. Author's interview, Beijing, June 2006.

241. Lewis and Xue, *Imagined Enemies.*

242. Thomas J. Christensen, "Posing Problems Without Catching Up: China's Rise and Challenges for U.S. Security Policy," *International Security* 25, no. 4 (spring 2001): 29.

243. "President Attends 'Formosan Association for Public Affairs' (FAPA)'s 25th Anniversary Celebration Banquet," Presidential Office Web site, March 4, 2007, http://www.president.gov.tw/php-bin/prez/shownews.php4?Rid=12655.

244. "Taiwan Reportedly Tests Missiles Capable of Hitting Shanghai, Hong Kong," Associated Press, March 6, 2007.

245. Chris Buckley and Ralph Jennings, "China Slams Independence Talk from Taiwan," Reuters, March 5, 2007.

246. For a pithy explanation of the importance of Taiwanese self-defense, see Holmes, "'Assassin's Mace' Is the PRC's Key in New Race."

247. Euan Graham, *Japan's Sea Lane Security, 1940–2004: A Matter of Life and Death?* (New York: Routledge, 2006).

248. Ibid.

249. Peng and Yao, *The Science of Military Strategy,* 67.

250. Liu, "Theory of the Command of the Sea."

Chapter 6

The views set forth here are the author's alone.

1. Luo Ping, "National Oil, Nationally Hauled: China's Energy Security Insurance Line" [*Guoyou Guoyun: Zhongguo Nengyuan de Anquan Baozhang Xian*], *Maritime China,* February 2005, 38–40.

2. "Hu Calls for Strong Navy"; "Chinese President Calls for Strengthened, Modernized Navy"; "Chinese President Calls for Strong Navy"; Lague, "China Airs Ambitions."

3. See Information Office of the State Council, *China's National Defense in 2006.*

4. Li Jie, "China's Oil Demands and Sea Lane Security" [*Shiyou, Zhongguo Xuyao yu Haidao Anquan*], *Jianquan Zhishi,* September 2004, 10–13.

5. Wu Lei and Shen Qinyu, "Will China Go to War over Oil?" *Far Eastern Economic Review* 169, no. 3 (April 2006): 38.

6. Qiao Enyan, "Petroleum Enterprises and Their Use in National Oil Security Strategy" [*Shiyou Qiye zai Guojia Shiyou Anquan Zhanlue Zhong de Zuoyong*], *Modern Chemical Industry,* July 2005, 9–12.

7. Ibid.

8. Yang Mingjie, ed., *Sea Lane Security and International Cooperation,* (Beijing: Current Affairs Publishing House, 2005), 123.

9. Luo Ping, "National Oil, Nationally Hauled," 38–40.

10. Ibid.

11. "The Development of Chinese Shipbuilding Industry in Recent Years," Organisation for Economic Cooperation and Development, December 15, 2006, http://www.oecd.org/dataoecd/18/38/37881499.pdf.

12. Li Shaojun, "Mahan's *Sea Power* and its Influence on China's Oil Security Strategy" [*Lun Haichuan dui Zhongguo Shiyou Anquan de Yinxiang*], *International Forum* 6, no. 4 (July 2004): 16–20.

13. Chen Angang, "Malacca: America's Coveted Strategic Outpost" [*Malike Haixia: Meiguo Jiyu de Zhanlue Qianshao*], *Modern Ships* [*Xiandai Jianchuan*], December 2004, 11–14.

14. Japan's interest in the Indian Ocean stems from the fact that most of its oil imports must also transit the Malacca Strait.

15. "China Gives Green Light to Myanmar Oil Pipeline," Agence France Presse, April 18, 2006, http://www.uofaweb.ualberta.ca/chinainstitute/nav03.cfm?nav03=45306&nav02=43617&nav01=43092.

16. Yang, *Sea Lane Security and International Cooperation,* 106.

17. Qin Xiao, "China's Energy Security Strategy and the Energy Transport Problem" [*Zhongguo Nengyuan Anquan Zhanlue Zhong de Nengyuan Yunshu Wenti*], *China Energy* [*Zhonguo Nengyuan*] 26, no. 7 (July 2004): 4–7.

18. "China Urged to Beef Up Ocean Oil Shipping," *Asia Pulse,* March 15, 2006, Lexis-Nexis, http://web.lexis-nexis.com. The tonnage figure cited here is significant in absolute terms, but reassigning these vessels to domestic firms would not help China's long-distance oil transport situation: few of these ships are the VLCCs needed to bring crude from the Middle East, Africa, and other distant locales.

19. Erica Downs, "The Chinese Energy Security Debate," *China Quarterly* 177 (March 2004): 21–41.

20. Ren Xiaoyu, "Analysis and Opinions on How PetroChina Markets its Equity Oil," *China Oil and Gas* 4 (2002): 50–52.

21. Yang, *Sea Lane Security and International Cooperation,* 123.

22. Zheng Changxing, "2005 China Shipbuilding Industry Development Characteristics," *Mechanical and Electrical Equipment* 2 (2006): 33–34.

23. Qin, "China's Energy Security Strategy and the Energy Transport Problem."

24. "Major Chinese Operator Calls for Maritime Oil Transport Development," BBC, March 10, 2006, Lexis-Nexis, http://web.lexis-nexis.com.

25. Yang, *Sea Lane Security and International Cooperation,* 124.

26. Ibid., 123.

27. "By Year End 2010, the Length of China's Oil Pipeline Network Will Grow by 25,000 KM," *Oil and Capital* (in Russian), February 26, 2007, www.oilcapital.ru/print/news/2007/02/261024_105757.shtml.

28. Zha Daojiong, "Three Questions About China's Future Oil Security" [*Sanwen Zhongguo Weilai Shiyou Anquan*], *China Petroleum Enterprise* [*Zhongguo Shiyou Qiye*]. Also see Zhang Wenmu, "China's Energy Security and Policy Choices" [*Zhongguo Nengyuan Anquan yu Zhengce Xuanze*], *World Economics and International Politics* 5 (2003): 11–16.

29. Zhang, "China's Energy Security and Policy Choices," 11–16.

30. Qin, "China's Energy Security Strategy and the Energy Transport Problem," 4–7. In 2002, Chinese tankers carried less than 4 percent of China-bound cargoes from the Middle East, none at all from West Africa.

31. This rough calculation assumes that Chinese seaborne oil import demand of approximately 3.3 million barrels per day would require two VLCCs/day to off-load in China. Thus, if one warship guarded a two-tanker group, the thirty-five-day round-trip between China and the Gulf would require thirty-five escorts in active service. (Chinese-flagged ships would be vulnerable traveling both to and from the Gulf, since they would be clearly marked as being in Chinese service). Assuming a 1-1 backup ratio, plus logistics vessels for refueling on the in- and outbound legs of the voyage, the PLAN would require upward of seventy highly modern ships to conduct such an operation. As Chinese information, surveillance, and reconnaissance improves, more focused operations to sanitize suspected subsurface and surface threat zones may become thinkable. Nonetheless, convoy operations would be highly asset-intensive while imposing high opportunity costs. Warships diverted to convoy duty would have to forego operations more directly related to the crisis that triggered the need for escorts in the first place. Counterblockade efforts would also suffer from the PLAN's lack of at-sea replenishment ships.

32. Yang, *Sea Lane Security and International Cooperation,* 119.

33. An attacker could theoretically try to close Indonesia's Lombok and Sunda Straits as well, but after a temporary disruption, energy shippers would likely bypass these chokepoints, finding new routes to key East Asian markets. By interdicting critical chokepoints, moreover, the attacking party might sacrifice its Asian allies' well-being and strain global tanker capacity, driving up tanker rates for oil consumers around the world. Japan and South Korea do have strategic oil stockpiles which, depending on the blockade's duration, could help them avoid supply shocks. Japan, for instance, has ninety-two days' worth of oil in its strategic petroleum reserve. Even so, diplomatic, economic, and political fallout of closing Malacca would be severe.

34. See High Seas Convention (1958), Article 8; United Nations Convention on the Law of the Sea (1982), Articles 32, 58(2), 95, and 236; A. Ralph Thomas and James C. Duncan, "Annotated Supplement to the *Commander's Handbook on the Law of Naval Operations*," *U.S. Naval War College International Law Studies* 73 (1999): 110, 221, 259, 390; Chairman of the Joint Chief of Staff Instruction 3121.01B (January 2005); Joel Doolin, "The Proliferation Security Initiative: Cornerstone of a New International Norm," *Naval War College Review* 59, no. 2 (spring 2006). The author thanks Prof. Peter Dutton for his guidance in this area.

35. A bill of lading, often abbreviated BOL or B/L, is a document issued by a shipper acknowledging that specific items have been received on board as cargo to be shipped to a designated destination for delivery to a consignee who is usually stipulated.

36. Yue Laiqun, "Unavoided Malacca Strait" [*Tupo Malike Kunju*], *China Petroleum Enterprise,* September 2005, 6.

37. For more information, consult William Murray and Gabriel Collins, "China's Counterblockade Options," in *Maritime Implications of China's Energy Strategy* (Annapolis, MD: Naval Institute Press, forthcoming).

38. Gary Dirks, "Energy Security: China and the World," speech at "International Symposium on Energy Security: China and the World," Beijing, China, May 24, 2006.

Chapter 7

The views voiced here are those of the author alone.

1. Rahul Roy-Chaudhury, *India's Maritime Security* (New Delhi: Knowledge World, 2000), xxii.

2. Arun Prakash, "Shaping India's Maritime Strategy—Opportunities and Challenges," Speech at the National Defence College, November 5, 2005, http://indiannavy.nic.in/cns_add2.htm (accessed February 21, 2007).

3. *The Indian Navy's Vision Document,* Admiral Arun Prakash, Directorate of Strategy, Concepts, and Transformation, Integrated Headquarters of the Ministry of Defence (Navy), New Delhi, May 25, 2006.

4. Indian Navy, Integrated Headquarters, Ministry of Defence, *Indian Maritime Doctrine,* INBR 8, April 25, 2004.

5. "CNO Calls for a New Maritime Strategy," *Today in the Military,* June 20, 2006, http://www.military.com/features/0,15240,101925,00.html (accessed February 18, 2007).

6. U.S. Government Accountability Office, "Defense Management: Comprehensive Strategy and Annual Reporting Are Needed to Measure Progress and Costs of DOD's Global Posture Restructuring, Appendix I," Report to the Subcommittee on Readiness, Committee on Armed Services, House of Representatives, September 2006, GAO-06-852.

7. Indian Ministry of Defence, "Indian Armed Forces: Security Environment: An Overview," http://mod.nic.in/aforces/welcome.html (accessed March 7, 2007).

8. C. Raja Mohan, "India and the Balance of Power: Will the West Engage?" *Foreign Affairs,* July/August 2006.

9. Barry R. Posen and Andrew L. Ross, "Competing Visions for U.S. Grand Strategy," *International Security* 21, no. 3 (winter 1996/97): 5–53.

10. James R. Holmes and Andrew C. Winner, "The United States, the Proliferation Security Initiative, and the U.S. Navy," *U.S. Naval Institute Proceedings,* May 2007.

11. Stephen Philip Cohen, *India: Emerging Power* (Washington, DC: Brookings Institution Press, 2001), 36–65.

12. Ibid., 39.

13. Roy-Chaudhury, *India's Maritime Security,* 125.

14. James Goldrick, *No Easy Answers,* Papers in Australian Maritime Affairs no. 2 (New Delhi: Lancer Publishers and Distributors, 1997), 19–20.

15. C. Raja Mohan, *Crossing the Rubicon: The Shaping of India's New Foreign Policy* (New York: Palgrave MacMillan, 2003), 204–7.

16. Goldrick's book provides an excellent history of the emergence of the navies of India, Pakistan, and Sri Lanka and the challenges they have faced, both politically and in terms of resources.

17. Roy-Chaudhury, *India's Maritime Security,* 127.

18. Sandeep Dikshit, "Defence Spending Moves Up," *Hindu,* January 3, 2007, http://www.thehindu.com/2007/03/01/stories/2007030105421200.htm (accessed March 5, 2007).

19. Rajat Pandit, "Quality of Russian Arms Worries India," *Times of India,* February 17, 2007.

20. Timothy D. Hoyt, *Military Industry and Regional Defence Policy: India, Iraq, and Israel* (London: Routledge, 2007).

21. "Panel to Consider Revamp of Premier Defence Research Body," *Nerve, News of India,* January 19, 2007, http://www.nerve.in/news:25350031141 (accessed April 29, 2007).

22. Draft Report of National Security Advisory Board on Indian Nuclear Doctrine, August 17, 1999, http://www.indianembassy.org/policy/CTBT/nuclear_doctrine_aug_17_1999.html (accessed January 12, 2006).

23. Robert S. Norris and Hans M. Kristensen, "India's Nuclear Forces, 2005," *Bulletin of the Atomic Scientists* 61, no. 5 (September/October 2005): 73–75.

24. Indian Navy, Integrated Headquarters, Ministry of Defence, *Indian Maritime Doctrine,* 49.

25. National Journal Group, "India Begins Developing Nuclear Missile Submarine Fleet, Former Naval Chief Discloses," Global Security Newswire, January 29, 2007, http://www.nti.org/d_newswire/issues/2007_1_29.html#4F4DDCF1 (accessed February 7, 2007).

26. Norris and Kristensen, "India's Nuclear Forces," 73–75.

27. Rahul Bedi, "Indian SSN Reactor Fully Online," *Jane's Defense Weekly,* August 30, 2006, 15.

28. Roy-Chaudhury, *India's Maritime Security,* 141.

29. Indiadefence, "Indian Navy Reveals Ambitious Expansion, Indigenization Programme," May 9, 2006, http://www.india-defence.com/reports/2460 (accessed August 18, 2006).

30. "Submarine Forces," *Jane's Underwater Warfare Systems,* September 19, 2005.

31. Norris and Kristensen, "India's Nuclear Forces," 73–75.

32. Bharat Karnad, *Nuclear Weapons and Indian Security* (New Delhi: MacMillan India Limited, 2002).

33. Indian Navy, Integrated Headquarters, Ministry of Defence, *Indian Maritime Doctrine,* 56.

34. Ibid., 63–64.

35. Ibid., 64.

36. "Procurement, Submarines," *Jane's Sentinel Security Assessment*—South Asia, March 13, 2005.

37. Rahul Bedi, "India Rejects P-3C Option," *Jane's Navy International,* March 1, 2006.

38. Rahul Bedi, "India Moves to Boost Airborne Surveillance," *Jane's Defense Weekly,* March 15, 2006.

39. Rahul Bedi, "Indian Navy Strives for Regional Dominance," *Jane's Defense Weekly,* December 21, 2005.

40. Mrityunjoy Mazumdar, "Indian Navy Regenerates its Fleet Air Arm," *Jane's Naval Intelligence,* December 1, 2005.

41. Hans de Vreij, "Terrorist Hunt on High Seas," Radio Netherlands, March 3, 2006, http://www.radionetherlands.nl/currentaffairs/ter060314?view=Standard (accessed March 22, 2006).

42. "India, France Begin Joint Naval Exercises," *Deccan Herald,* February 27, 2005, http://www.deccanherald.com.

43. P.S. Suryanarayana, "Aircraft Carrier on a Friendly Mission," *Hindu,* August 3, 2005.

44. "USS Trenton Procurement Approved," *Indian Express,* August 24, 2006.

45. CNS Press Conference on Navy Day, New Delhi, December 2, 2005.

46. Press Information Bureau, Government of India, Ministry of Defence, "India and Oman Set Up Joint Military Cooperation Committee," March 11, 2006.

47. Daniel Goure, "The Tyranny of Forward Presence," *Naval War College Review* 54, no. 3 (summer 2001): 11–24.

48. Sudha Ramachandran, "Delhi All Ears in the Indian Ocean," *Asia Times,* March 3, 2006.

49. Juli A. MacDonald, *Indo-U.S. Military Relationship: Expectations and Perceptions* (Washington, DC: Booz Allen Hamilton, 2002).

50. Rahul Bedi, "Is Privatization the Panacea for India as it Grapples with the Spectre of Obsolescence?" *International Defence Review,* December 1, 2005.

Chapter 8

The views voiced here are those of the author alone. This chapter first appeared in the summer 2006 issue of the *Naval War College Review.*

1. For more on Boyd's thought, consult the Defense and the National Interest Web site, http://www.d-n-i.net.

2. See, for instance, Julian S. Corbett's analysis of geographic factors in the 1904–5 Russo-Japanese War. Julian S. Corbett, *Maritime Operations in the Russo-Japanese War, 1904–1905,* ed. John B. Hattendorf and Donald M. Schurman (Annapolis and Newport: Naval Institute Press and Naval War College Press, 1994), esp. 1–10.

3. For a detailed contrast between Japan and Britain on geography and history, see Peter J. Woolley, *Geography and Japan's Strategic Choices: From Seclusion to Internationalization* (Dulles: Potomac, 2005), 1–6.

4. Peter J. Woolley, *Japan's Navy: Politics and Paradox 1971–2000* (Boulder: Lynne Rienner, 2000), 8.

5. Toshi Yoshihara and James R. Holmes, "China, a Unified Korea, and Geopolitics," *Issues & Studies* 41, no. 2 (2005): 119–70; Robyn Lim, *The Geopolitics of East Asia: The Search for Equilibrium* (London: RoutledgeCurzon, 2003).

6. Duk-ki Kim, *Naval Strategy in Northeast Asia: Geo-strategic Goals, Policies and Prospects* (London: Frank Cass, 2003), 168–69.

7. See Kaijo Jieitai 50-nenshi Hensan Iinkai [MSDF 50th Anniversary Editorial Board], *Kaijo Jieitai 50-nenshi* (Tokyo: Boeicho Kaijo Bakuryo Kanbu, 2003), 126.

8. Mahan, *Influence of Sea Power,* 71. For more on Mahan, see Philip A. Crowl, "Alfred Thayer Mahan: The Naval Historian," in *Makers of Modern Strategy: From Machiavelli to the Nuclear Age,* ed. Peter Paret, Gordon A. Craig, and Felix Gilbert (Princeton: Princeton University Press, 1986), 444–77; Russell F. Weigley, *The American Way of War* (New York: Macmillan, 1973), 167–91; Jon Tetsuro Sumida, *Inventing Grand Strategy and Teaching Command: The Classic Works of Alfred Thayer Mahan Reconsidered* (Washington, DC: Woodrow Wilson Center Press, 1997), 80–98; Rolf Hobson, *Imperialism at Sea: Naval Strategic Thought, the Ideology of Sea Power and the Tirpitz Plan, 1875–1914* (Boston: Brill Academic Publishers, 2002). On Mahan's influence outside the United States, see John B. Hattendorf, ed., *The Influence of History on Mahan* (Newport: Naval War College Press, 1991).

9. Margaret Tuttle Sprout, "Mahan: Evangelist of Sea Power," in *Makers of Modern Strategy: Military Thought from Machiavelli to Hitler,* ed. Edward Meade Earle (Princeton: Princeton University Press, 1943), 415–45; James R. Holmes, "Mahan, a 'Place in the Sun,' and Germany's Quest for Sea Power," *Comparative Strategy* 23, no. 1 (2004): 27–62.

10. James R. Holmes and Toshi Yoshihara, "The Influence of Mahan upon China's Maritime Strategy," *Comparative Strategy* 24, no. 1 (2005): 53–71; and James R. Holmes and Toshi Yoshihara, "Command of the Sea with Chinese Characteristics," *Orbis* 49, no. 4 (2005): 677–94.

11. Alfred Thayer Mahan, *The Problem of Asia* (New York: Harper's New Monthly Magazine, 1900; reprint, Port Washington: Kennikat Press, 1970), 15.

12. Notes one analyst of Mahanian theory, "Central to the theory of sea power was the expectation of conflict. When a nation's prosperity depends on shipborne commerce, and the amount of trade available is limited, then competition follows, and that leads to a naval contest to protect the trade." George W. Baer, *One Hundred Years of Sea Power: The U.S. Navy, 1890–1990* (Stanford: Stanford University Press, 1994), 12. See also Pekka Korhonen, "The Pacific Age in World History," *Journal of World History* 7, no. 1 (1996): 41–70.

13. Mahan, *Problem of Asia,* 33.

14. Ibid., 124.

15. Ibid., 26, 124.

16. Mahan, *Influence of Sea Power,* 138.

17. Alfred Thayer Mahan, *The Interest of America in Sea Power, Present and Future* (Boston: Little, Brown, and Company, 1897; reprint, Freeport: Books for Libraries Press, 1970), 198.

18. Ibid., and Alfred Thayer Mahan, *Lessons of the War with Spain,* quoted in Sprout, "Mahan: Evangelist of Sea Power," 433.

19. John Keegan, *The Price of Admiralty: The Evolution of Naval Warfare* (New York: Viking, 1989), 101–2, 109, 170.

20. Alfred Thayer Mahan, *From Sail to Steam: Recollections of Naval Life* (New York: Harper & Brothers, 1907; reprint, New York: Da Capo, 1968), 3.

21. David C. Evans and Mark R. Peattie, *Kaigun: Strategy, Tactics, and Technology in the Imperial Japanese Navy, 1887–1941* (Annapolis: Naval Institute Press, 1997), 67–71.

22. "The Chino-Japanese War," *Pall Mall Gazette* (London), August 18, 1894, 7.

23. Ronald H. Spector, *Eagle against the Sun: The American War with Japan* (New York: Free Press, 1985), 293.

24. Woolley, *Geography and Japan's Strategic Choices,* 11, 17.

25. Richard W. Turk, *The Ambiguous Relationship: Theodore Roosevelt and Alfred Thayer Mahan* (Westport: Greenwood Press, 1987), 4.

26. S.C.M. Paine, *The Sino-Japanese War of 1894–1895: Perceptions, Power, and Primacy* (Cambridge: Cambridge University Press, 2003), 150.

27. Spector, *Eagle against the Sun,* 43; Evans and Peattie, *Kaigun,* 2, 133–51. See also Sun Tzu, "The Art of War," in *The Seven Military Classics of Ancient China,* trans. Ralph D. Sawyer (Boulder: Westview, 1993), 145–86. Akiyama, who served as an observer on board Adm. Sampson's flagship during the Spanish-American War and later talked with Mahan, introduced many of the staff planning and war-gaming techniques he saw in Newport when he returned to the Naval Staff College.

28. Sprout, "Mahan: Evangelist of Sea Power," 415. Mahan's contemporary, the theorist Sir Julian Corbett, was biting. On one occasion he derided Mahan's work as "shallow and wholly unhistorical." Grove, "Introduction," xxx.

29. Roger Dingman, "Japan and Mahan," in *The Influence of History on Mahan,* ed. John B. Hattendorf (Newport: Naval War College Press, 1991), 50.

30. Ibid., 56.

31. Schencking, *Making Waves,* 2–6.

32. Evans and Peattie, *Kaigun,* 134.

33. Ibid., 134–35.

34. "Without a doubt," declares S.C.M. Paine, "Japan had absorbed Captain Mahan's lesson concerning the necessity of the command of the sea" by the early 1900s. Paine, *Sino-Japanese War,* 327.

35. Evans and Peattie, *Kaigun,* 139–40.

36. Mahan, *Influence of Sea Power,* 71.

37. Evans and Peattie, *Kaigun,* 140–41.

38. Evans and Peattie, *Kaigun,* 64. See also Darrell H. Zemitis, "Japanese Naval Transformation and the Battle of Tsushima," *Military Review* 84, no. 6 (2004): 73–75.

39. Alfred Thayer Mahan, "Discussion of the Elements of Sea Power," in *Mahan on Naval Strategy,* ed. John B. Hattendorf, intro. (Annapolis: Naval Institute Press, 1991), 31.

40. Paine, *Sino-Japanese War,* 150–53.

41. Tsunoda Jun, "The Navy's Role in the Southern Strategy," in *The Fateful Choice: Japan's Advance into Southeast Asia, 1939–1941,* ed. James William Morley, trans. Robert A. Scalapino (New York: Columbia University Press, 1980), 241–95; Evans and Peattie, *Kaigun,* 514–16.

42. Observes Samuel Eliot Morison, the United States spent "a much too big slice of the thin appropriation pie" on battleships in the interwar era, "due, fundamentally, to Captain Alfred Thayer Mahan's teachings to the effect that all other classes of warships would be so outranged and outgunned by them in fleet actions as to be useless." Samuel Eliot Morison,

The Two-Ocean War: A Short History of the United States Navy in the Second World War (Boston: Little, Brown, 1963), 11; Spector, *Eagle against the Sun,* 19, 33, 47, 58.

43. Turk, *The Ambiguous Relationship,* 1–6, 101–7. Henry Adams described TR as "pure act." Henry Adams, *The Education of Henry Adams,* intro. James Truslow Adams (New York: Modern Library, 1931), 417.

44. Evans and Peattie, *Kaigun,* 136–37.

45. Dingman, "Japan and Mahan," 61.

46. Spector, *Eagle against the Sun,* 47. See also David C. Evans, ed., *The Japanese Navy in World War II: An Anthology of Articles by Former Officers of the Imperial Japanese Navy,* 2nd ed. (Annapolis: Naval Institute Press, 1986), 505, 507.

47. Dingman, "Japan and Mahan," 65.

48. Yoji Koda, "The Russo-Japanese War: Primary Causes of Japanese Success," *Naval War College Review* 58, no. 2, 2005, http://www.nwc.navy.mil/press/review/documents/NWCRSP05.pdf.

49. Author interviews with retired JMSDF flag officers and academic specialists from the Okazaki Institute, Tokyo, February 2006.

50. Given the extensive mining both by the Japanese defenders and the U.S. Navy, de-mining operations lasted for decades—making the Japanese navy one of the most capable minesweeping forces in the world.

51. James Auer observes, "By 1949, after Allied Occupation force reductions, the Japanese minesweeping force was the largest and most capable in the Western Pacific." For more, see James E. Auer, *The Postwar Rearmament of Japanese Maritime Forces* (New York: Praeger, 1973).

52. Auer, *Postwar Rearmament of Japanese Maritime Forces,* 64–67.

53. John Lewis Gaddis, *Strategies of Containment: A Critical Appraisal of Postwar American National Security Policy* (Oxford: Oxford University Press, 1982).

54. The three major straits are the Tsugaru Strait (dividing Honshu and Hokkaido islands), the Tsushima Strait, and the Soya Strait (between Sakhalin and Hokkaido). Beyond the archipelago, the Luzon (Bashi) Strait between the southern tip of Taiwan and the northern Philippines is deemed a critical chokepoint.

55. See Kaijo Jieitai 50-nenshi Hensan Iinkai, *Kaijo Jieitai 50-nenshi,* 27–28.

56. See James Auer and Tetsuo Kotani, "Reaffirming the 'Taiwan Clause': Japan's National Interest in the Taiwan Strait and the U.S.-Japan Alliance," in *Japan–Taiwan Interaction: Implications for the United States,* ed. Roy Kamphausen (Seattle: National Bureau of Asian Research, October 2005), 58–83.

57. Auer, *Postwar Rearmament of Japanese Maritime Forces,* 161–68.

58. For details of the debate, see Auer, *Postwar Rearmament of Japanese Maritime Forces,* 132–47.

59. For details on the NDPO's conceptual framework, see Christopher W. Hughes, *Japan's Re-emergence as a "Normal" Military Power* (New York: Oxford University Press), 67–68.

60. Kaijo Jieitai 50-nenshi Hensan Iinkai, *Kaijo Jieitai 50-nenshi,* 124–25.

61. For an excellent account of the debate on sea-lane defense, see Woolley, *Japan's Navy: Politics and Paradox,* 65–87.

62. See Christopher W. Hughes and Akiko Fukushima, "U.S.–Japan Security Relations: Toward Bilateralism Plus?" in *Beyond Bilateralism: U.S.–Japan Relations in the New Asia-Pacific,* ed. Ellis S. Krauss and T.J. Pempel (Stanford: Stanford University Press, 2004), 67.

63. Toru Ishikawa, "Japan Maritime Self Defense Force's Enduring Relationship with the U.S. Navy," Navy League, December 2002.

64. See especially Corbett, *Some Principles of Maritime Strategy.* See also William R. Sprance, "The Russo-Japanese War: The Emergence of Japanese Imperial Power," *Journal of Military and Strategic Studies* 6, no. 3 (2004): 1–24.

65. The 1995 NDPO, the first in nearly two decades, revised its predecessor's parameters for the post–Cold War strategic context. The NDPO accurately anticipated the new security responsibilities Japan would be called upon to shoulder.

66. The apparent lack of enthusiasm stemmed in part from Chinese opposition to combined patrols.

67. For details about Japan's antipiracy activities, see John F. Bradford, "Japanese Anti-Piracy Initiatives in Southeast Asia: Policy Formulation and the Coastal State Responses," *Contemporary Southeast Asia* 26, no. 3 (2004): 480–505.

68. Embassy of Japan Web site, http://www.us.emb-japan.go.jp/english/html/press releases/2005/042505a.htm.

69. Japanese Ministry of Foreign Affairs Web site, http://www.mofa.go.jp/policy/terrorism/measure0510.html.

70. Japanese decision-makers were deeply conflicted over the Aegis deployment, worrying that Japan would become embroiled in any combat that might ensue.

71. U.S. Department of State, "Proliferation Security Initiative," http://www.state.gov/t/isn/c10390.htm.

72. Jamie Miyazaki, "Japan Deploys Self-Defense Forces to Aceh," *Jane's Intelligence Review,* March 1, 2005.

73. "SDF Mission in Full Swing; But Tsunami Relief Exposes Flaws in Overseas Deployments," *Yomiuri Shimbun,* February 8, 2005, 4.

74. Government of Japan, "National Defense Program Guidelines, Approved by the Security Council and the Cabinet on December 10, 2004," provisional translation.

75. Yuki Tatsumi, "National Defense Program Outline: A New Security Policy Guideline or a Mere Wish List?" *CSIS Japan Watch,* December 20, 2004.

76. Speculation that the ship would be named the *Akagi,* after the World War II flagship that led the attack on Pearl Harbor, stirred a controversy over Japanese intentions.

77. Hughes, *Japan's Re-emergence as a "Normal" Military Power,* 82.

78. Koyu Ishii, "Heisei no Hinomaru Kubo '16DDH' no Opeleshon," *Sekai no Kansen,* April 1, 2005, 106–9.

79. Martin Fackler, "A Reef or a Rock? Question Puts Japan in a Hard Place," *Wall Street Journal,* February 16, 2005, A1.

80. "Japanese MSDF Spots Five Chinese Naval Ships Near East China Sea Gas Field," Kyodo World Service, September 9, 2005.

81. According to the report, "The Chinese Navy aims to extend the space for offshore defensive operations while integrated combat capabilities are enhanced in conducting offshore campaigns, as mentioned above. In addition, it is pointed out that the country aims to build a so-called blue-water navy in the future. Therefore, it is important to monitor Chinese movements and identify Chinese strategies underlying them." Japan Defense Agency, *Defense of Japan 2005* (Tokyo: Japan Defense Agency, 2005), 14.

82. We use Carl von Clausewitz's maxim that war's "grammar, indeed, may be its own, but not its logic" as a device. Carl von Clausewitz, *On War,* trans. and ed. Michael Howard and Peter Paret (Princeton: Princeton University Press, 1976), 605; James R. Holmes and Toshi

Yoshihara, "Mao Zedong, Meet Alfred Thayer Mahan," *Australian Defence Force Journal* 171 (October 2006): 33–50.

83. Kim, *Naval Strategy in Northeast Asia,* 173.

84. Ni Lexiong, "Sea Power and China's Development," *Liberation Daily,* April 17, 2005, 2, U.S.-China Economic and Security Review Commission Web site, http://www.uscc.gov/ researchpapers/translated_articles/2005/05_07_18_Sea_Power_and_Chinas_ Development.pdf. See also Holmes and Yoshihara, "The Influence of Mahan upon China's Maritime Strategy," 53–71.

85. Ni, "Sea Power and China's Development," 1–2. On Germany's quest for sea power, see Holmes, "Mahan, a 'Place in the Sun,' and Germany's Quest for Sea Power," 27–62.

86. Ni, "Sea Power and China's Development," 4.

87. Ibid., 5.

88. Andrew J. Nathan and Robert S. Ross, *The Great Wall and the Empty Fortress: China's Search for Security* (New York: W.W. Norton, 1997), 24–26.

89. See, for example, Ryohei Oga, "What the PRC Submarine Force Is Aiming For," *Sekai no Kansen,* July 1, 2005, 96–101; and Toru Kizu, "Japan and China—A Comparison of Their Sea Power," *Sekai no Kansen,* November 1, 2004, 84–91.

90. "China Bringing Okinawa 'within Range'—What Underlies Oilfield Development in the East China Sea," *Sentaku,* January 1, 2006, 46–47.

91. Yoshiko Sakurai, "Proposal to Prime Minister Koizumi—The Enemy Is within Japan," *Sankei Shimbun,* January 12, 2006.

92. Bill Gertz, "China Builds Up Strategic Sea Lanes," *Washington Times,* January 18, 2005, http://www.washingtontimes.com/national/20050117-115550-1929r.htm.

93. Hideaki Kaneda, "The Rise of Chinese 'Sea Power,'" *Philippine Daily Inquirer,* September 22, 2005.

94. Yoichi Funabashi, "Japan's Waters: Vast in Size and Potential," *Asahi Shimbun,* January 13, 2004.

95. Jun Kitamura, "The U.S. Military's Perception of Japan and National Strategies That Japan Should Have: Proposal for the Future of the Japan–US Alliance," *Seiron,* February 1, 2006, 298–307.

96. JDA, *Defense of Japan 2005,* 43.

97. See "JDA to Step Up Vigilance against PRC; GSDF to Conduct Joint Exercises with U.S. Military; MSDF Developing New Torpedo," *Nihon Keizai Shimbun,* December 31, 2005, and "Japan, U.S. to Simulate Defense for Outlying Islands in Map Exercise," Kyodo World Service, August 4, 2005.

98. "Maritime Self-Defense Force News," *Sekai no Kansen,* December 1, 2005, 160–61.

99. "Jieitai vs. Chugoku Gun: Jieitai Wa Kakutatakaeri," *Bessatsu Takara jima,* September 1, 2005.

100. John B. Hattendorf and Donald M. Schurman, "Introduction," in Corbett, *Maritime Operations in the Russo-Japanese War,* v–xvii.

Chapter 9

1. *International Energy Outlook 2005* (Washington, DC: Energy Information Agency, 2005); *British Petroleum Statistical Review of World Energy, June 2005* (London: British Petroleum, 2005).

2. *Energy Security Initiative: Some Aspects of Oil Security* (Tokyo: Asia Pacific Energy Research Center, 2003), 4.

3. Steven W. Lewis, Conference Report, "The Future of Energy Security and Energy Policy in Northeast Asia: Cooperation Among China, Japan and the United States," http://www.rice.edu/energy/research/asiaenergy/docs/UFJ_conferencereport_web.pdf, accessed April 29, 2007.

4. L. Wu, "China's Oil Security Challenges and its Countermeasures," *Geopolitics of Energy* 26, no. 11 (2004): 2–5, in Pable Bustelo, "China and the Geopolitics of Oil in the Asian Pacific Region," Working Paper 38/2005 (Madrid: Elcano Royal Institute, 2005), 22–23.

5. Bustelo, "China and the Geopolitics of Oil," 25.

6. U.S. Department of Energy, "South China Sea," *Country Analysis Briefs,* March 2006, http://www.eia.doe.gov.

7. Peter Kien-Hong Yu, "The Chinese (Broken) U-Shaped Line in the South China Sea: Points, Lines, and Zones," *Contemporary Southeast Asia* 25, no. 3 (2003): 405–31.

8. "South China Sea Region," U.S. Energy Information Administration, *Country Analysis Briefs,* August 1999, and Greg Austin, *China's Ocean Frontier: International Law, Military Force, and National Development* (Sydney: Allen & Unwin, 1998), http://community.middlebury.edu/~scs/scs-intro-t7.html.

9. Ralf Emmers, "Maritime Disputes in the South China Sea: Strategic and Diplomatic Status Quo," Institute for Defense and Disarmament Studies, Singapore, September 2005, 6–7.

10. Liselotte Odgaard, "The South China Sea: ASEAN's Security Concerns About China," *Security Dialogue* 34, no. 1 (2003): 22.

11. Chris Chung dissertation; Stein Tonnesson, "Sino-Vietnamese Rapprochement and the South China Sea Irritant," *Security Dialogue* 34, no. 1 (2003): 55–56.

12. Sam Bateman, "Sea Change: Resolving East Asia's Maritime Disputes," *Jane's Intelligence Review,* March 2007, 1–2.

13. Ibid., 2.

14. Stein Tonnesson, statement at Norwegian Institute of International Affairs-IDSS Workshop on Maritime Security in Southeast Asia, June 14–15, 2005, Oslo, Norway, in Emmers, "Maritime Disputes in the South China Sea," 15, n. 37. The discovery of large deposits in the Berents Sea, together with higher energy prices, has magnified the diverging claims of Russia, which bases its claims on a meridian line extending to the North Pole, and Norway, which bases claims on the median-line principle.

15. Alice Ba describes four phases, Kuik Cheng-Chwee three. Alice D. Ba, "China and Asean: Renavigating Relations for a 21st-Century Asia," *Asian Survey* 43, no. 4 (July/August 2003): 622–47; Kuik Cheng-Chwee, "Multilateralism in China's ASEAN Policy: Its Evolution, Characteristics, and Aspiration," *Contemporary Southeast Asia* 27, no. 1 (2005): 102–23.

16. Ba, "China and Asean," 623–27.

17. Cheng-Chwee, "Multilateralism in China's ASEAN Policy."

18. Christopher R. Hughes, "Nationalism and Multilateralism in Chinese Foreign Policy: Implications for Southeast Asia," *Pacific Review* 18, no. 1 (2005): 119–35.

19. Denny Roy, "Southeast Asia and China: Balancing or Bandwagoning?" *Contemporary Southeast Asia* 27, no. 2 (2005): 305–22.

20. State Council, *China's National Defense in 2006* (Defense White Paper), 3.

21. Roy, "Southeast Asia and China," 310.

22. Hughes, "Nationalism and Multilateralism," 130.

23. Peter Kien-Hong Yu, "Setting Up International (Adversary) Regimes in the South China Sea: Analyzing the Obstacles from a Chinese Perspective," *Ocean Development and International Law* 38 (2007): 147–56.

24. Mark J. Valencia, Jon M. Van Dyke, and Noel A. Ludwig, *Sharing the Resources of the South China Sea* (Honolulu: University of Hawaii Press, 1997).

25. David C. Kang, "Hierarchy, Balancing and Empirical Puzzles in Asian International Relations," *International Security* 28, no. 3 (2003/04): 165–80; Yuen Foong Khong, "Coping with Strategic Uncertainty: The Role of Institutions and Soft Balancing in Southeast Asia's Post–Cold War Strategy," in *Rethinking Security in East Asia: Identity, Power and Efficiency*, ed. J.J. Suh, Peter Katzenstein, and Allen Carlson (Stanford, CA: Stanford University Press, 2004); Amitav Acharya and See Seng Tan, "Betwixt Balance and Community: America, ASEAN, and the Security of Southeast Asia," *International Relations of the Asia Pacific* 6, no. 1 (2006): 37–59.

26. Stephen Brooks and William Wohlforth, "Hard Times for Soft Balancing," *International Security* 30, no. 1 (2005): 72–108.

27. Ian James Storey, "Creeping Assertiveness: China, the Philippines and the South China Sea Dispute," *Contemporary Southeast Asia* 21, no. 1 (1999): 95–118.

28. Michael Doyle, *Ways of War and Peace* (New York: Norton, 1997).

29. Richard N. Rosecrance, *The Rise of the Virtual State: Wealth and Power in the Coming Century* (New York: Basic Books, 1999).

30. Thomas Friedman, *The Lexus and the Olive Tree* (New York: Anchor, 2000), 253.

31. David M. Rowe, "The Tragedy of Liberalism: How Globalization Caused the First World War," *Security Studies* 14, no. 3 (2005): 407–47.

32. Alex Liebman, "Trickle-down Hegemony? China's 'Peaceful Rise' and Dam-building on the Mekong," *Contemporary Southeast Asia* 27, no. 2 (2005): 281–305.

33. John Ravenhill, "Is China an Economic Threat to Southeast Asia?" *Asian Survey* 46, no. 5 (September–October 2006): 653–74. Ravenhill finds the picture on FDI quite mixed.

34. See Aaron Friedberg's "The Future of U.S.–China Relations: Is Conflict Inevitable?" *International Security* 30, no. 2 (2005): 7–45. See also U.S. Department of Defense, *The Military Power of the People's Republic of China 2005* (Washington, DC: Government Printing Office, 2005).

35. *Jane's Defence Weekly,* April 25, 2007; *Jane's Sentinel Security Assessment—China and Northeast Asia,* March 22, 2007 (accessed April 25, 2007). PRC defense expenditures remain at approximately 1.5 percent of GDP.

36. *Jane's Defence Weekly,* April 25, 2007; *Jane's Sentinel Security Assessment—China and Northeast Asia,* March 22, 2007 (accessed April 25, 2007); "PLA Navy Facilities," Federation of American Scientists Web site, www.fas.org/man/dod-101/sys/ship/row/plan/index.html (accessed April 25, 2007).

37. Timothy Hu, "China—Marching Forward," *Jane's Defence Weekly,* April 18, 2007.

38. David Shambaugh, "China Engages Asia: Reshaping the Regional Order," *International Security* 29, no. 3 (2005): 64–99, 86.

39. Yu, "Chinese (Broken) U-Shaped Line," 405–31.

40. Michael Leifer, "ASEAN as a Model of a Security Community?" in *ASEAN in a Changed Regional and International Political Economy,* ed. Hadi Soesastro (Jakarta: Centre for Strategic and International Studies, 1995), 141, in Emmers, "Maritime Disputes in the South China Sea," 9.

Index

ABOUT THE CONTRIBUTORS

Bernard D. Cole is a faculty member at the National War College, in Washington DC. He served thirty years in the U.S. Navy as a Surface Warfare Officer, commanding a frigate and a destroyer squadron. Cole has authored numerous articles and chapters, as well as four books: *Gunboats and Marines: The U.S. Navy in China; The Great Wall at Sea: China's Navy Enters the 21st Century; Oil for the Lamps of China: Beijing's 21st Century Search for Energy;* and *Taiwan's Security: History and Prospects.* He is currently writing a book on energy security in Asia. Cole holds an AB degree in History from the University of North Carolina, MPA in National Security Affairs from the University of Washington, and a Ph.D. in History from Auburn University.

Gabriel Collins is a research fellow in the U.S. Naval War College's China Maritime Studies Institute. He is an honors graduate of Princeton University (AB, 2005) and is proficient in Mandarin and Russian. His work focuses on energy and the shipping industry and has been published in *Oil & Gas Journal, Geopolitics of Energy, Oil & Gas Investor, and The National Interest.*

Andrew S. Erickson is an assistant professor in the Strategic Research Department at the U.S. Naval War College and a founding member of the department's China Maritime Studies Institute (CMSI). Erickson previously worked for Science Applications International Corporation (SAIC) as a Chinese translator and technical analyst. He has also worked at the U.S. Embassy in Beijing, the U.S. Consulate in Hong Kong, the U.S. Senate, and the White House. Proficient in Mandarin Chinese and Japanese, he has traveled extensively in Asia. Erickson graduated magna cum laude from Amherst College with a BA in history and political science, received an MA from Princeton University in international relations and comparative politics, and completed his Ph.D. dissertation at Princeton University on Chinese aerospace development. His research, which focuses on East Asian defense, foreign policy, and technology issues, has been published in *Journal of Strategic Studies, Comparative Strategy, Undersea Warfare, Space Policy,* and *Naval War College Review.*

John Garofano is Jerome Levy Chair of Economic Geography and Professor, National Security Affairs, and Professor in the Strategy and Policy Department at the U.S. Naval War College where he also teaches electives on Asian security issues. Dr. Garofano's research interests include military intervention, Asian alliances and security problems, and the making of U.S. foreign policy. His writings have appeared in *International Security, Contemporary Southeast Asia, Asian Survey, and the Naval War College Review* among others. Prior to joining the War College Dr. Garofano was Senior Fellow at the Kennedy School of Government, Harvard University, and has taught at the U.S. Army War College, the Five Colleges of western Massachusetts, and the University of Southern California. Dr. Garofano received the Ph.D. from Cornell University and an MA from the Johns Hopkins School of Advanced International Studies.

James R. Holmes is an associate professor in the Strategy and Policy Department at the U.S. Naval War College. He is a Phi Beta Kappa graduate of Vanderbilt University and earned graduate degrees at Salve Regina University, Providence College, and the Fletcher School of Law and Diplomacy at Tufts University, where he was awarded a Ph.D. in 2003. Dr. Holmes graduated from the Naval War College with highest distinction in 1994 and was the recipient of the Naval War College Foundation Award, signifying the top graduate in his class. Before joining the Naval War College faculty, he was a senior research associate at the University of Georgia Center for International Trade and Security, Athens, GA; a research associate at the Institute for Foreign Policy Analysis, Cambridge, MA; and a U.S. Navy surface warfare officer, serving in the engineering and weapons departments on board the battleship *Wisconsin,* directing an engineering course at the Surface Warfare Officers School Command, and teaching Strategy and Policy at the Naval War College, College of Distance Education. He is the author of *Theodore Roosevelt and World Order: Police Power in International Relations,* co-author of *Chinese Naval Strategy in the 21st Century: The Turn to Mahan,* and co-editor of *Asia Looks Seaward: Power and Maritime Strategy.*

John Curtis Perry is Henry Willard Denison Professor of History at the Fletcher School of Law and Diplomacy, Tufts University. Dr. Perry is currently the director of the Oceanic Studies Program and was formerly the director of the North Pacific Program at the Fletcher School. He is a senior advisor to the Japan Society of Boston and a consultant to South Korea's Ministry of Foreign Affairs. His works include *Facing West: Americans and the Opening of the Pacific* (Westport, CT: Praeger, 1994) and *Flight of the Romanovs: A Family Saga* (New York: Basic Books, 1999). He holds a BA and MA from Yale University and a Ph.D. in History from Harvard University.

Nicholas Evan Sarantakes is an associate professor of Joint and International Operations at the U.S. Army Command and General Staff College. He has a Ph.D. in history from the University of Southern California. He also holds the MA degree in history from the University of Kentucky. He did his undergraduate work at the University of Texas. He is the author of *Keystone: The American Occupation of Okinawa and U.S.–Japanese Relations* (2000) and *Seven Stars: The Okinawa Battle Diaries of Simon Bolivar Buckner, Jr. and Joseph Stilwell* (2004). He is currently finishing a book that examines allied strategy and joint international operations at the end of World War II tentatively titled *Allies to the Very End: The United States, the British Nations, and the Defeat of Imperial Japan.* He has published a number of articles that have been appeared in outlets like *The Journal of Military History* and *Joint Forces Quarterly.* He is a Fellow of the Royal Historical Society and has previously taught at Texas A&M University—Commerce, the Air War College, and the University of Southern Mississippi.

Andrew C. Winner is an associate professor in the Strategic Research Department at the U.S. Naval War College. His areas of focus are, South Asia, the Middle East, nonproliferation, maritime strategy, and U.S. national security issues. Prior to his current appointment, he was a senior staff member at the Institute for Foreign Policy Analysis, Cambridge, MA, where he conducted research and analysis on South Asia, the Middle East, nonproliferation, the use of force, and coalition politics. Prior to joining the Institute, he was executive assistant to the Assistant Secretary of State for Political-Military Affairs and special assistant to the Under Secretary of State for Arms Control and International Security Affairs where he worked on nonproliferation, security in the Persian Gulf, arms transfer policy, bilateral security dialogues, NATO enlargement, and security assistance. He holds a Ph.D. from the University of Maryland, College Park, an MA from the Johns Hopkins University School of Advanced International Studies (SAIS), and an AB from Hamilton College.

Toshi Yoshihara is an associate professor in the Strategy and Policy Department at the U.S. Naval War College. Previously, he served as a visiting professor in the Strategy Department at the U.S. Air War College, Montgomery, AL. Dr. Yoshihara was also a senior research fellow at the Institute for Foreign Policy Analysis, Cambridge, MA. His current research focuses on the influence of geopolitics in Asia, China's naval strategy, and Japan's maritime strategy. He has co-authored journal articles on Chinese maritime strategy that appeared in